A John Catt Publication

HEAD STRONG

11 LESSONS OF SCHOOL LEADERSHIP

BY DAME SALLY COATES

WITH STEVE ADCOCK & MICHAEL RIBTON

First Published 2015

by John Catt Educational Ltd,
12 Deben Mill Business Centre, Old Maltings Approach,
Melton, Woodbridge IP12 1BL

Tel: +44 (0) 1394 389850 Fax: +44 (0) 1394 386893
Email: enquiries@johncatt.com
Website: www.johncatt.com

ISBN: 978 1 909717 268

Set and designed by Theoria Design.

CONTENTS

Foreword

by Roy Blatchford,
Director of the National Education Trust

I first went to the school at the centre of this book in 1974. I was a young teacher in charge of a South London school football team. In those days, to travel by tube on a Saturday morning into West London to play football on the Scrubs was an adventure into another's territory – for boys and teacher alike. These were heady years in the Inner London Education Authority (ILEA). The combination of teacher shortages, militant union action, political members' ideological differences and a sprawling bureaucracy led to some of the larger comprehensives simply being ungovernable. I was teaching in one in Brixton.

Burlington Danes offered an alternative picture, one not immediately apparent to the visiting footballers looking up at the forbidding walls of the infamous Wormwood Scrubs prison which dominate the local area. With its proud grammar school and Church of England traditions, here was a school in the mid-1970s which teachers aspired to belong to. At a time of teacher shortages, I remember talking to the one of the deputy heads on the touchline and being told how competitive it was to secure a teaching post at the school. In essence, its grammar school halo was still in place as London's schools went comprehensive.

Thirty years later in 2004 I entered the school as one of Her Majesty's Inspectors. The school was in special measures and I was the lead HMI, monitoring its progress. A combination of factors had led to the school's decline and students were being poorly served. I remember distinctly standing at the school gates one November morning and counting in just on a third of the total student population, late for registration. The next decade is the story of this book.

In my experience of leading, coaching and inspecting great schools around the world, the following key ingredients are present: they excel at what they do in a consistent manner; they have strong values and clear expectations; their achievements do not happen by chance but through deeply reflective, carefully planned strategies; there is a high degree of internal consistency; leadership is well distributed and ambitious to move the school forward.

In essence, the cocktail is disarmingly simple: the virtuous combination of well-qualified, skilled teachers motivated by clear, fair-minded and knowledgeable leadership, collectively focused on students' well-being and all-round achievement – achievements which sometimes and often surprise the learners themselves.

Yet no school I know is better than the ambition of its leadership, in the same way that no classroom is better than the skills of its teacher. Schools rise or fall on the quality of leadership, particularly that of the head. This is especially true in areas of social challenge, where heads need to lead from the front in a highly visible way. The principles of the head determine the principles of the school.

The title of this book risks misleading the reader who takes its meaning too literally. Being 'headstrong' isn't about being macho. It's about being committed to your values and resilient in the face of challenges. The narrative of *Headstrong* is not just one of school improvement by an inspiring headteacher. Importantly it is a tale of the joy and fulfilment which the role brings.

Roy Blatchford,
February 2015

Preface

I write this in the autumn of 2014, two months into my new role as director of academies for a national network of schools. I'm now looking at areas of deprivation across the south of England and overseeing intervention strategies to ensure that all young people receive the quality of schooling they deserve. I've relished the chance to get out of London and immerse myself in schools across the south of England: from Swindon to Ashford; Kettering to Poole. My two months in this regional role have reaffirmed my view that every school is unique: a delicate compound of several elements including its students, its teachers, its history, the local community, the curriculum and the facilities. Such is the diversity of our schools that an identikit approach to school improvement will never work.

I began work on Headstrong in 2010 and these pages were written during my time at Burlington Danes. I wrote from the perspective of a headteacher attempting to do the best for her school, amid the various factors and influences from inside and outside the school gates.

I was reminded that all schools have a life of their own in my final weeks at Burlington Danes. I was inundated with messages of support and gratitude from parents, teachers, students and governors. Students made me a tribute video and colleagues performed a stirring rendition of 'One Day More' from *Les Miserables* in staff briefing on my final day. But life went on, and continues to do so, in that pocket of West London. I remain in close contact with my successor, Michael Ribton, and I have no doubt that Burlington Danes will continue to flourish long into the future. The organisational memory of the school has been wiped and rebooted; success has become the norm.

Yet it's precisely because each school is unique that the role of the headteacher is so important. It falls on the head of each school to select the best ingredients and pull the most promising levers to ensure success for his or her students. As we approach another General Election it seems that once again educational policy is in limbo, with teachers and school leaders across the land bracing themselves for another flurry of directives from the Department for Education. There is no better time therefore to remind ourselves that as headteachers it's our job to proactively set the agenda for our schools, to steer the ship in the direction of our choosing rather than simply keep it afloat as the waves rise around us. I hope that the pages that follow provide inspiration to school leaders eager to lead transformational schools up and down the land.

Introduction:
The tragedy of a
failing school

'In large states public education will always
be mediocre, for the same reason that in large
kitchens the cooking is usually bad'
– Friedrich Nietzsche

I was in the furniture department of John Lewis on Sloane Square in December 2007 when I received a call from the chief executive of Ark Schools offering me the role of principal at Burlington Danes Academy. As my husband Serge wandered off into the crowds of Christmas shoppers I sunk into a sofa and found myself accepting the offer as I read the sign on the wall of the store – 'Never Knowingly Undersold' – with a large dose of irony.

I immediately regretted it. I was extremely happy in my role as principal at Sacred Heart Catholic School – a smaller but similarly gritty school in South London where I had worked for over 20 years. I had been head at Sacred Heart for four years, and in that time we had been judged 'Outstanding' by Ofsted, the government inspectorate. I knew all the students by name; I had even taught some of their parents. I enjoyed strong relationships with an inspiring team of teachers and was quite happy to see out my career at the school that I had joined as head of English 20 years earlier. My husband was one of my deputies at Sacred Heart, I met him there when he joined as head of PE in 1988 and I was content with the convenient routines we had developed over the years; busy but fulfilling days bookended by Serge's impatient chauffeuring through busy London traffic.

One of the most valuable trappings of headship is having your own PA, and it was my PA at Sacred Heart who took the calls from a very persistent head-hunter in the autumn of 2007. The head-hunter was acting on behalf of Ark, an educational charity which had just taken over Burlington Danes. I was clear from the start that I wasn't interested, but we had a few conversations and before long I received a phone call from Sir Michael Wilshaw, head of the renowned Mossbourne Academy in Hackney and Ark's director of education (and now head of Ofsted). Michael spoke with conviction, telling me that the job at Burlington Danes was a job worth doing. He came to Sacred Heart to describe the school to me, and a week or so later I accompanied him on a visit to Burlington Danes where I saw for myself the sorry state it was in, combined with the potential for improvement. So I submitted a hastily-completed application form, but in truth I still felt uncertain about the role. I was up against a popular internal candidate. Teachers at Burlington Danes were jaded by the turbulence they had endured in recent years and it was clear that they favoured the internal applicant for the stability that he offered. It was strange going to the school for the 'assessment day', vying for a job I didn't really want and meeting staff who didn't really want me. Hence my words to Serge on the top floor of John Lewis after I accepted the role just a few weeks later: 'what the hell have I done?'

Taking the Burlington Danes job was a risk because of the success and relative comfort of my job at Sacred Heart, and the size of the challenge seven miles west. The school was described to me as unruly, chaotic and lacking basic discipline and, while I've never been a pushover, I wouldn't class behaviour management as a particular strength: I had Serge for that. The salary I took at Burlington Danes was no better than my previous one, and then there was the risk of working for an academy – at that time a new model of school governance which had aroused the ire of the teaching unions. The jury was out on whether academy status made much difference. When you see a successful leader it's easy to assume that they always carried that air of success, but the fact is that whatever stage you get to in your career you never lose the doubts and uncertainty that you brought with you on your first day. So I doubted whether I could transform this struggling academy in west London. I had only worked at two schools, and I had surrounded myself with wonderful teams who complemented my strengths and weaknesses. Perhaps I had bitten off more than I could chew?

Extracts from Ofsted's Monitoring Visit to Burlington Danes Academy in March 2008, one month before my arrival

The Academy was rated 'satisfactory' (following a review of Ofsted ratings, this was later changed to 'requires improvement')

'There are a high number of surplus places which make the academy vulnerable to casual admissions throughout the year.'

'A larger number of staff than is typical left the academy last year, but it is now almost fully staffed. However, as a result about a quarter of teaching staff are inexperienced and consequently require significant support.'

'The achievement of students last year was inadequate and there were an extremely high number of fixed term exclusions, largely due to inappropriate and disruptive behaviour. The academy attributes these difficulties to the problems caused by the reorganisation of the faculty structure.'

'This visit has raised some concerns about the standard of education provided and the academy's performance will be monitored.'

'The academy rightly judges that standards were low and achievement inadequate last year. Senior leaders attribute this to the difficulty of maintaining clear lines of accountability and communication through the new faculty structure. Whilst this was certainly a contributory factor, a more fundamental reason is the low expectations of student achievement. During this visit progress seen during lessons varied considerably because a number of lessons were based on an inaccurate understanding of students' achievement, prior knowledge and potential.'

'...a significant proportion of their lessons are affected by low-level disruption.'

'Attendance last year was inadequate.'

'...a number of students are late to the start of lessons and some teachers do not routinely take registers.'

'The development of the academy has been hampered by the duplication of responsibilities and accountabilities at senior level. This has led to confusion for both students and staff. Middle managers are unclear about their role in improving the quality of teaching and learning.'

Full inspection reports can be found at: reports.ofsted.gov.uk

Burlington Danes Academy was blessed with a grand name, but in all other respects it was a deeply troubled school. It lies in the shadow of the Wormwood Scrubs prison perimeter wall. Burlington School and St Clement Danes had once been selective grammar schools for girls and boys respectively, and in their heyday they enabled young people from West London to acquire a proud education. The playwright Dennis Potter and MP Frank Field both attended St Clement Danes in the 1950s, while Burlington School for Girls could trace its history back to Christmas Day 1699 when it was established on a small site on Carnaby Street with a bold mission: 'to teach sixty poor girls to read, write and cost accounts… and instructing them knowledge of the Christian religion.' In the 1970s the two schools, which were by now located just off Wood Lane in West London, merged to form Burlington Danes Church of England School. Standards slipped, and by the time Burlington Danes became Ark's first academy in 2006 the rot had set in. Behaviour was poor: less than one third of students gained the government's benchmark of five decent GCSEs and the local community was voting with its feet by sending their children to other schools in the area.

The composition of students at Burlington Danes is similar to the make-up of young people that I worked with in South London. Over 50% of students at Burlington Danes receive free school meals, meaning that their household income is less than £16,000 per year. This in a city where the average rent in 2014 was £1,412 per month. A large proportion of our students live in neighbourhoods which feature in the bottom 1% of the government's Income Deprivation Affecting Children Index (IDACI). Beyond this material disadvantage many of the young people that I work with suffer from a social dislocation which is every bit as damaging. The area surrounding Burlington Danes typifies this. A patch of north Kensington just a stone's throw from the school gates is home to politicians, lawyers and media executives. Walk another 15 minutes and you'll encounter the stunning Georgian villas of Portobello and Notting Hill, or the graceful elegance of Holland Park mansions. Yet on the way you would struggle to miss the drab blocks of social housing which provide homes to many of the young people in my care.

The riots of 2011 revealed some of the latent tensions lying below the surface of modern cities such as London. Some of our students live on the nearby Peabody estate which harboured one of the terrorist cells responsible for the 2005 London bombings. Gun and knife crime, gang culture and drug-related incidents form part of a significant number or our students' experience. The causes of riots, terrorism and violent crime are of course complex, but particularly in the summer of 2011 it was clear that many young Londoners lacked a sense of belonging in their city, and were oblivious to the rights and responsibilities that sit alongside true citizenship.

So it was with great trepidation that I left behind the comfort of Sacred Heart for the challenge of transforming Burlington Danes. However, in my two visits to its sprawling site in West London I had captured a glimpse of its potential. The 1930s art-deco listed building, once home to the girls school, would soon be overshadowed by a three-story £20 million state-of-the-art English, maths and science block. Plans were also in place for the five acres of fields to be embellished with a performing arts centre, an all-weather sports pitch and a sixth form centre, which would enable us to retain students for the crucial two years between GCSEs and university. The staff I met on my visits were earnest and compassionate, albeit demoralised. The students I encountered struck me as ambitious and determined, yet thoroughly disillusioned with the education they were receiving. The 'Danes' in the school's name derives from the fact that the boys' school was established by wardens of St Clement Danes Church, founded on The Strand to serve medieval London's Danish community. Burlington Danes now served a wonderfully diverse West London community: white British students made up 15% of the school population whilst Moroccans, Afghans, Somalians, Bangladeshis, Egyptians and Poles, amongst others, made up the rest. I had come to relish such diversity and vitality since moving to London from Kent in the 1970s.

First impressions

I vividly recall my first visit to Burlington Danes. I took the tube to White City on a crisp autumn morning and found myself at a bus stop outside BBC Television Centre asking a group of school girls how to get to Burlington Danes. "Follow us," was their response. So I climbed aboard the 220 bus for the pointlessly short journey along Wood Lane to the gates of Burlington Danes, but at least my journey gave me a chance to hear about the school from those who knew it best. The girls I spoke to weren't happy. They breathlessly explained to me that their friendship group had been torn apart by the introduction of 'small-schools' – schools within schools intended to provide a more intimate student experience. I'm not sure if those girls remember accompanying me on my first visit to Burlington Danes, but I'm sure that one of them had a glint in her eye when I announced in an assembly on my first day as head that I would be abandoning the small-school model.

My own education had opened my eyes to the unique power bequeathed to schools to shape the lives of those who pass through them. I grew up in Maidstone, Kent, with a brother and sister who were much older as well as a younger brother. I went to a private convent school at the age of seven until I was 16, a fate that saved me from the vagaries of the 11-plus – an examination taken at 11 which determined whether you would go to a high achieving grammar school or a grossly inferior 'secondary modern'. The pages that follow will reveal my belief in rigorous testing, but subjecting 11-year-olds to a single test of such huge gravity, with life chances being dictated by the outcome, seemed to me then, and now, as rather unfair.

Entrenched school failure is a scar on civil society. John F. Kennedy remarked that 'our progress as a nation can be no swifter than our progress in education'. Yet on both sides of the Atlantic we're still grappling with the challenge of creating great schools, especially in deprived areas. Should it be that difficult? Schools have existed for thousands of years and you would have thought that by now we would have cracked the code of their success: strong leadership; dedicated and talented teachers; decent facilities and resources; personalised support – it's a blueprint that you could copy and paste from the website of any academy chain. Yet these tenets are so startlingly obvious that Socrates himself might have offered them when creating the original Academy in Athens. Perhaps the crucial difference is that those eager scholars in ancient Greece enrolled in his academy through choice. Two-and-a-half thousand years later, western states are still floundering for the alchemy required to deliver effective *compulsory* education, a challenge made even harder when dealing with deprived urban communities.

The German philosopher Nietzsche suggested that 'In large states public education will always be mediocre, for the same reason that in large kitchens the cooking is usually bad'. But it needn't be like this. In his book *Hope and Despair in the American City: Why there are no bad schools in Raleigh*, Professor of Education Gerald Grant talks of a 'democratic bargain' whereby we tolerate the inequalities of capitalism as long as we have a strong education system for all. It's no different to the American dream, or 'equality of opportunity' as we prefer to call it in Europe: everyone in society should have a fair crack at making it to the top if they are willing to work hard. Yet we are plainly failing to deliver on this democratic bargain. The statistics make grim reading, and you've probably heard them before, so here's just a few. Just 7% of young people in England go to private school, yet 46% of students at Oxford University were privately educated. Seventy-five per cent of judges in England were privately educated, along with 70% of finance directors ('The Educational Background of the Nation's Leading People', The Sutton Trust, November 2012). Indeed, *The Times* reported that: 'In ten professions or careers more than half of the most prominent figures were privately educated. They include national or local government (68 per cent), law (63 per cent), senior armed forces (60 per cent) and business (59 per cent)' ('How so many of Britain's elite class all sat in the same elite classrooms', 20 November 2012). The same report went on to say that, 'Only 10 per cent of the elite attended comprehensives, including Daniel Craig, the actor, and Robert Peston, the BBC journalist, while 1 per cent went to non-selective secondary modern schools. Among these were the actor Colin Firth and Sir Steve Redgrave, the Olympic rowing champion.' So it seems that the guile of 007 is required to ascend the social ladder. I agree wholeheartedly with the former education secretary Michael Gove who described the persistent supremacy of a privately educated elite as 'morally indefensible'.

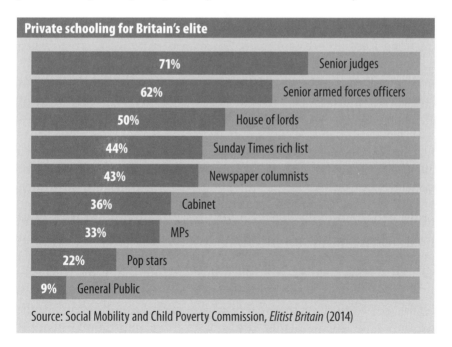

Private schooling for Britain's elite

71%	Senior judges
62%	Senior armed forces officers
50%	House of lords
44%	Sunday Times rich list
43%	Newspaper columnists
36%	Cabinet
33%	MPs
22%	Pop stars
9%	General Public

Source: Social Mobility and Child Poverty Commission, *Elitist Britain* (2014)

Translating this moral imperative into decisive action is tough, but it can be done. Take this graph for example:

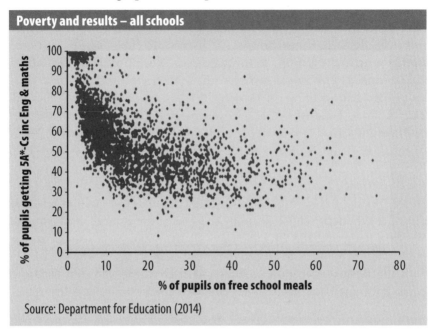

Poverty and results – all schools

% of pupils getting 5A*-Cs inc Eng & maths / % of pupils on free school meals

Source: Department for Education (2014)

Bertrand Russell once said that, "the mark of a civilised human being is being able to read a column of numbers and weep" – passing this particular test with the graph above is scant consolation for the injustice revealed by the all-too predictable scattering of those dots. Put simply, the graph shows a strong correlation between wealth and pupil attainment, with students on free school meals far less likely to gain a good set of GCSEs than their more affluent peers. The tragedy is that we've known about the pernicious link between social background and achievement for decades. The Coleman Report of 1966 concluded that in America 'schools bring little influence to bear on a child's achievement that is independent of his background and general social context; that this very lack of an independent effect means that the inequalities imposed on children by their home, neighbourhood, and peer environment are carried along to become the inequalities with which they confront adult life' (Coleman *et al.*, 1966, p. 325). Nearly 50 years on, a 2010 OECD report ('A family affair', p. 185) suggests that in Britain a father's income determines the earnings of his son more than in any other rich country. Yet for those of us committed to the fact that it doesn't have to be like this, the diagram above offers hope, for if you home in on the outliers – the schools with high levels of free school meals and high levels of student performance – you'll see that some schools are bucking the trend. And if some schools are doing it, then why can't all? That's the challenge faced by leaders of schools in deprived communities, and it's a challenge that inspired me to become principal of Burlington Danes Academy in 2008.

This chapter in a tweet: Burlington Danes was in a funk; reluctantly I agreed to try to rescue it.

Lesson 1:
Lead from the front

'When I had my first meeting with him, it was like he had walked in with a bag of confidence, opened it and flooded the room with it.'

The challenge of leadership is to create a sense of purpose for an organisation and to equip those within the organisation with the means to pursue that purpose. The leader must lead from the front. Of course there's a place for all sorts of leaders; there are plenty of introverts and reflective types who become successful leaders by creating systems and procedures which ensure operational efficiency. But schools are tribal organisations; urban schools especially so. So an urban school in a state of crisis requires a leader who leads from the front by establishing a personal grip on the organisation. Out goes the leadership textbook and in comes the confidence, resilience and authenticity to transform a ragged organisation into a thriving learning community.

Such a transformation requires meticulous planning. I visited Burlington Danes a few times in those early months of 2008 and had key staff from Burlington Danes visit me at Sacred Heart. Few staff at Burlington Danes had any experience of working in an effective school and I wanted to whet their appetite. I wanted them to hear the patter of footsteps on calm corridors, to see smiling teachers enjoying their craft and to feel the wonderful sense of justice being administered by a calmly managed detention! The staff at Burlington Danes had become battle-weary; their faces revealed the exhausting struggle of life in a failing school, where a toxic culture of low expectations and mistrust saps the life out of every initiative, every policy and every lesson. Many of the teachers and leaders at Burlington Danes had never seen a thriving school. Their visits to Sacred Heart stoked their optimism and quashed the defeatism that they had come to accept.

As well as hosting visits to Sacred Heart I spent my evenings and weekends planning meticulously for my arrival in West London. In his 2012 book *Education, Education, Education*, the former Schools Minister Andrew Adonis reflected: 'In government, it is hard to reform successfully unless you have largely worked out your reform plan beforehand. Once in office, even as a special adviser, let alone as a minister, there is precious little time and space to research and think through a subject' (p. 11). It was vital that I hit the ground running at Burlington Danes and the detail of my planning was microscopic as I scheduled to the minute the conversations that I needed to have, the messages that I had to convey to staff, the decisions that I had to make and the meetings that I should arrange. I left nothing to chance as I planned for the takeover of a failing school. 'Failing' is a potent term but the truth was that I didn't have much to go on as I prepared for Burlington Danes. Everyone I consulted offered a different opinion on the place beyond the fundamental issues of poor behaviour, low morale and below-par exam results. So my plans were not particularly clever, subtle or bespoke: I prepared for the swift transformation of a failing school. By the time term began on Monday 21st April 2008 I knew exactly what had to be done and my meticulous planning gave me the confidence to deliver.

Planning the first steps of headship

The key questions are:

- What is good about the academy?
- What isn't good and requires changing or scrapping?
- What do you expect of the principal?

If you want to make an instant impression, revamp the toilets and look at the food that's served! Change the uniform in a subtle way, especially if students are consulted and can help with the design.

Talking is important: meet teams for lunch or afternoon tea, meet students, meet parents, identify your challenging students and see them with their parents, identify your weaker staff and see them for a professional conversation. Get to know your leadership team: identify all those hidden talents and let them loose. Be visible but importantly be visible with purpose.

Accountability really matters: do organisational structures allow for effective decision-making? Does the curriculum engage students? What is behaviour like – and not just of students? Is there an appropriate formality?

Focus on learning, not behaviour. Call in sets of workbooks. Look at teaching and learning diagnostically. Look at display. Analyse the data systematically and relentlessly but value all that is immeasurable about the school: purpose, diligence, communication, pride, the sense of mission, the sense of community and collegiality, ethos, tone, rigour, persistence, clarity, the look and feel of the school and expectations. These are the things that make ordinary schools extraordinary.

My task was to reinvigorate the school. It needed a shot in the arm, an injection of warmth and positivity. The school had received a monitoring visit from Her Majesty's Inspectorate just a month before my arrival. I recall the inspectors gravely passing on the dismal comments of students about their school – and these were the students who had been handpicked to meet the inspectors. It's imperative that children are proud of their school: it should be the best school in the world as far as they're concerned. So I came in and talked about the school in a manner it wasn't yet: a good school, where teachers deliver engaging lessons and happy young people acquire the skills required for future success. In doing so I lifted the expectations of the school. Anyone unsure of the power of expectation should remember the last time they walked onto a stationary escalator, expecting it to be moving. Even when you can see that an escalator is off you intuitively walk differently, only to correct yourself after a few steps. My job in the summer term of 2008 was to correct the gait of students and staff at Burlington Danes. The heavy trudge of the staff had to be turned into a spritely bounce, while the discordant pounding of students' feet on the long, narrow corridors had to be channelled into a calm, quick, stride.

Step by step, progress was made.

Term began with a staff meeting in which I shared my impression of the school's strengths and weaknesses. The positives were the fantastic facilities and a core of talented and dedicated staff. This last point sounds like an expedient one, but I really meant it. In the same way that the students were underachieving I could tell that the majority of teachers were eager to do well and would flourish given half a chance. The list of weaknesses that I shared with teachers on that April morning was longer. I was the third head in three years, and there was no sense of unity amongst the staff, exemplified by a pervasive blame culture. There were dozens of supply teachers, teachers on short-term contracts and weak teachers. Line management systems were confusing, and perhaps most damaging of all: expectations of students were woefully low. I told staff that we would double the number of students gaining five or more decent GCSEs within two years, leapfrogging the national average on the way. I shared my simple mantra that teachers should plan, teach and mark.

Three points for a new headteacher to get across in the first staff meeting

I was asked in my Ark interview what three things I would say to staff in my first staff meeting. My responses were:

1. Teaching and Learning is the most important activity. Teachers are the most important resource. Everything I do, we do, we must measure against the impact on our classroom practice. I will see everyone teach. I will meet with every employee.

2. Sort out student behaviour: it must be conducive for learning. Renegotiate the behaviour management policy.

3. I am unable to do this alone; it is a collective effort: on the corridors, playgrounds and in the classroom. Only together can we make a difference.

It might not have been the rousing call to arms of a Hollywood movie, but it struck a chord. I was crystal clear when I reassured the teachers that I knew what an outstanding school was like, and I knew how to make Burlington Danes an outstanding school. I assured everyone – staff, students, visitors – that I was here to stay. Stability matters. One thing you learn in teaching is that most people want to be led. There's nothing more discombobulating for a child than the squabble for supremacy in a classroom where the teacher is struggling to assert herself. Equally, in the staff room people want to know where they stand, and they crave the stability provided by a confident leader. Confidence is critical as a head teacher, and I did all I could to spread this confidence with my jaded new colleagues. I was reading a *Sunday Times* article about the former England manager Fabio Capello in which someone described him thus: 'When I had my first meeting with him, it was like he had walked in with a bag of confidence, opened it and flooded the room with it.' That was my job in the summer of 2008.

In those early days I deliberately ignored all the peripheral stuff and focused on the urgent task at hand: the challenge of dragging this school out of its prolonged malaise. There are countless decisions that have to be made when you lead a complex organisation, but I tried to focus on those that resonated with our core mission. Nothing is more fundamental in a school than the quality of lessons being delivered in classrooms so I asked the heads of department to collect lesson plans from their team for the week ahead on the Friday of each week. These lesson plans were submitted to me for checking. I was looking for challenging, engaging lessons which stretched and supported all students. This raised the profile of teaching and learning and ensured that in those opening weeks teachers were planning carefully. It also meant that senior staff could check that our message of high expectations was influencing classroom practice. We checked that tasks were being differentiated for higher and lower ability students; we checked that lessons gave students a chance to hit and exceed their target grades; we checked that homework consolidated the foundations laid in class.

Also on that first day I held assemblies with all students, year group by year group. I had been warned against doing this, with some staff saying that the children would be openly defiant, but the reality was much different. They filed in and listened to my message, which again was one of high expectations: this is where we're heading; this is how we're going to get there; this is what I need you to do to help us. At the end of the assembly 15-20 students from each year group were called to the front and sent home with a letter saying that they shouldn't return to school without their parents. These were students who my senior team had identified as persistently causing disruption. These students duly returned over the following days with their parents in tow, and my meetings with them filled my diary during that first week and enabled me to share my expectations with parents. I've had four children – my youngest is currently doing his A levels – plus three step-children, so I know that parents want the best for their kids. The challenge for a head is convincing parents that you share this desire and that if they trust you and the school, you'll be able to make good on the deal. We permanently excluded one student who showed no signs of being able to adapt to the new way of doing things, but the other 72 returned with our full support and we've not had to repeat this exercise since.

Above all, I needed the students to realise that things were different from now, and a few environmental changes would have conveyed this message from the moment they arrived on that spring morning. The previous year I attended a headteachers' conference in Amsterdam and I found myself impressed by some all-weather table tennis tables that I saw in a cramped playground there. The tables were hugely popular at Sacred Heart so during the Easter break I had ten of them installed in the playground at Burlington Danes. I can't think of a better sport than table tennis for young people to play at break. It's incredibly accessible, you make rapid progress, it doesn't take too much space and once the tables are in place it doesn't require much equipment. My PA and I sold balls and bats at cost price and within days friendly crowds were gathering around the tables every break and lunch, as well as before and after school. Those same tables are still standing six years later and we've developed quite a reputation for our ping pong prowess: the Mayor of London, Boris Johnson even popped in for a game of 'whiff whaff' a couple of years ago.

A few further physical changes reinforced the message that things were different. Door stops from a £1 shop in Shepherds Bush were distributed one morning, encouraging staff to keep their doors open while they were teaching – a policy I've always adopted with my own office too. The door stops were also useful on the corridors; our main building was listed due to its architectural significance as a 1930s art deco structure, but this left us with heavy iron doors forever swinging in students' faces. It's only a small thing, but when you've got 1,000 young people dashing between lessons six times a day it makes sense to ease their passage. Pot plants and hanging baskets were installed around the site, while a few hundred metres of carpet made the corridors feel more homely. An eye for detail is so important.

The opening months

First term, day one:

- Met staff; school closed to pupils
- Set out the vision and engaged with staff, but also set out clear and expected behaviour: dress code, planning, display, attendance, staff briefing, staff bulletins, new systems
- Allocated temporary SLT roles, shared my expectation of collegiality

Day two

- Saw all pupils throughout the day in assemblies
- Set out expectations, challenged misbehaviour

- Explained the new way of doing things, shared my high expectations and emphasised the benefits: improved results, calmer classrooms, table-tennis in the playground
- Sent targeted students home with a letter informing them not to return without their parents

Day three

- On corridors, smiling, positive
- Sold table tennis bats and balls
- Met with parents of targeted students
- New behaviour policy in place: Behaviour Officer Tony Rumble roaming the corridors

First half-term

- Chose a new uniform with a blazer and school bag
- Installed a tannoy system so that I could speak to the whole school at once. I used it sparingly: it should always feel like something of an event.
- Got rid of supply teachers; existing teachers took up the slack (many were under-contracted hours)

Second half term

- All parents received the new blazer for free, but they had to come to school to collect their voucher. I used this as a chance to talk to all parents, and to tell them about exams, new class groups, rank orders *etc*
- SLT weekend away, new SLT roles and responsibilities in place

September 2008

- Waited in anticipation as pupils lined up in new class groups. Would they all have blazers and bags? Sent about 20 children home but most did. Phew!
- Opened door to my office for students and staff

Leaders are always under the spotlight, and this was especially true when I arrived at Burlington Danes. I was an outsider, and teachers at Burlington Danes had seen heads come and go. Authenticity is paramount as a leader. You have to be comfortable in your shoes and you need to be able to speak to parents, teachers and students with absolute confidence and clarity. This conviction is impossible to fake. Organisations such as Future Leaders and the National College of School Leadership do a great job of helping aspirant school leaders develop the competencies of headship, but so much of school leadership is about character. Children can spot a fake in a flash. This leaves headteachers with no choice but to be themselves, I guess Churchill meant something like this when he said, "I have nothing to offer but blood, toil, tears and sweat." This is where experience comes in handy; I had led a department and had delivered on almost every aspect of school leadership, from writing a timetable to recruiting staff. I had led an outstanding school. Such experience gave me the confidence to lead from the front at Burlington Danes. The conversation that I had most often in those early days involved reassuring teachers, middle leaders and senior leaders that I knew the ingredients of an outstanding school and I knew exactly how to turn Burlington Danes into one.

During these early days as a leader, while the spotlight still shines bright, it's important to allow people to see your character and to gain a sense of your passion and motives. Ark recently launched a series of leadership lectures, with the first one delivered by the highly impressive former Foreign Secretary David Miliband. He championed the importance of sharing your passion and motivation, revealing the drive that burns within, rather than hoping that because you're a progressive politician, or because you've chosen to work in a challenging school, people will know and understand your motives. I tell my students that they deserve the best, that they should be every bit as successful as the private school students who tread the pristine turf on the playing fields next to our school, and I tell them that my desire for them to succeed keeps me up at night. I've worked with teachers and school leaders who try to leave their character at home each morning but more often than not I think this leads to an aloof and detached professional manner, at odds with the buzzing human vitality of a modern school.

Why be a headteacher?

According to a National College for School Leadership (NCSL) 2010 study, 'What's good about leading schools in challenging circumstances':

'...headteachers display professional characteristics focused on personal conviction and respect for others, tenacity in advocacy for young people and resilience in standing by them. These are tempered by a degree of personal humility. They combine high levels of emotional intelligence and a confidence in risk taking with a passion for the development of the pupils, for the school and for the role of headteacher.'

I cannot put it any better myself.

1. As a head, you can shape the future for more than 1,000 children: it is the ultimate position in education. In my view you need vision, drive, passion, commitment and an eye for detail. You need emotional intelligence to read the subtext of others and to be a 'people person' *ie* interested in the lives, motivation and hopes of others. Quality relationships are key to retaining and developing your staff. A 60-hour week is normal and you have to be able to shoulder the overall accountability. Yet you can make such a hugely significant difference to young people's lives. You have to possess egalitarian instincts, a respect for individuals and a profound concern for their needs. A deep belief that all can succeed whatever their background or circumstances is essential.

2. It is an opportunity to shape a school in your way: your ideas, your vision and your values put into action: I find that deeply satisfying. There is a lot of talk at present about the 'moral purpose' of leadership, as if outstanding leadership can have anything but moral purpose. I went into teaching because I loved English and wanted to share my enjoyment of literature with young people: this love and sense of purpose has never left me though I rarely teach young people anymore; it is at the root of all I believe and grounds me in the fact that it is in the classroom where the school succeeds or fails. This is the moral purpose: that it is the classroom where leaders must focus: all else is peripheral.

3. It is the ultimate test of professional credibility. True, in Hargreaves and Fullan's *Professional Capital* they say: 'When the classroom door is closed, the teacher will always remain in charge. Where students are concerned, the teacher will always be more powerful than the principal, the president or the prime minister. Successful and sustainable improvement can therefore never be done to or even for teachers. It can only ever be achieved by and with them' (2012, p. 45) ... but teachers rely on headteachers to provide the right environment in which to deliver quality lessons: behaviour, community, tone, ethos.

4. It is autonomous: you set the rules, you determine your working day. I love the fact that there is no single 'style'. Setting the pace, leading by example, building links with outside interests, meeting parents, teaching classes, creating teams and devolving responsibility: these are the levers at a headteacher's disposal and a savvy leader uses them all in good measure.

Michael Fullan states: 'Judge the quality of leadership in a headteacher by the leadership s/he develops in others'. This is so right – and the best leadership is that of the teacher in front of a class.

Schools have a vitality of their own and they stir into life each morning from the moment the caretaker unlocks the padlock on the front gate to the first strike of the bell at 8.30am. Jumpy, caffeinated teachers gather round photocopiers, site staff set out chairs for assembly and a handful of eager students (normally the same ones every day) drift through the gates before finding solace in a quiet corner of the school. Between 7.30am and 8.30am 1,000 children will have strolled through our gates – nonchalantly at first, then with increasing pace as the bell approaches and the threat of detention looms. Each one of these young people brings with them a heady mix of hopes, dreams, troubles and anxieties. That's the joy of working in a school; the jumble of energy we encounter each day. I love also their limitless ambition: the student who can barely write wanting to be a lawyer or medic; the student who strives to be a professional footballer or winner of a TV talent show. Throw adolescence into the mix, add a sprinkling of social strife and you gain a sense of the challenge schools face in channelling this energy into something purposeful and harmonious. I have the utmost respect for teachers in all types of school – I know that affluent youngsters need every bit as much love, care and attention as anyone else – but having worked in tough London neighbourhoods for nearly 40 years I'm acutely aware of the tension that some of our students carry with them when they leave home in the morning.

Perhaps the trickiest challenge I faced when arriving at Burlington Danes was gaining the support of my new SLT (strategic leadership team). I had received mixed reviews about the quality of the leadership team, but my own impression of them was positive. One by one most of them had visited me at Sacred Heart so I was beginning to form my own judgement. Once at Burlington Danes I could see that they all had a decent presence in front of the students, which is a prerequisite for senior leadership in a school. It was a stroke of luck that I inherited a competent team because with my husband taking the helm at Sacred Heart there was no chance that I could plunder my previous team! It's tempting for any leader to bring trusted allies with them into a new role but as it turned out I'm glad my hands were tied, and in any case it's an important principle that I work and develop talent from within the organisation, rather than recruit from outside. I have a large SLT of 12 people in total, all of whom have been promoted from within.

The one ally that I did appoint was my senior vice principal Michael Ribton. I didn't know Michael before but he was an established deputy head at Holland Park School and his CV indicated that he could be the strategist I was after. So after a few interviews and conversations, Michael was offered the role of my 'right hand man'. He joined me for my first ever meeting with staff before the start of that spring term, and he's been at my side since. We're both at school from soon after six each morning, talking shop over our Weetabix and porridge. He's a man of great intelligence, insight and humour, with the guts to challenge me and others when he disagrees with something. As the years have progressed, and other commitments have pulled at my time, Michael's become increasingly visible and vital to leading the academy. It proved to be an astute appointment. I also brought in a new PA, Debbie, who continues to be a crucial support to me six years later. Like Michael, Debbie had no vested interest in the *status quo* so her loyalty was to me, and no-one else. A good PA is vital for any leader. You need to be able to trust them so that they can become your confidante with whom you can think aloud, offload your frustrations and sound out your ideas. They're also faced with the task of managing your diary, so it's vital that they understand your priorities. I was well supported by Ark in those early days. As a leader it's difficult to be an expert in law and HR, so it's vital to surround yourself with good sources of advice and information.

We were moving in the right direction from the start: smiles started returning to the faces of staff and we held exams for every subject in every year group, which sent out a clear message that we were in the business of equipping young people to excel in exams. Data is so critically important: assessment can drive up standards and generate the self-awareness of understanding where you are and how to get to the next level. Formal exams for all students also had a calming effect, and showed pupils the important lesson that hard work yields success. No-one who visits Burlington Danes can accuse us of being an exam factory: we're a vibrant, warm community where a plethora of talents are celebrated, but passing exams is the bread and butter of school life and we set about drilling students to take exams seriously. Filing into the exam hall in silence, using no other colour pen but black, calculating how many minutes you should allocate to each available question: these habits continue to serve our students well and we cultivated them from the start.

My response to our weekly newsletter interview '54321'

5 people you would love to have round for dinner:

Billie Holliday – she could sing for us as well

Stephen Fry – for his witty conversation and he would have us all laughing

Nelson Mandela – a freedom fighter who believed in using peace not violence

George Clooney – just for the fun of his Hollywood gossip and his good looks of course

Queen Elizabeth I – a powerful and single-minded women in an age when women had few rights

4 books and films you will never forget

Hamlet – I love Shakespeare and this is my favourite play

Wuthering Heights – a book with passion and drama set in the bleakest of landscapes

Snow White and the seven dwarfs – the first film I watched at the cinema

The Exorcist – this film gave me sleepless nights for about a week when I first saw it

3 foods you would have for your last meal

Panfried scallops and prawns – I love seafood

Chicken Madras – you can't beat a curry

Strawberries and cream

2 countries you would love to visit

India – a land with so much to see and so much culture and history

Tibet – I have wanted to go here since I read a book called 'Seven Years in Tibet'. It seems so mysterious and hidden

1 day you will always remember

Teaching my first lesson at a school in Peckham as a young teacher. I faced a class of Year 9s none of whom had a pen or the slightest interest in having an English lesson. How things have changed!

Behind closed doors we had conversations with teachers who were underperforming. Evidence from lesson observations, along with our own analysis, suggested almost a third of the teachers weren't up to scratch. We encouraged a handful of teachers to find work elsewhere, and by and large they got the message. At the same time that we tackled our underperforming students, and staff I took swift action to retain our best teachers. A brilliant PE teacher and a gifted young English teacher had received job offers from other schools, so I spent time convincing them of my confidence in transforming BDA, and reassuring them of the part they were to play on the journey. Both of these teachers went on to become key members of staff; one of them advancing to assistant principal having served as head of year from Year 7 through to Year 11, and the other one taking the lead of a thriving English department. Getting staff onside is probably my greatest strength. Confident people can come across as arrogant or aloof, but my self-confidence is of the inclusive sort: 'stick with me and you will thrive'. They normally do.

Conversations with under-performing teachers

In my first week at BDA, I asked the SLT (except for Michael, as he joined the school with me) to list those who they thought were inadequate teachers. Twenty-three out of 65 or so teachers were listed. A meeting was held with each member of staff on the list, either with Michael or myself – or both of us. The conversation would go like this:

"I am sorry but you have been identified by the leadership team as inadequate."

"What do you mean? I am not. You haven't seen me teach!"

"No, you're right, I haven't and you are correct to infer that I should make my own mind up on this issue. I will see you teach, look at your lesson planning, review student workbooks and look at your marking and markbooks."

As the conversation continued the member of staff slowly began to absorb the reality of the situation. Twenty-one of the staff we had identified resigned and left that same year, and the remaining two left the following year. The academy was a challenging place, I told myself, to calm my moral qualms about passing on underperforming staff – perhaps they could succeed in a smaller, more orderly school?

On reflection, teachers do have to know the minimum responsibilities of the post: the required competencies and standards and to whom they are accountable. These conversations are an example of my direct style of management. When you are direct you give people a chance to make the right decision about their career.

Challenging conversations are part of a headteacher's daily diet; I try to be direct, open, frank and honest. I do not judge the whole person, but describe their behaviour and performance. An evidence base is essential, and it is most important to be assertive. Teachers are the most valuable resource a school has. But always, always put the pupil first and foremost.

There were some difficult moments too as we raised the bar of expectation throughout the school. One of my assistant heads compiled a revision guide for Year 11 students ahead of their summer exams, but the formatting was woeful, with each subject using a different font and page layout. So we binned the boxes of booklets and I asked my senior deputy to start afresh. My philosophy, as always, is putting out the best and not accepting sub-standard. A new head has plenty of currency in bringing about change and it's important to spend it well, especially at the beginning. You're aided by the fact that most teachers have chosen teaching because they care about children and want them to do well, so there's a common purpose that you can leverage. Then you've got the fact that most people crave a stable, purposeful workplace, and as you're at the helm it's probably in their interest to at least comply, but more likely be positively supportive. The restrictive stranglehold of union militancy was already loosening which gave me a bit more wiggle room with staff, so the only barriers we faced were the bad habits, low morale and low expectations that had formed during the years of prolonged underachievement. None of these barriers were insurmountable. It's not as if I was taking over a football team bottom of the premier league, with 19 other teams desperate to keep you there, or a failing business where rapacious rivals would gladly watch you fold. Everyone wanted us to flourish; we just had to get everyone pulling in the same direction.

I learnt a lot about leadership in those early days of re-energising a flagging organisation. People are wary of change, and leaders are wary of unleashing reform, but I learnt for myself that if an organisation needs to be transformed then there's no place for timidity, you should think your plans through and then execute them, with all your energy. I learnt to take calculated risks, to be resilient and to have high expectations of those around me; most people want to be successful and are capable of being so. I was careful to judge people for myself, and I prepared thoroughly for the difficult conversations that I had to have. I was wholly proactive in those early weeks, with a clear plan for each day and each hour. I applied common sense, and trusted my judgement. My days at school felt like crisis management, and there were not enough minutes in the day to deal with all the issues that emerged. This is where it's vital to delegate, and to fight tooth and nail for the breathing space to think strategically; to plan ahead for a better future rather than be battered by the needs of the present. So each evening I would go home, consult my journal and re-plan for the following day. I rehearsed key conversations, cast aside issues that didn't really matter and focused solely on the fundamental challenge of creating an environment conducive to fertile teaching and rich learning. Above all, I reassured myself that everyone – pupils, parents, teachers, Ark, governors – wanted the school to be a success. All I had to do was pull the right levers.

Napoleon is said to have remarked that "a leader is a dealer in hope" and it did feel in those early days that my biggest challenge was lifting the spirits of a demoralised organisation. As an English teacher I love the line that became famous during President Obama's election victory in 2008: 'You campaign in poetry but you govern in prose'. It was a mixture of hope-filled poetry and mundane prose in those early days. The poetry came from the encouragement and praise I heaped on staff and students, both collectively and in the privacy of my office. The prose came from the multitude of small changes we made to the daily rhythms of school life. I insisted that female staff were referred to not as 'miss' but as 'madam' – the proper equivalent of 'sir'. Manners matter – it's not old-fashioned to hold doors open and to show special courtesy to older people. Rewards were offered to teachers with 100% attendance throughout the term, we would publicise residual marks for teachers of key year groups, showing how students performed across all their classes. This meant that if they did better in their English class than in their other classes, the English teacher would gain a positive residual. We tweaked the uniform, bringing in tartan skirts for girls, which I've always liked. Heads of faculty were appointed (enabling me to promote and retain key staff) and the convoluted small school structure was replaced with a more traditional year group arrangement. Classes would be set by ability and every year group would be examined at regular points throughout the year, with their results publicly displayed as rank orders. Some of it was drastic, but in my view we weren't tweaking around the edges, we were reinforcing the new way of doing things: high expectations, rigor, professionalism, pride.

The Transformation Agenda in a nutshell

On my arrival, I found:

- poor behaviour
- high rates of exclusion
- high staff absence rates

- lack of consistency
- haphazard/non-existent line management; the small school model
- poor attendance rates
- demoralised staff
- systems which suited staff, not students or parents *eg* early closure every Wednesday
- uncared for environment
- poor/unsatisfactory teaching
- poor results
- unmotivated and 'sad' students

The four key themes

1. Ethos and tone setting

- Emphasis on the Christian values of the academy/charities/community
- Two assemblies every day with an emphasis on SLT assemblies reflecting a weekly theme
- Staff briefing every day, including a staff-led 'reflection'
- Areas of the building decorated and smartened – bar football/table tennis/student photographs
- Weekly staff bulletin highlights good practice and gives guidance on aspects of teaching to colleagues
- Comprehensive staff handbook as part of staff induction
- Student leadership scheme established

2. Collegiality and consistency

- New uniform
- Form period at end of day
- Line-up every morning
- Newly devised templates *eg* for policies, observation, schemes of work *etc* in a 'house style' – even a decision on the BDA 'font' (Century Gothic)
- Celebration of achievement in new bi-annual magazine 'The Griffin'
- Raising expectations of parents: questionnaires/communication/open-door policy/ revision guides/parent newsletter
- SLT weekend residential determined Academy Improvement Plan/bonded team
- Staff events
- New Academy-Home Agreement

3. High expectations and accountability

- Dismantling of school structure and restructuring of staff
- Met with parents of seriously misbehaving students in first two weeks
- All teachers identified as underperforming seen in the first month
- Programme of scheduled observation/workbook reviews/scheme of work reviews
- Newly devised performance management with some value-added common targets
- All performance of students and staff data driven
- All classes set by ability
- Published rank orders of effort and achievement
- Outstanding teachers identified
- Recruitment of quality staff in key positions, especially English and science
- Recruitment of subject specialists and pruning of temporary and supply staff along with peripheral positions *eg* 'learning mentors' and 'behaviour consultants'
- New behaviour management policy

4. Plan, teach, mark

- Short-term: all staff to submit lesson plans to heads of faculty in a newly devised format one week in advance
- Data analysed at regular six-week intervals
- Subject self-evaluation
- Strategic emphasis primarily on learning and not behaviour
- Excellent Teacher Scheme/Lead Teacher appointments initiated
- Raising achievement programmes
- Observation: Learning Walks and SLT observation
- Assessment/rank order
- Imparting a heightened sense of the accountability of classroom teacher

So it was the combination of poetry and prose which enabled us to stop the rot. Abraham Lincoln once said that, "He who moulds public sentiment goes deeper than he who enacts statutes or pronounces decisions", but we worked on both simultaneously. And it's impossible to separate the two: you need the tangible changes to make a positive difference, which in turn lifts morale. Jim Collins, author of the 2001 book *Good to Great*, writes powerfully on this, arguing that collective success is the most powerful way of getting colleagues on side. It reminds me of that line 'nothing succeeds like success'. We gained some early wins in the summer of 2008. Teachers revelled in their new sense of purpose, students were motivated by the profile we had given to their success in the classroom, and before long it felt like we had unity at Burlington Danes. In his wonderful book *The Learning Game,* Jonathan Smith reflects on a career in teaching by remarking 'if the head, the staff and the pupils all feel that they are, broadly speaking, in the same boat, you are in a happy school' (p. 208). So despite all the tangible successes of that first term, perhaps the poetry resonated more powerfully than the prose. We were becoming a happy, harmonious school, and with your staff, students and parents behind you, there's not much that can get in your way as a head. I think Abraham Lincoln had something similar in mind when he said, "With public sentiment nothing can fail, without it nothing can succeed".

Leading from the front in those early days involved taking the stage, front and centre, to reinvigorate the school. I had to be professional, decisive, boundlessly optimistic and energetic, while also being calm, authoritative and brutally honest about the moribund state the school was in. This is the yin and yang of school leadership: the iron first in the velvet glove. A headteacher in a failing school has to be the bravest of the brave, visibly leading the charge, flying the flag for your SLT and your teachers to follow. Failing schools can't be cajoled back to life, they have to be pummelled into shape. Throughout this transformative process the leader is exposed, open to criticism, ridicule and blame. You have to be completely professional, never forgetting that the job of the head is to role model the job of the head, treating your teachers as if they will one day be leading a school.

This chapter in a tweet: Headteachers must show the confidence to set the agenda and invigorate the school. This requires visibility, authenticity and resolve.

Lesson 2:
Be courageous –
have high expectations of all

'To build a better world we need to replace
the patchwork of lucky breaks and arbitrary
advantages that today determines success – the
fortunate birthdates and the happy accidents
of history – with a society that provides
opportunity for all.'

All leaders would claim to have high expectations. The challenge is to constantly reinforce these expectations in your daily contact with stakeholders, which in my case comprise of students, parents, teachers and senior leaders. Transforming schools in tough neighbourhoods starts with the belief that children from such backgrounds really can succeed – a belief that is written into Ark's genetic code like the letters that run through a stick of rock. Such expectations were lacking at Burlington Danes in 2008. Few teachers there could remember the school being a good school, and the students had become accustomed to the fug of anger and frustration which permeated the corridors. Teachers had come to accept that 'these kids' would always struggle to learn, and the best you could hope to do was to contain their bad behaviour. For their part, the students had come to accept that teachers would come and go and that the culture of the street would inevitably infiltrate the culture of the corridors. These low expectations had to be shattered from the start and challenged every day. My high expectations were based on the success I had seen at Sacred Heart. I had seen for myself that students from the toughest of backgrounds can be successful if the conditions are right, and I was convinced that I could transport these conditions to Burlington Danes. Ultimately, my optimism was based on what Harvard psychologist Carol Dweck calls 'the growth mindset' (2006): the belief that intelligence is not fixed and, consequently, that every child has the potential to flourish.

Great expectations

Pupils respond to the expectations that you have of them. If you really believe something will happen then you increase the probability that it will!

This is exemplified by Rosenthal and Jacobson's *Pygmalion in the Classroom*. In 1968, Robert Rosenthal, a Harvard professor, and Leonore Jacobson, an Elementary School principal, borrowed the term 'Pygmalion effect' from George Bernard Shaw's play to describe an experiment that they carried out in an elementary school, which the authors called Oak School, to test the hypothesis that in any given classroom there is a correlation between teachers' expectations and pupils' achievement.

In the experiment, Rosenthal and Jacobson gave an intelligence test to all of the pupils at the beginning of the school year. After the test had been completed they randomly selected 20% of the pupils, without any reference to their test results, and reported to the teachers that these particular pupils were showing 'unusual potential for intellectual growth' and could be expected to 'bloom' in their academic performance by the end of the year. Eight months later, at the end of the academic year, they came back and re-tested all the pupils. Those that they had labelled as 'ready to bloom children' showed significantly greater increase in the new tests than the other children who were not singled out for the teachers' attention.

Even before teachers have seen a pupil deal with academic tasks in the classroom they are likely to have some expectation for their behaviour. If they are to teach a 'lower group' they will have different expectations than if they are to teach a 'fast group'. If they believe that children from working class or specific ethnic backgrounds are less interested in progressing academically than others then, once again, they will have different expectations.

It goes to show that teacher's expectations matter and that pupil labelling is founded on quicksand, reinforcing existing class, ethnic and gender inequalities by establishing a classroom climate in which some pupils are systematically encouraged to succeed whereas others are systematically disencouraged. Conversely, a change in teachers' expectations can lead to an improvement in intellectual performance from those who are usually expected to achieve the least.

Believe and it can happen! Or as Shaw wrote it: 'You see, really and truly, apart from the things anyone can pick up, the difference between a lady and a flower girl is not how she behaves, but how she's treated. I shall always be a flower girl to Professor Higgins, because he always treats me as a flower girl, and always will; but I know I can be a lady to you, because you always treat me as a lady, and always will'.

In *The Spirit Level*, a recent study of the impact of income inequality, Wilkinson and Pickett suggest how selfish behaviours can emerge in young people trying to cope with a stressful upbringing: 'the emotional make-up which prepares you to live in a society in which you have to fend for yourself, watch your back and fight for everything you can get, is very different from what is needed if you grow up in a society in which you depend on empathy, reciprocity and co-operation' (2010, p. 211). Such claims are echoed by Annette Lareau in her book *Unequal Childhoods*: 'for working class and poor families, the cultural logic of child rearing at home is out of synch with the standards of institutions' (p. 3). She cites the all too familiar example of parents supporting their offspring in breaking school norms: 'Billy Yanelli's parents were proud of him when he beat up another boy on the playground, even though Billy was then suspended from school' (2003, p. 6). In *Bowling Alone*, Robert Putnam laments the decline of social capital: 'social capital refers to connections among individuals – social networks and the norms of reciprocity and trustworthiness that arise from them' (2000, p. 18). Co-operation, reciprocity, trust: these are the exact ingredients required for a social institution such as a school to function. If young people arrive through our gates without these characteristics then the school must work even harder to establish order and purpose.

In his 2012 book *How Children Succeed*, Paul Tough applies such findings to the world of education:

> We know from the neuroscientists and the psychologists that students growing up in these [low income] homes are more likely to have high ACE [Adverse Childhood Experience] scores and less likely to have the kinds of secure attachment relationships with caregivers that buffer the effects of stress and trauma; this in turn means they likely have below-average executive-function skills and difficulty handling stressful situations. In the classroom they are hampered by poor concentration, impaired social skills, an inability to sit still and follow directions, and what teachers perceive as misbehaviour (p. 192).

As a mother I know that the development of *all* children is dependent on a complex mix of physical and emotional stimuli, and I get frustrated with the idea that middle class children are born onto a conveyer belt leading to success and fulfilment. But while admitting the vulnerability of all young people, Paul Tough helps to reveal the lengths that teachers and schools in poor areas must go even to create conditions conducive for learning. At Burlington Danes we invest huge energy in creating a calm, orderly, positive environment, where hard work leads to recognition and pride. All teachers, whichever the school, must plant and nurture delicate seeds, but in some schools these seeds are scattered on fertile ground, and a bountiful harvest is the default and most likely outcome, barring some kind of negative intervention. In the schools that I know best the environmental factors create a very different default outcome. Our seeds have fallen on rocky ground. The land is parched and the wind can be fierce, but with intensive care and perseverance we can still yield a decent crop.

In practice, 'high expectations' means securing the best possible outcomes for all students through relentless personalised support. A few years ago I might have agreed that intervention should be targeted on those failing to meet benchmark standards. As we've evolved we've cast our net wider and I'm now proud to say that all students at Burlington Danes receive intervention to enable them to meet personalised targets, irrespective of national norms and expectations. Intervention cuts to the heart of the mission of running a school in a challenging area for it involves proactively meddling with the life chances dictated by accident of birth. Malcolm Gladwell puts it like this: 'To build a better world we need to replace the patchwork of lucky breaks and arbitrary advantages that today determines success – the fortunate birthdates and the happy accidents of history – with a society that provides opportunity for all' (2009, p. 268).

I was reminded of the power of fortune just a few weeks ago when we analysed the number of September and October birthdays in our top two sets in Year 7 compared to the number of September and October birthdays in our bottom two sets in Year 7. A completely even spread of birthdates would suggest that approximately 16% of students would be born in any two-month period. We found that our top two sets contained 24% September-October birthdays whereas our bottom two sets contained 8%. This suggests that age, rather than ability, has a significant impact on the sets that students find themselves in and reminds us of the need to provide frequent opportunities for growth and progression throughout the 'ability' range. It's also a reminder of the arbitrary nature of some of the labels that we apply to students. Take this passage from Paul Tough's *How Children Succeed*:

When white students at Princeton were told before trying a ten-hole mini golf course that it was a test of natural ability in sports (which they feared they didn't possess), they scored four strokes worse than a similar group of white students who were told it was a test of their ability to think strategically (which they were confident they did possess). For black students, the effect was opposite: when they were told the mini golf course was a test of their strategic intelligence, their scores were four strokes worse (p. 96).

These findings shatter the illusion that intelligence (or sporting prowess) is fixed, and also remind us of the importance of using a range of measures and tests to measure student progress, rather than rely on one-off, all-or nothing assessments.

The phrase 'growth mindset' has become something of a buzzword in education circles of late and rightly so. It's the opposite of the fixed view of intelligence: that some people have it and others don't. The growth mindset focuses instead on practice and opportunity, suggesting that everyone can succeed given the right conditions. In his recent book *Bounce: The Myth of Talent and the Power of Practice*, the journalist and former Olympian Matthew Syed provides a devastating critique of the talent view of expertise: 'world-class performance comes by striving for a target just out of reach, but with a vivid awareness of how the gap might be breached. Over time, through constant repetition and deep concentration, the gap will disappear, only for a new target to be created, just out of reach once again' (2010). For Syed, focused engagement is critical. Someone might drive a car for ten years without necessarily becoming a better driver, he says, if that person hasn't focused on improving and received feedback and tuition to help him do so. The implications of this growth mindset are immense for schools. Syed asks his readers to 'Think of the thousands of potential Wimbledon champions who have never been fortunate enough to own a tennis racket or receive specialized coaching'. For those of us working in challenging schools the tragedy cuts a little deeper than the absence of working class children at the all-England club. In order to encourage practice and the focused development of talent, Syed urges schools to praise effort rather than ability: 'intelligence-based praise orientates its receivers towards the fixed mindset; it suggests to them that intelligence is of primary importance rather than the effort through which intelligence can be transformed; and it teaches them to pursue easy challenges at the expense of real learning'.

Exemplifying 'high expectations' of students

What do high expectations really look like?

Outstanding teachers with high expectations:

- have a focus on learning, not behaviour
- have high and challenging standards of learning
- understand precisely the ability level of their students
- continually assess, throughout the lesson, their students' learning to ensure that teaching objectives are being met
- have structured, collaborative group work which improves students' communication and dialogue and increases students' motivation
- mark work at least every two weeks with clear guidance on how to improve it
- have classes with workbooks that are neatly presented, organised, are made up of completed tasks and demonstrate a range of taught, differentiated activities. Books are free of graffiti/doodles; students are proud of their work.
- promote self-control and positive behaviour; independence and a sensitivity to others; social values and attitudes; attendance, punctuality and appropriate dress (partly by modelling it themselves)
- use routines and procedures so students are aware of what to expect and how to behave without having to be told
- develop students' higher order thinking skills through the use of questioning by the teacher
- often plan outstanding lessons
- have a range of activities to develop critical thinking
- utilise a range of different styles of learning allowing students to the opportunity to exceed target grades
- set tasks that extend beyond the classroom and that encourage independence

Syed's theories resonate with those espoused by Malcolm Gladwell in his book *Outliers: The Story of Success*. In this book he proposes 'the 10,000 hour rule': the notion that it takes 10,000 hours of practice to develop expertise in a particular area. He supports this with examples of The

Beatles, Bill Gates and Ice Hockey players: 'We all know that successful people come from hardy seeds, but do we know enough about the sunlight that warmed them, the soil in which they put down the roots, and the rabbits and lumberjacks they were lucky enough to avoid?' (p. 20). Like Syed, Gladwell applies his theories to schools, arguing that effort and persistence are the key determinants of success. This is especially true for maths, according to Gladwell, claiming a direct correlation between countries who value effort and hard work and countries where children excel at mathematics: Singapore, South Korea, China, Hong Kong and Japan.

It's difficult to think that any teacher would disagree with the growth mindset – it defeats the object of teaching to assume that talent is purely natural – but in challenging schools it's an absolute prerequisite, because we're working with young people who often haven't had a chance to develop their potential talents. But it's one thing saying that as teachers and as a school we're committed to the growth mindset of development, and another thing to embed this viewpoint in the daily workings of the school.

Teaching is an intensely human endeavour, and I've noticed on many occasions in my career that teachers impose their own impressions and expectations on young people, for better or worse. A recent story that a teacher shared in our staff briefing captures the power of expectation, and it's a lesson that anyone involved in schools would be wise to recall.

The Story of the Boatman

Once there was a man leaving his village for the other side down the long river. The boat journey is slow and lengthy, so he struck a conversation with the boatman.

He asked, "What are the people like at the far side of the river?"

The boatman asked, "What are the people like on the side you came from?"

The man replied, "Oh, they're mean, good for nothing, unfriendly and generally bad people. Some of the worst people I've ever met. I'm really very glad I'm leaving them for the far side!"

The boatman paused and then said, "Oh, I wouldn't be so quick to celebrate if I were you. You'll find that the people on the far side are just about the same".

On another day, another man was also leaving from the same village for the other side of the river. He also struck up a conversation with the boatman.

He asked, "What are the people like at the far side of the river?"

The boatman asked in return, "What are the people like on the side you came from?"

The man replied "Oh, they're so warm, nice, friendly and generally great people. Some of the best friends I've made. I'm going to miss them so much, I may never meet such nice people anywhere else!"

The boatman paused and then said with a smile, "Oh, I wouldn't worry much if I were you. You'll find that the people on the far side are just about the same".

Of course, high expectations work both ways, and stretching students to fulfil their potential means pulling them up when they fail to meet agreed standards. And so it is that at 3.45 on a Friday afternoon, as 95% of the school population cheerfully file through the school gates onto Wood Lane, clutching the weekly newsletter as they go, the remaining 5% of the student body are being taken by their tutors into the main hall for our weekly SLT detention. These 50 students (the numbers change a little each week) will have to wait another two hours for their weekend to begin. Members of SLT and heads of year take it in turns to run the detention, with at least two people sharing the task each week. It provides a memorable end to the week. The hall is laid out as if for an exam. On each table lies four pieces of lined A4 paper and a laminated sheet with instructions for the detention. The school day finishes at 3.40pm and after a few minutes students will start to arrive. Many of them will protest their innocence, so heads of year are always on hand to explain the reason, resolve disputes, and reassure students that parents have been informed. Mr Rumble, my behaviour manager, orchestrates the seating arrangements, demonstrating an uncanny knack for group dynamics as he seeks to separate some of our more mischievous detainees. It normally takes about 15 minutes for all the students to arrive, by which point boys and girls from Year 7 to Year 11 have been sprinkled around the hall, slowly accepting their fate. Those who haven't yet started writing their lines will be prompted to do so. As the laminated sheet informs them, in two hours they're expected to fill their eight sides of lined paper with the line that best suits the reason they've been detained. A few of the more common ones are listed below (note the similar length of each line, reducing the incentive to pick the shortest one).

1. I will arrive to school fully equipped for every lesson.

2. I will take responsibility for my actions and attend detentions.
3. I will strive to avoid earning three or more demerits in a week.
4. I will not fight or show aggression to other students in school.
5. I will respect school resources and property at all times.
6. I will arrive on time for school and for lessons.
7. I will treat members of staff with respect at all times.
8. I will complete all of my work in every lesson.
9. I will not disrupt or hinder the learning of others.
10. I will attend every lesson, every day, every week.

The laminated instructions provide a good lesson in the difference between a necessary cause and a sufficient cause, something I was only taught at sixth form: 'Completing eight sides is a necessary but not sufficient condition for passing this detention. You must write eight sides and serve your two hours.' Not surprisingly we still have students gleefully informing us that they've completed eight sides half way through the detention, expecting to be released before the ink has dried on the eighth side.

During the two hours an elaborate dance is played out between the 50 students and the two senior teachers leading the detention. Just as in the classroom, the numbers are stacked against the teachers. Each week there are students looking to pounce on a momentary lapse of concentration from the teachers at the front. Nods and winks are their weapons, combined with the coughs, sniffles and giggles which occasionally break the silence of the stagnant hall. This is where senior teachers earn their stripes. You can be 99% sure that the suspiciously dry cough that suddenly emanated from the front row was a deliberate attempt to break the silence, but that 1% of doubt can be enough to stop you going over and reprimanding the coughing culprit. It's one of the hundreds of judgement calls made by teachers every day, but an experienced teacher will be able to follow either path – confront the suspect, or give a knowing look which says 'we all know it was you, and if you test me again there will be consequences' – without losing face. The third option, and one that I wouldn't recommend to inexperienced staff, is to punish the whole group by increasing the length of the detention by five minutes for any interruption caused by any student. It's a high-stakes tactic. In any case, coordination between the two teachers in charge is essential. The unwritten code of detentions states that one teacher will always remain front and centre, casting their gaze over the sea of transgressors before them. The other teacher is free to roam, checking that lines are being completed in the correct manner. Attempts to hasten the writing of eight sides are legion, and sometimes quite impressive. Students might opt for a thick nib so that the single line on the laminated sheet fills two lines on their page. Others will hold two pens in their hand at the same time, which with a steady poise and a correctly angled grip can enable two lines to be written at the once. It's a wonder we catch these students committing misdemeanours in the first place such is the guile they display in detention.

Professional pride amongst members of the SLT ensures that the two hours are always served in full. No-one wants to be seen as a soft touch. In truth, the ability to implement effective detentions is a good test of the stability of a school. There's nothing more demoralising for a teacher and damaging for a school than students misbehaving in a detention. It shows a complete lack of understanding of the purpose of a detention, and leaves the authority of the teacher in charge shot to pieces. It's vital that a detention feels like a punishment, not in an oppressive, vindictive way, but in the sense of justice being delivered, penance being paid. A detention should remind the students that in joining our community they have signed up to an agreed code of conduct, and that at this point in time they're in the small minority who have failed to deliver on this promise. A detention is the last option they have to put this right before we need to involve their parents. As such, a detention should be seen as a test to pass, rather than an ordeal to endure. In addition to these whole school detentions, teachers run their own detentions and we also have a daily homework detention. The guiding principle behind detentions, and indeed all sanctions, is that they should be delivered promptly and students should be absolutely clear why they are being punished. It's an old maxim in teaching that what matters is the certainty, not the severity, of the punishment. Students must know that if they're late, they'll serve a detention that same day. If they fail to do their homework, they'll be given a detention by their teacher for the following day.

Some readers might be surprised to hear that we issue a same-day, one-hour detention for students who are late in the morning. By 'late' we mean any time, even a few seconds, after the bell goes at 8.30am. I'm aware that this sounds rather harsh, not least given the transport problems that we regularly face in Europe's biggest city. The rationale behind the sanction is that it compels students to ensure that they are on time in the morning. We tell students that every minute counts at school, so we're betraying our own advice if we fail to sanction tardiness in the morning. There's nothing wrong with a school being strict as long as the sanctions imposed are clear, consistent and transparent. Readers will be reassured that most of our students live within walking distance of the school so don't strictly rely on public transport.

I should also reassure readers that detention is only one side of the coin when it comes to responding to poor conduct, the other side being correction. Every detention is accompanied by a conversation from the person who issued it, informing the child of why they're in detention and what they can do to avoid another one. My vice principal in charge of behaviour monitors the lists of students placed in detention to check for regular offenders. He will then liaise with heads of year to support these students, perhaps through harnessing the advice and support of the school counsellor, and often by engaging with parents. One of the themes that emerges from analysis of detention lists is that the vast majority of students placed in detention (81% in 2012) are boys, greatly surpassing our admittedly skewed gender ratio of 59% male, 41% female (there are popular all-girls schools in the area). I'm pleased to say that no other particular trends emerge from detention lists *eg* ethnicity, family income, special educational needs but the predominance of boys continues to concern me. Beyond the detention hall, high expectations must be reinforced every lesson.

A September 2014 Ofsted report ('Below the radar: low-level disruption in the country's classrooms') highlighted the problem of low-level disruption. Low-level disruption includes students being late for lessons, checking their phones, chatting in class and failing to bring the correct equipment. It can easily slip under the radar but its cumulative effect can be pernicious. Not only does it absorb precious time in the classroom and prevent the mood of focused engagement that teachers seek to cultivate, but it's energy sapping for teachers to constantly remind students to comply with basic norms. The report suggests that 'many teachers have come to accept some low-level disruption as a part of everyday life in the classroom' and that 'too many school leaders, especially in secondary

47

schools, underestimate the prevalence and negative impact of low-level disruptive behaviour' (2014, p.5). It's another reminder that school leaders have to be tuned in to the daily challenges faced by teachers. It can seem almost unfashionable to focus on behaviour as a school leader: teaching and learning, assessment, data and curriculum are all more strategic points to focus on. Yet if you can eliminate this low-level disruption, this background crackle of discord, everything that teachers and leaders do in a school on a daily basis will be more effective. Leading a school where low-level disruption is the norm is like driving with the handbrake on, and for a new headteacher it's the first issue to tackle.

The problem of persistent low-level disruption

If the curse of education is not poor teaching but satisfactory, dreary teaching then with students it is not rampantly awful behaviour but persistent low-level disruption (LLD).

The sobering reality is that it is the teacher that is the decisive element in the classroom.

The teacher sets the tone; creates the 'climate'; makes it all happen. Teaching in the school has to be positive to address the national difficulty of persistent, annoying, low-level silliness that interrupts – or even destroys learning.

When addressing persistent LLD the place to start is with the teacher's practice:

- is it consistent?
- is there a clear seating plan?
- are higher order learning objectives shared with the class?
- does learning have an obvious contextual flow, *ie* the students know what they have done and where they are going?
- has the work been regularly marked and valued by the teacher?
- are expectations suitably challenging?
- is the plenary set up at the start of the lesson: how will students know what they have achieved?
- how will the students learning be assessed throughout the lesson?
- are tasks varied and engaging?
- are skills being developed?
- do students know where they are at and how to reach the next level up?
- does the teacher share examples of excellent work with the class?
- is the learning environment modelling your expectations?

- is the teacher welcoming and friendly, modelling the expected behaviour?

Perhaps more sobering is the reality that managing student behaviour is as much about changing one's own behaviour and strategies.

In spite of all that, disruption may continue, however. Consider these overheard commands:

- Why are you chewing/yapping/late/not wearing your tie?

All of these invite debate, taking time out of your planned lesson. It is more effective to describe the reality: *eg* 'You are late but I do not want to waste the class's time. Please see me after the lesson' or 'There is a class rule about respecting others. Please listen'.

Another strategy is to implant in the student's mind a scenario where s/he had acted differently and so the consequences are different and positive, *eg* 'What would have happened if you had arrived on time?' This way the student describes a situation where his/her behaviour had been positive and they had behaved well. It dismantles confrontation. Outstanding teachers do this all the time without realising it.

After the teacher has given an instruction, secondary behaviours can appear worse than the primary behaviour, *eg* muttering or swearing under the breath. The skill here is to ensure that the primary task is being followed and to deal with the secondary behaviour at the end, away from the class. But do deal with it; always follow up and follow through and get parents onside.

Secondary behaviour from a student normally serves to elicit response. Agree and then return to original instruction, *eg* 'I hate this' – 'I'm sure that you do and I'd like you to sit down'; 'This lesson is boring' – 'it may well be and I'd like you to get back to work'. Try to do these commands with calm authority: less intrusion results in less confrontation.

Rebuilding and repairing, nurturing and moulding are the tools of an outstanding teacher. Remember that students are far from the finished article and that with your support you can make a significant difference to their lives.

Sanctions will only work if they're built on a foundation of trust between students and staff. Students must trust that you have their best interests at heart and that you will apply the school's rules consistently and fairly. I recently hosted a group of school leaders from Michigan, USA. As I took them round the school I came across a student wearing a hat: a clear contravention of school uniform policy. I took the hat from the child's head which prompted one of our guests to say that in America I wouldn't be able to get away with that; that students and parents would complain about their rights being infringed. The difference here is that if you've established a culture of trust and respect then students know that they must comply with our expectations. When I first arrived at Burlington Danes I probably couldn't have taken the hat from the child; earning the trust of the children gives you this freedom.

Raising parents' expectations

Parents matter. We often talk in schools about raising pupil expectations, but how often do we undertake the vital task of raising parental expectations? In my view there is a deep underlying problem in British schooling, exacerbated in the inner-city: we have encouraged parents to be consumers of education rather than participants in it.

Parental engagement is a powerful lever for raising achievement in schools, so how is it achieved?

- Most importantly, seek their views: parental surveys at parent evenings school plays *etc* are powerful indications of how well you are doing as a school. Publish survey findings and write to any aggrieved parents if you can, following up their concerns. Be at the school gate for pick-up: ensure this is regular so parents know and expect you there.

- Be dogged in pursuing those parents who fail to attend parents' evenings.

- Have 'postcards of success' or similar quick notes fired off to parents of successful pupils.

- Write home regularly. Teachers should be regularly communicating with parents, photocopying exemplary work, praising achievements *etc.*

- Parents want to support their child to learn more effectively: offer workshops to facilitate that; ask parents want they would like support with.

- The school library is an important part of our provision: hold events for parents there, reading workshops *etc.* Some school libraries allow parents to borrow books and engage parents that way.

- The Parent Teacher Association should be highly valued, driven by SLT, it needs a decent budget and annual strategic direction. Working towards a common goal – *eg* funding an aspect of school life gives purpose to their fundraising.

- Hold parent evenings for a particular ethnic group if they are well represented in your school, arrange for translators *etc.*

- Be professional and precise about dates *etc* in student planners and on your website. Have clear systems regarding snow days *etc.* Rarely, if ever, close the school unexpectedly.

- Communication – showcase student talents as often as possible: school plays, artwork, team sports and so on. It is good to have plenty of opportunities for parents to come into the school rather that to be asked to come in for negative reasons.

- Always see parents who visit the school even if you are desperately busy: they have taken the time to come in. Make it clear in every meeting that you want the same thing as them: success for their child.

- Be clear about data: hold evenings to explain this. Parents like to know how their child is doing in comparison to others so ensure you can put all data into a current national context. All children must know their working at current level and target level. We hold a 'parents learning with their child' evening which helps to enforce school expectations of pupils' work.

- A group of hard to reach parents might come in for tea with the SENCO and principal, for example, to discuss issues surrounding dyslexia or behaviour for learning.

- Homework is such an obvious performance indicator for a school and yet so often it is poor and ill-thought out, as if setting it is enough. Get rid of turgid worksheets; set substantial work to be completed at home, such as research projects that require independent learning. Display great work. And ensure it is marked promptly. We've recently subscribed to 'Show My Homework' which enables parents and students to check their homework for each subject through a link on the school website.

A fundamental tenet of our behaviour policy is that when students misbehave we don't blame them as individuals, or explain their conduct in terms of character flaws. We seek to help them improve by giving them the skills to correct their behaviour and the opportunity to invest their energy in more fruitful pursuits. You only have to look at the literacy levels of adult prisoners. *The Guardian* reported that that 'More than three-quarters of them [UK prison population] cannot read, write or count to the standard expected of an 11-year-old' ('Illteracy and innumeracy are the UK's dirty little secrets', 3 May 2010) to see the impact that schooling can have on individual conduct, for better or worse.

Having worked in London schools for four decades I feel well placed to comment on trends in the behaviour of young people over the years. I'm sceptical of claims that behaviour is getting worse, and put such views down to a hyperactive media and misplaced nostalgia. Feelings towards young people often reflect the views expressed here:

They [young people] have exalted notions, because they have not been humbled by life or learned its necessary limitations; moreover, their hopeful disposition makes them think themselves equal to great things – and that means having exalted notions. They would always rather do noble deeds than useful ones: Their lives are regulated more by moral feeling than by reasoning – all their mistakes are in the direction of doing things excessively and vehemently. They overdo everything – they love too much, hate too much, and the same with everything else.

Yet I'm sure some readers will have guessed that such comments aren't from the opinion pages of a modern newspaper. They are the words of Aristotle, and they were uttered two-and-a-half thousand years ago. It would seem then that castigating the younger generation has a long history, and is perhaps explained by older people failing to understand young people and feeling alienated and perplexed as a result – a problem all the more pertinent given the current pace of change in society. Evidence would appear to be on the side of today's younger generation when it comes to judging against previous generations. Under the headline 'Why are vandalism rates falling?' a BBC news article in January 2013 revealed that since 2007 incidents of vandalism had declined by 37% in England and Wales. Meanwhile *The Economist* reported that between 2003 and 2010: 'The proportion of 11-to-15-year-olds who had drunk in the previous week halved' ('The British love affair with the bottle appears to be ending', 6 October 2012). A key feature of this book has been the power of expectations, and as a society we must be careful not to cast young people in the role of spoilt, anti-social, drug-taking vandals, not least when the evidence offers an alternative view. I recall behaviour being awful when I started teaching almost 40 years ago. Schools are now far more systematic and structured, enabling us to pick up on poor conduct much more quickly.

But arguing that, on the whole, young people are no worse than in the past does not preclude us from recognising that times have changed, and that young people today face different challenges, and present different types of misbehaviour, than in the past. The internet is at the heart of these differences. Like all new forms of technology, we should recognise that the internet is simply a medium of communication, just like books, and it's worth remembering that when books were first introduced in the 15th century they were banned by some governments, churches and schools for fear of the dangerous ideas that they would spread. Similar concerns have led to some schools banning YouTube, which I find strange given the wealth of engaging and informative videos that can be found on the site. To ban books, or to criticise the internet, is to shoot the messenger, rather than tackle the message. Indeed the ease with which students can access inappropriate content on the internet is troubling. It seems bizarre that sexually explicit images are banned from daytime television, restricted in films and kept on the top shelf of newsagents, yet accessible with just a couple of clicks on the internet. Obviously such sites are blocked from the school system, but most of our students have access to the internet at home and on their phones and it's high time that the government stepped in to regulate access to adult content on the internet, for example by making families 'opt in' to this type of content rather than 'opt out' (an example of the behavioural nudges I will refer to later).

Beyond the proliferation of adult content, I think the biggest danger presented by modern technology is the opportunity it gives young people to send messages to each other, often under the cloak of anonymity. I'm sure there's not one school in the country which hasn't had to deal with the repercussions of 'cyber-bullying'. Once again, we can't blame the internet for an age-old problem, but there's no doubt that the internet and mobile phones have made it easy for young people to message each other. Even if the communication isn't malicious, there's a risk of overkill when it comes to instant messaging. Many of our students admit to being awake through the night using WhatsApp and other instant messaging services to communicate with their friends, and as a parent of teenagers myself I know how difficult it is to monitor this. In short, there is so much for students to do these days rather than read a book! I should also note that mobile phones enable students to contact friends and family outside of school, seeking support for school bust-ups which in a previous age would have fizzled out without external involvement. Our strict approach to mobiles in school makes this a rare occurrence, but it does happen. The ubiquity of mobile phones and laptops is indicative of that other modern day phenomenon: materialism. I'm no luddite – I enjoy tweeting and I make fairly good use of my iPad – but we have a duty as educators to show young people that there's more to life than the possession of the latest phone, trainers or laptop. Of course it's in the interests of high street retailers to give young people the opposite message, so we've got our work cut out. If it seems like our young people have grown up in a land of plenty, the sting in the tale is that the recent economic outlook makes it doubtful that current living standards can be bettered or even maintained in the future. What does seem clear is that the well-paid jobs for unskilled workers are a thing of the past thanks to the irrepressible forces of globalisation. Take these facts from the blog of BBC's home editor Mark Easton: 'Go back to 1984 and ONS labour market data shows that 44% of UK jobs were unskilled or low skilled jobs. Now it is about 27%. People working in the knowledge industries accounted for 31% of jobs in 1984. Now it is close to 45%' ('Graduating for the 21st century', 2 March 2011). These changes, replicated throughout the rich world, make it all the more important that we equip our students to challenge for competitive, high-status employment.

What are the skills pupils need for work?

A US research project by the National Association of Colleges and Employers (NACE) in 2013 found that in spite of the reliance on IT skills in modern life, the old-fashioned virtues of team work, initiative, self-organisation and face-to-face communication are what employers crave most. It is schools' responsibility to provide opportunities for pupils to demonstrate these skills though: sport, working in the library, supporting a local primary, hosting a tea dance for senior citizens, running a school fair *etc.*

It is an interesting list of desired qualities and one I share with pupils at assemblies. Ranked in true BDA style from the most important at number one they are:

1. Ability to work in a team
2. Ability to make decisions and solve problems
3. Ability to plan, organise and prioritise work
4. Ability to communicate verbally with people inside and outside an organisation
5. Ability to obtain and process information
6. Ability to analyse quantitative data
7. Technical knowledge related to the job
8. Proficiency with computer software programmes
9. Ability to create and/or edit written reports
10. Ability to sell and influence others

It's perhaps worth considering differences in conduct and social pressures between students from low income inner city backgrounds, and those from more affluent middle class backgrounds. Again I only have to draw on my experience as a parent to note that adolescence presents challenges for all those who experience it, regardless of family income. Many of my friends who work at more affluent schools suggest that sex, drugs and alcohol, for example, are far bigger issues in the suburbs, small towns and in the countryside than we face in the inner city. Perhaps my own experience is tainted by the fact that since the 1980s I've worked in a Catholic school and now a Church of England school with a large Muslim population. One issue that does affect us in the inner city though is the grip of gangs. My darkest day in teaching was at Sacred Heart when a girl was stabbed in the playground by another student. As I said to the national media at the time, this was a disagreement that got out of hand and it had absolutely nothing to do with gangs, but this didn't stop one national newspaper describing it as a 'gang feud'. Journalists from *The Sun* came down to the school, and I was on live TV defending the name of the school and making it clear that this was an isolated incident, as indeed it was. We were an outstanding school before the incident, securing brilliant results for our students, and our results continued to improve afterwards. Gangs are a real and present threat for some young people today though. The grip of gangs was especially strong at the two South London schools that I've worked in, and throughout London there's an obsession with territory, with young people displaying almost tribal loyalty to that most arbitrary of territorial divisions: the postcode. In my recent spell as executive principal of a school in Brixton I was astonished to meet students from SW9 (Brixton) who wouldn't dream of setting foot in SW2 (Tulse Hill), despite these locations being a ten-minute walk from each other. I've previously noted the desire that young people possess for acceptance, belonging and amusement, and if schools fail to provide this then gangs, and even postcodes, might.

So high expectations means believing that a young person's future is not dictated by her present or past. It means creating systems which track the progress of all students and intervening when this progress fails to meet expectations. High expectations means establishing a culture of discipline and compliance with agreed norms, with sanctions in place for those students who fall short. These high expectations must be set out on day one and reinforced every day thereafter. They are underpinned by courage: the courage to take risks and to face up to the reality, however grim; the courage to take the ethos of the school into the street beyond; to have frank conversations with staff and tackle issues head-on; the courage to be vigilant and resilient, avoiding the distractions and complacency that will throw you off course.

This chapter in a tweet: Claiming to have high expectations is the easy bit; they must be constantly reinforced by the way you support all students.

Lesson 3:
Create a professional culture of good will and mutual support

'All it takes is one teacher – just one – to save us from ourselves.'

A clumsy distinction is sometimes made between heads who prioritise teachers and those who prioritise students. It's clumsy because as a head you can only deliver benefits for young people if you have a talented, harmonious, motivated team of teachers. So this chapter will explore how headteachers can develop and maintain a positive staff culture. I feel honoured to stand before the Burlington Danes staff each day. I look around the staff room and I think of the other occupations that could have lured these talented men and women. Let's start with those who have previously pursued other careers. We've got a science teacher who developed a knack for spotting talent as a head-hunter in the city, a history teacher who once toured the country as a professional golfer, a maths teacher who honed his communication skills by working in advertising, another maths teacher who applied her eye for detail to the role of a corporate lawyer, an assistant principal who joined us from the engineering sector, and a geography teacher who led expeditions around the world. Of those teachers who came straight into teaching from university I see potential TV presenters, politicians, web designers, consultants and architects. The career choice of talented graduates provides a snapshot of the health of a society and I'm extremely proud that teaching now attracts some of the best: Teach First, for example, is now the biggest recruiter of graduates from Oxford and Cambridge (*Times Educational Supplement*, 10 April 2009).

Teach First is based on the notion that (a) teacher quality has a huge impact on student performance; and (b) top graduates (*ie* those who have excelled academically) are more likely to be great teachers than those of a mediocre academic pedigree. More on the second point later, but it's difficult to dispute the first. In his book *How Children Succeed*, Paul Tough claims that researchers have agreed that of all the factors affecting student success, teacher quality is the most important:

> ... education reformers have mostly united around one specific issue: teacher quality. The consensus of most reform advocates is that there are far too many under-performing teachers, especially in high-poverty schools, and the only way to improve outcomes for students in these schools is to change the way teachers are hired, trained, compensated and fired (p. 189).

Headteachers in challenging schools have to create goodwill with staff because we ask so much of our teachers. Twelve-hour days are common and most of our teachers think nothing of working at weekends and in their holidays. Appointing teachers is one of the most important roles for a headteacher so I insist that I personally interview all candidates, whatever role they've applied for. Once teachers have been appointed it's my job to create the conditions which allow them to thrive. I get paid to absorb the stress so that others can relax and focus on their work. In the same way that when you get home with your family you think 'I can relax now, I'm home', I want teachers to feel this when they arrive at school. I view the school as a family, with me watching over it. So I'm protective of my teachers and I take pride in their development. I encourage open and honest dialogue and I seek to be the anchor during the inevitable ups and downs that affect all families. This approach is symbolised by my open door policy. I'm happy for teachers to come and see me to discuss any issues they have. Of course a headteacher can't be too close to his or her staff. That question of whether leaders should be liked, respected or feared is obviously too simplistic to capture the complexity of leadership, but all three elements play their part. Being liked isn't essential, but it helps, especially given the warm, familial atmosphere that we've sought to build here. A head lacking the respect of the staff will struggle to lead effectively, and I guess being a little bit feared does no harm, though it's not a facet of my character that I actively cultivate.

Leading a team of teachers is the essence of the headteacher's role. Just as there's no set formula for teachers when it comes to winning over their classes, the same is true for heads trying to win over their staff, and again the challenge is to identify your strengths and play to them for all their worth. One of my strengths is my confidence: my conviction that I know what it takes to make a school succeed. So I share this confidence with my staff, and make them aware of the part they have to play in our future success. When things go wrong I take responsibility and pick people up. When things go well, I heap praise on others. I think it was President Truman, who said, "It is amazing what you can accomplish if you do not care who gets the credit."

Borrowing a phrase from Jim Collins, author of *Good to Great*, getting the right people on the bus in the first place is obviously the first challenge of HR. When I meet potential recruits I look for interpersonal skills, a winning smile and professional enthusiasm; someone who has researched the school and knows what we're about. Relationships are vital in schools and I'm keen to see candidates who can demonstrate the ability to forge strong and positive relationships. During interviews I always start by asking the candidate why they have applied, and what attributes they will bring to the school. I ask them what makes a great teacher, and I'm keen to hear what they do in their spare time. I must also confess that I take interest in the way that candidates walk into the room, along with what they are wearing. I know this sounds superficial but if someone has prepared for the interview with care and really wants the job then that comes through in the way they walk towards you and shake your hand. Of course there's a risk of favouring your own type of person, which you have to guard against. I do this by keeping students in mind as I judge the merits of different applicants, thinking about which applicant the students would respond most positively to. Such is my desire to recruit great teachers that I've been known to take a flexible approach to the staffing structure. For example two years ago we had a vacancy for a history teacher, but with two outstanding candidates I took both, and the 'extra' one is now a very strong head of year, as well as a brilliant classroom teacher. It's thrilling to see recruits go on to prosper, especially when you've taken a chance on them.

Let's pause for a moment to discuss the importance of intelligence in the armoury of a teacher. I mentioned before that Teach First, by seeking candidates with a 2:1 degree or above and 300 UCAS points, is committed to the notion that intellect aids teaching. Obviously in any job you would rather employ someone with top grades than someone with average grades, all else being equal. Most of our teachers are of high intellectual calibre and it is a powerful message for a teacher to remind students that she has thrived in her own education, and that she has actively chosen to become a teacher rather than pursue other prestigious careers. It's not a particularly intellectual word to use, but I would say that I want my teachers to be 'bright', rather than 'intelligent', because I think 'bright' captures that sense of being sharp, on the ball and sparky. It's important to raise the bar when seeking to attract new teachers, but I wouldn't want to exclude people who failed to achieve a 2:1 in their degree. Some of these would-be teachers without a 2:1, or without straight As at A level, might have struggled somewhat in their own education, which perhaps fuels their motivation to be a teacher. Plus, of course, a teacher who found things difficult at school might be well placed to help students in a similar situation. Such is the variety of ability in a comprehensive 11-18 school like Burlington Danes that there is plenty of scope to match teachers to suitable classes. Some teachers thrive with low achieving Year 7 students, while other teachers develop an expertise with sixth form students. I've seen enough Oxbridge graduates struggle in the inner city classroom to remind me to look beyond the 'education' section of the CVs that land on my desk.

Of course, recruitment is not an exact science, not least in teaching, where there's a massive discord between the challenge of teaching a standalone lesson on interview and then managing a full timetable of classes day in, day out. The challenge is all the greater in inner city schools, and in my experience it soon becomes apparent when I've appointed someone ill-suited to the intensity of urban education, where the pace is fast and expectations are high. Most years we have one or two new recruits who struggle to meet these expectations, and we act quickly to offer support and find a solution. Support will come from the head of department and, if the teacher is a trainee, from the assistant principal responsible for trainee teachers. The support will consist of help with lesson planning, strategies for individual students and classes, and frequent drop-ins to the classroom in question. I've even been known to take some paperwork into classes and sit at the back of the room to aid a new teacher in that initial establishment phase. More often than not the problem is that the new teacher is struggling to control the class. I mentioned earlier that compliance is not always the default setting with our students, and five years after my arrival I'm still frustrated when students test the mettle of a new teacher. Supporting teachers in this phase is a delicate operation. If I, or other senior colleagues, intervene too much, then we risk undermining the authority of the new teacher, and the students will continue to view the new teacher warily. But if we do nothing it won't take long for a classroom culture of disengagement, apathy and disruption to emerge: a state from which it's difficult for the new teacher to recover. So we monitor new recruits closely, and at times we've had to utilise Ark's six-month probationary period which enables the school and the teacher to cut ties more easily within that six-month period than we can afterwards.

Overseeing the process of embedding new staff into the school community reminds me of those wildlife programmes you see where a family of chimpanzees are encouraged to adopt a stray chimp from another troupe. Wildlife experts prepare for the transition by familiarizing both parties with their respective scents, but ultimately you have to step back and hope that the family take to the new addition, just as I hope our students take to their new teachers. Of course, references from previous employers, as well as the interview and application process described above, help make the process of teacher recruitment less of a lottery. On the whole I trust the references written by other heads: there's a good deal of professional integrity amongst principals. When we seek references we use a numbered scale to gauge the views of headteachers on various facets of a teacher's aptitude. I find that this type of question generates a more reliable response than if we just ask for a reference in prose form, which often yields a bland response. One question we ask is whether the current head teacher would go out of his/her way to appoint the candidate again. If it seems that I'm rather obsessive when it comes to recruiting the right teachers, perhaps I should console myself that a teacher who seems pretty average to one student might be the teacher who transforms the life of another. And most of us only need one or two teachers who we really connect with for our lives to be enriched, a point neatly captured by Daniel Pennac in *School Blues* (2010): 'All it takes is one teacher – just one, to save us from ourselves and make us forget all the others' (p. 221).

Such is the energy required to work in a challenging school that motivation and resilience would feature high on my list of requirements for new recruits (and both facets are of course tough to gauge on interview). Motivation is a curious thing. As a teacher it's one of the toughest characteristics to nurture in students, and it's no easier with staff. The truth is that you need teachers to bring a certain level of motivation to the table, and then we'll provide the context where that motivation can be put to good use. I'm honest with teachers on interview about the challenge of working in a complex urban school, and I'm lucky that now we've established a reputation for rigour and high expectations, potential recruits tend to know what they're signing up to. That said, there are things we can do as heads to cultivate the motivation of our teachers. I constantly remind our staff how important they are and what a difference they make to the lives of our students. It's widely recognised that teachers do change lives, but the fact is that it's rare for students to tell teachers about the impact they're having (not least because the students themselves will probably come to appreciate that impact several years from now). So it can be easy for teachers to lose site of the end goal, and that's why I frequently remind them that by consistently teaching excellent lessons we are improving the life chances of our students. I also show goodwill to teachers, allowing time off for weddings, funerals and unavoidable appointments. I strive to be cheerful and positive in my daily interaction with colleagues, making them feel good about working here. Amidst the maelstrom of human emotions on show in a busy school corridor it's amazing how far a smile goes.

On a personal level, my own motivation remains strong nearly 40 years after I first stepped into the classroom. I love the job of working in a vibrant school. I relish the sense of community, and value the relationships that bind the school. I like spending time with the students, the staff, and my senior team; I don't think I'll ever run out of new ideas and initiatives that might just add another percentage point to our exam results. I often make to-do lists at home in the evening so by the time I arrive at school in the morning I'm keen to see people and share my new ideas. Being a headteacher obviously gives me freedom to generate and implement new methods, but in truth one of the joys of teaching is the freedom to innovate which is granted to every classroom teacher. In his 2009 book *Drive*, Daniel Pink questions the impact of rewarding staff performance. Yet unlike Pink I think that there is a place for extrinsic rewards in teaching, and I've spoken publicly of my support for performance-related pay rather than automatic annual progression. I think that when performance pay is applied constructively it rewards and motivates teachers. The danger of course, is that it encourages a fixation with a narrow set of outcomes, but if the measures used to judge performance are sufficiently robust and varied, such as lesson observations, exam results and contribution to the school community, then I think we can ensure that rewards are appropriately allocated. Teachers' pay has improved markedly in recent decades which has helped to restore the status of the profession. To further enhance the status of teaching I would raise the starting salary of new teachers, a measure which would be cost-neutral when combined with phasing out automatic annual pay progression.

One thing that I couldn't get my head around when I first visited Burlington Danes was the absence of a staff room. It's no surprise that the spirit of teachers was fractured when there was no space for them to gather together. In my previous schools, staff rooms were the hub of the organisation, a meeting point for laughter, refreshment and support during the stresses and strains of a tough day. So I requisitioned one of our biggest classrooms and made this our staff room, kitted out with the usual soft furnishings, coffee-making facilities and of course a pigeon hole for every teacher. While students arrive in the morning we gather together each day in the staff room to share announcements for the day ahead. Our daily staff briefing has become my favourite part of the day: 100 bright, determined teachers gathering for a daily act of fellowship. We start with a moment of reflection, led by a different teacher on rotation – before moving on to notices and announcements.

The reflections were quite simple to start with – The Lord's Prayer or a memorable poem – but they've since become quite competitive as staff vie to outdo each other with the poignancy, humour or ingenuity of their message. One courageous young teacher had 100 teachers on all fours doing yoga stretches for her reflection. It was met with bewilderment by some colleagues, but four years on we have a weekly staff yoga club. Other teachers have used their moment of reflection to share something about their personal story. We've had teachers talk about losing loved ones, their wedding day, and battling personal demons. I never expected the staff reflection to acquire such poignancy when I first suggested it (one teaching assistant described giving his reflection as the most frightening thing he's ever done), and it might seem a bit much to take in at 8.15 in the morning when everyone's keen to tackle the day ahead. Admittedly, it can be a relief to hear a colleague read a simple poem, or share a warming tale from the classroom. Yet, over time, these reflections have helped to build a powerful sense of trust amongst colleagues and having this daily opportunity to touch base with my staff has become crucial to the way I lead the school: we gather together, gain strength from each other, then disperse, energised and informed.

The Goose Story

This is one of my favourite briefing reflections that we've had over the last five years. I think it was shared by science teacher Ms Stanger. The author is unknown.

Next autumn, when you see geese heading south for the winter, flying in their familiar 'V' formation, you might be interested in knowing why they fly that way. Science has learned that, as each bird flaps its wings, it creates an uplift for the bird immediately behind it. By flying in a 'V' formation, the flock together gains over 70% more flying range than if each bird flew on its own.

Like the geese, people who share a common direction and a sense of community can get where they are going quicker and easier, because they are traveling on the thrust of one another.

Whenever one goose falls out of formation, it suddenly feels the drag and resistance of trying to go it alone. It will quickly try to get back into formation to take advantage of the lifting power of the birds in front. If we have as much sense as a goose, we will stay in formation with those who are headed the same way we are going.

When the lead goose gets tired, it rotates back in the wing, and another goose takes over the point position – it pays to take turns doing hard jobs!

The geese from behind honk constantly, as you've no doubt heard whenever a flock passes overhead. They do this to encourage those up front to keep up their speed – an encouraging word goes a long way!

Finally, when a goose gets sick or is wounded by gunshots, and falls out of the formation, two geese follow it down to stay with it and protect it. They stay until the goose is either able to fly again, or dies.

They then launch out on their own or with another formation to catch up with the group. If we have the sense of a goose, we will stand by each other. Simple. Perfect.

If our staff briefing sounds a little emotionally excessive, it's worth recognising that inner city schools are hubs of intense human interaction. On any given day a school of 1,000 students and staff will be home to millions of personal exchanges: student to student, teacher to student, teacher to teacher. Given the intensity of the interaction, I encourage teachers to be themselves, to reveal their character and to engage with their emotions rather than seeking to adopt a cold, clinical manner. Our moment of reflection at staff briefing provides a chance for teachers to show something of themselves in the staff room, and I like to see teachers take this honesty and passion with them to their classrooms. The honesty and humility contained in the daily messages also serve to nurture trust between teachers. We often talk about trust and fear in the classroom, with great teachers replacing the latter with the former. So too in the staff room, the challenge for the head is to eliminate fear and create a spirit of mutual trust between colleagues.

The joy and tears expressed in staff briefings remind me how far we've come as an organisation. Yes, the attainment of students was poor, yes behaviour was challenging, but above all Burlington Danes was a desperately sad place. The children were angry, short-tempered, vying for respect in the absence of respected authority figures. The teachers were beleaguered, demoralised and sceptical. It was a dysfunctional organisation. Staff sickness was rife – in the year before my arrival we were spending over £150,000 per year on supply teachers. So nothing gives me more pride than a happy, energised staff room. As a headteacher you're forever trying to gauge the state of staff morale, like a doctor checking the pulse of his patient. Plenty of SLT time is devoted to discussing the mood of the staff, and it's a fine line to tread. I believe teachers want to work hard, and willingly go the extra mile, but teaching in a tough school is energy-sapping, and burnout is a constant risk. In the course of an average day I will have traversed our sprawling site several times, taking straggling students to lessons, perhaps covering the class of an absent colleague, supporting a new teacher in establishing routines. It's not particularly strategic, but being visible is crucial for a headteacher, and I'm well supported in roaming the site by my SLT. The SLT follow a 'walkabout rota', so for each of the 35 periods in a week one member of SLT is roaming the site. The word 'walkabout' conjures images of aimless strolls through the outback, but in truth we follow a set route around the school, putting at least a foot in the door of every single classroom and lingering, if needs be, over our more volatile classes. It's a good way of ensuring that senior leaders are seen to be supportive of classroom teachers. It's easy to forget the challenge faced by a teacher with a full timetable, not least since one of the ironies of progressing to senior leadership is that some of your best teachers are taken out of the classroom to focus on 'management'. This can dull them to the intensity and pressure of a six-period day, and a damaging discord can emerge between a senior leader's perception of the organisation and the perception of teachers in the classroom.

I've worked with senior leaders who argue that the weight of responsibility they carry means that they have the toughest job in the school. I disagree. The further you advance up the school hierarchy the more control you have over your day and your time, and the less you're at the mercy of the moods of teenagers, which could be dictated by something as random as one sip of Lucozade too many, or a careless word from one student to another. I remember on one occasion I was sitting with my senior team discussing plans for the day ahead. We had a school concert to attend at 6.30pm and one of my team wondered aloud how we should fill the 'dead time' between the end of school and the start of the concert. He was quickly howled down by the rest of the team who pointed out that they were regularly on site until seven, eight, even nine at night, and that this is typical of classroom teachers at the school. So it's vital that senior teachers remain connected to the experience of a classroom teacher. The English teacher in me recalls Shakespeare's *Henry V*, when the young king disguises himself as an ordinary soldier on the eve of the Battle of Agincourt in order to gauge the morale and the concerns of his weary troops. Tesco executives do it by spending a week per year on the shop floor; we do it by roaming the corridors and visiting classes on a daily, sometimes hourly basis.

Once the right staff have been appointed and they've found their correct seats on the bus, the challenge is to enable these teachers to thrive by providing opportunities for personal development. As I've mentioned above, I look for motivated teachers, and such teachers tend to develop themselves. So it's common for staff to give me books which they've been inspired by, or they'll bring ideas to me for initiatives they want to introduce. We also try to give teachers time for self-development. So on inset days we'll allow plenty of free time for teachers to mark, plan and collaborate. But no organisation can wash its hands of staff development, and we've taken a few measures to ensure that the talents of our teachers are actively nurtured. I remember going to Ebury Street near Victoria station for professional development when I was an English teacher in Peckham. The Inner London Education Authority was responsible for staff development at this time, and this was the base for English teachers. On one occasion, within minutes of our arrival, myself and other fledgling English teachers from across London were asked to write a poem and then read it aloud to the strangers in our midst, who duly critiqued the quality of our stumbling stanzas. Obviously I felt quite uncomfortable about reading my poem to complete strangers, but it made me realise that we often ask students to do the same in our lessons, so I adjusted my classroom activities appropriately. Training days should provide more positive lessons than this however, and it's partly because of my own experiences of external training that at Burlington Danes we tap into the talent within and ask our own teachers to lead inset to their colleagues.

Typically we'll start each of the six half terms in the school year with an inset day in which teachers will deliver training to their colleagues before free time is provided for planning and marking. I write this on the final day of the Christmas holidays in January 2014. Tomorrow we return to school and staff will choose from a carousel of the following activities, each led by a teacher in the school: cultivating extended writing, embedding independent learning at sixth form, collaborative learning in Key Stage 3, bringing current affairs into the curriculum, using CCR (our student tracking database); analysing cohort data and developing departmental cohesion. Sure enough, all of the success stories mentioned in this book, such as assertive mentoring, the Venn diagrams, aggregation of marginal gains, plus plenty that I haven't mentioned here, have been championed internally, even if they originated from external courses or resources. The process of establishing a sixth form revealed the importance of allowing teachers time to nurture their own development rather than send them off on expensive courses. One of the reasons for improved exam performance in England in recent years is the wealth of material available to teachers (and students) on the internet. So a teacher setting up an A level in history has access to past papers from the last five years, complete with mark schemes and examiners' reports, in which the exam board gives specific feedback on the performance of students for each question. The canny teacher will make a note of all recent questions for every topic on the syllabus, and soon enough will be able to embed these questions into her lessons to provide challenge and focus throughout the year. It's a far cry from when I started teaching when teachers were oblivious to the workings of exam boards.

Our inset days provide a valuable opportunity for teachers from different departments and different levels of the school to work together to improve their classroom practise. In recent years we've used members of the SLT to model good practice to the rest of our teachers. One activity involved senior leaders teaching a mini lesson to a group of teachers. Another senior leader then gave feedback based on the quality of the lesson observed. This reinforced the transparency that we seek to cultivate amongst teachers and broke down barriers between teachers and leaders in the school. I am the only member of our leadership team who doesn't teach a regular class (I frequently take cover lessons when we're short) and it's absolutely vital that our leaders keep their own pedagogical practice sharp.

It's easy to underestimate the importance of subject knowledge, and in my experience schools in challenging environments have sometimes advocated the view that generic pedagogical skill, rather than subject knowledge, makes the difference in the classroom. Certainly when you look at a school's programme of professional development you're far more likely to see sessions on literacy, questioning, assessment, behaviour management or pastoral care, rather than subject-specific issues. Teachers have been left to fend for themselves to develop not only their subject knowledge, but also their awareness of the difficulties that students face in their particular subject. Schools should give departments more time for professional development within their teams, and school leaders should explore measures to encourage teachers to sharpen their own subject knowledge, perhaps through regular 'expert briefings': lunchtime lectures led by teachers and open to students and staff.

The purpose of our professional development programme is to ensure that teaching and learning take centre stage in the school. I want to hear teachers talking about a great lesson they've delivered as they walk down corridors, and I want to see teachers share resources and ideas as they grab a coffee in the staff room. It's easy to become distracted by the social issues that our young people bring to school, and it's true that at times we feel more like social workers, counsellors and police officers than teachers. So it's important that the culture of the school directs teachers' attention back on the craft of pedagogy. In the same way that all students should know how they can improve in each of their subjects, I want teachers to be striving for constant improvement by testing new strategies and sharing great ideas. There are some fantastic blogs on teaching and web resources which can help classroom teachers and each week one of our vice principals emails our teachers a list of the best web resources and blog posts in order to keep our staff in tune with developments in the profession.

Another key element of our staff development programme is a weekly teaching and learning reflection in our Tuesday staff briefing. This replaces our usual staff reflection and provides a chance for a teacher to share a 'golden nugget' of pedagogical advice. Teachers can volunteer to take one of these slots, or we'll ask our more experienced and specialised teachers to take the lead. The teaching and learning reflection that I remember most fondly was one led by assistant principal Chris Fairbairn. Chris is a mesmerising maths teacher (he once entered his Year 10 maths class for their GCSE exam one year early and 29 pupils gained A and A* grades) and on this occasion used his moment of reflection to emphasise the importance of students being aware of the assessment criteria on which they are judged. He asked all teachers to sketch a house in 30 seconds, revealing that they would be judged on the quality. He then awarded marks for minor details such as chimneys, windows, curtains, a knocker on the front door. This delighted one or two eager teachers who had embellished their doodles with the required details, but frustrated the rest of us who didn't know the terms on which we would be judged (little did I know at the time but I would experience a similar sense of deception when the GCSE English grades boundaries were shifted in 2012!). Mr Fairbairn's message, of course, was that judging students without sharing the terms on which they are judged breeds frustration and disillusionment, and that students should be just as familiar with mark schemes and assessment objectives as their teachers. A memorable lesson, and testament to the value of scheduling a weekly moment of pedagogical reflection.

One of the key ways in which we invest in staff development is through offering a subsidised Masters in Education Management, delivered by King's College London. I took a Masters myself in Education when I was at Sacred Heart and most of my Strategic Leadership Team now have a Masters, which enables us to keep an eye on the bigger picture that a post-graduate course in education tends to provide. It's vital that if we want a talented and motivated workforce that we provide opportunities for teachers to study to Masters level. It's always difficult to provide examples of the practical application of a Masters in the daily life of a school – after all, Masters courses are designed to stimulate critical debate rather than to offer practical nuggets – but it's natural and healthy that after working in schools for a sustained period professionals seek to deepen their knowledge by discussing some of the big questions concerning education.

A chapter on nurturing a team of teachers would be incomplete without reference to the issue of staff absence. Most schools remain completely unaffected by recent workplace reforms such as flexi-time and working from home. We need our teachers in the classroom in front of their charges, and it's a huge problem for schools when sickness, childcare issues, tube strikes and broken boilers prevent this from happening. Staff absence was flagged as one of the key problems when I arrived in 2008. There were days in the winter term of that year when more than 20 teachers were off sick, leaving the school crawling with supply teachers. Supply teachers serve their purpose – I've met a few good ones in my time who I've recruited on a full-time basis – but the reality is that they have no connection to the school and very little incentive to ensure that their lessons are well delivered. There's nothing worse for a school leader than seeing a supply teacher search desperately for the room they've been sent to only to be met by whooping teenagers delighted that the rules that their usual teacher has worked so hard to establish won't apply for the next hour. It's quite common for this same supply teacher to finish the hour with a list of names of students who have misbehaved, leaving a head of department or head of year with the unenviable task of sanctioning students without knowing if the supply teacher applied school systems consistently and fairly.

So in my first term at Burlington Danes I made the decision to do away with all supply teachers. At the time, the academy was spending £150,000 per year on cover staff. It was too easy for teachers to call in sick as there was a dedicated 'cover telephone' that staff would leave messages on. I explained to all staff the disruption cover teachers caused to the academy and how it unsettled the pupils. It would be to all our benefit if we were to do the cover ourselves. If it got particularly heavy, I explained, then SLT would do block cover in the hall. I detailed Michael, my senior vice principal, to lead the system in our first term. Staff had to telephone between 6.30 and 7am and were not allowed to leave messages, they were required to have a conversation. Neither were partners, spouses or friends allowed to call in on a member of staff's behalf. Perhaps more importantly, the good will that was beginning to develop amongst staff, combined with the fact that lessons would have to be covered by colleagues on their free periods, encouraged teachers to drag themselves to school where previously they might have called in sick. Staff with frequent absences, particularly those who had the odd day off here and there, triggered an absence review meeting, part of our newly drafted absence policy. Attendance improved enormously within a few weeks. Now most cover is generated by trips and journeys, or staff training. The cover telephone is disconnected in Michael's office, in part because supply agencies pleading for work are the only callers.

Using teachers for cover is a prickly issue as far as the unions are concerned. We ensure that teachers aren't used more than once a week and that the load is shared fairly, with SLT taking more than anyone else. The vast majority of teachers are more than happy to oblige, knowing that we all benefit from a stable, orderly school. For me it serves as an example of where the unions have placed themselves on the wrong side of the argument. They campaign vociferously against staff being used for cover, but in doing so they forego the stability of the school and place the rights of teachers over the needs of students, which seems at odds with the vast majority of our staff who have actively chosen to work in a school which serves a social purpose. I feel very fortunate that recent industrial action has left Burlington Danes unaffected, such is the lack of union militancy amongst our teachers. In addition to using teachers to cover lessons we employ two cover supervisors to take the classes of absent colleagues. I'm proud to add that six years after my first half term at Burlington Danes a supply teacher has not set foot in the building.

Reducing staff absence

When I started at Burlington Danes staff absence was a big problem. The school was spending over £150,000 a year on supply staff. The real cost though was in other, less measurable terms: low staff morale, disrupted classes, the quality and continuity of teaching disrupted and the words 'free lesson' often resounding around the corridors. This was a problem that required both an immediate and long-term fix.

Short-term strategies

- Get rid of all supply teachers – there are good ones but most have little if any investment in the school. Explain that departments will cover each other in the first instance. Appoint your own Higher Level Teaching Assistant cover supervisors: ensure they are strong on behaviour management and have a good relationship with the pupils.

- Relaunch your staff absence policy. For example, ten days sick in any one year ought to be a referral to Occupational Health.

- At the same time, launch your cover policy: staff need to be clear about the guidelines and parameters of cover. Have a senior colleague answer all sickness calls. It is simply too easy to text or leave a message: I insisted that they speak to my senior vice principal to explain the problem in confidence. This had an immediate effect of reducing absence.

- Have follow-up meetings with all staff who have been absent. It takes time, but makes a powerful point. Look for patterns of absence (*eg* Mondays or Fridays) and be forthright about asking them. Indeed, being frank and honest is key to any dealings with staff. Describe the problem their absence is causing and the effect it has on the pupils.

- Use SLT for cover and use it as an opportunity to thoroughly review the absent member of staff's exercise books, room and display.

Long-term strategies

- Contentiously, I reward staff with 100% attendance at the end of year – just a bottle of wine or book tokens *etc*

- Report staff absence to governors

- Try to reduce CPD during the daytime, when it is necessary try to ensure cover is done in-house in the affected department

- Within reason, support staff who need time off for weddings/family events *etc* – a bit of generosity goes a long way!

It's a controversial view, but my opinion on industrial action is that we should be a non-striking profession, just like the police. We must find ways to express our concerns about government policy without denying a day of schooling to the children placed in our care. I've met with many union reps over the years and in dealing with the unions I always put the onus on them – 'surely you don't want to defend poor practice?' We must always act in the interests of the students, and I welcome the emergence of organisations like Edapt which provide legal support for teachers without pursuing a political agenda.

Occasional treats and benefits help to raise the spirits of our teachers. We can hardly compete with Google, where staff receive free massages and as much food as they can eat, but every break time we serve tea and coffee in the staff room, providing a chance for teachers to catch their breath and enjoy the company of their colleagues. Every Friday, cakes and pastries are added to the tea trolley – one of the vice principals collects them on his way to work. We also try to provide regular collegial experiences. Chair of governors Lord Fink is extremely generous in supporting our Christmas gathering, and we try to end most terms with some kind of social event for staff, like a trip to a local restaurant. This was a tradition that I started in that first summer term of 2008 with a trip to the London Eye followed by dinner at a restaurant in Chinatown. We brought everyone – lunchtime supervisors, maintenance staff, the office team – it was a powerful reinforcement of my message of gratitude to staff for the incredible effort they make on a daily basis. We also hold a staff quiz once a year, invariably won by the SLT (probably on account of being the only team with an average above age above 30). These benefits are trivial compared to the sweat and tears given by staff each week but I hope they're seen as a small token of my genuine appreciation of their efforts.

The combined impact of staff reflections, a Christmas gala and termly treats is that a rich patchwork of school life begins to develop which creates a sense of unity and common purpose. I've heard headteachers say that their role is to develop within young people a desire to live for something beyond themselves. I agree that pursuing a higher purpose than your own satisfaction fulfils a deep human need and as a headteacher I'm grateful for the opportunity to galvanise a workforce behind a common purpose. The rituals that I've described in this chapter reinforce this community spirit and one of the reasons that our staff stay with us is their attachment to the patchwork of shared experiences that we've woven into the school calendar.

Throughout my career I've noticed how important it is that teams are balanced rather than being composed of individual superstars. You can't work too long at a school without realising that groups of people constitute more than the sum of their parts. Teamwork guru Meredith Belbin puts it like this: 'Teams are a question of balance. What is needed is not well balanced individuals but individuals who balance well with one another' (1996 p. 73). The surest means of ensuring a balance is by recruiting people who put the team first. Especially within my senior team it's vital that members leave their personal ego at the door. It's tiresome when people fight their own corner and defend their own projects, rather than see the bigger picture. From the leader's perspective it's important to be comfortable to appoint and promote people who possess more talent than you in specific areas. A leader unsure of his own abilities might be wary of surrounding himself with talented deputies, but a confident leader must harness all the talent at his or her disposal. If you can't command authority within your senior team then it's in everyone's interest for this to be exposed.

The open door to my office symbolises the open, direct, warm, rigorous staff culture that I've tried to build at Burlington Danes. In a recent staff survey more than two-thirds of respondents cited their fellow teachers as the best thing about working at the school, commenting on the talent, dedication and support amongst the staff body. A headteacher can only impact students' lives through his/her teachers, so it's vital that I attract talented teachers to Burlington Danes and then retain and develop them through fostering a positive culture where effort and talent is recognised, praised and rewarded. There's nothing more galvanizing for an organisation than sharing a common external goal, and for us the glue that binds us is our desire to impact the lives of the students we serve. A daily staff briefing in which all teachers can contribute, combined with the occasional staff outing, all serve to reinforce this precious *esprit de corps*. I've already noted the intensity of the task of working in a challenging school and we constantly monitor the morale of teachers and tweak deadlines and expectations appropriately. Again, Jim Collins offers good advice on minimising the bureaucratic burden on staff, suggesting that organisations should nurture discipline rather than bureaucracy: 'most companies build their bureaucratic rules to manage the small percentage of wrong people on the bus, which increases the need for more bureaucracy to compensate for incompetence and lack of discipline, which then further drives the right people away, and so forth' (p. 121). Collins goes on to use the analogy of an airline pilot who enjoys freedom and responsibility within a strict system, which I think chimes with the balance of structure and freedom that we try to provide for our staff.

Yet, in honesty, striking the balance between discipline and freedom, and trying to ensure that we are rigorous but not ruthless, is a constant challenge. I've already noted that most years we lose one or two new teachers during the first term, often because they struggle to cope with the pressure of the daily school routine. I'm sure that my teachers would have their own ideas on whether we achieve that balance between trusting them to deliver, and holding them to account. I can honestly say though that I'm critically aware of the pressures on staff and I'm conscious to avoid the situation faced by some urban schools in America, where highly motivated and energised 20-somethings throw themselves into their work for a decade or so, only to leave the profession or move to a more comfortable school once they approach their thirties, seeking a more settled family life. Teaching requires so much energy and it's vital that teachers have fulfilling lives beyond school to refuel them for the challenge of the classroom.

Ultimately we do sometimes reach a point with teachers where we want them to leave. In my experience it's easier than a headteacher might think to secure the departure of an underperforming teacher, you just need to have the stomach for it. That starts with a conversation, explaining that you're not happy with the quality of work that a colleague is currently producing. In these situations I will outline the support that we've already offered, and explain how I expect this to continue, but I'll often suggest that it's in the interest of the teacher to look for work elsewhere. Explaining this to a colleague is one of the toughest challenges that a head can face. No-one likes criticism, and professionally it doesn't get much worse than being told by your boss that you're no longer wanted. Such conversations have become easier for me over time because my feelings about what children need have strengthened. I'm more passionate than ever about the importance of every lesson being led by a talented, dedicated teacher, so by focusing on the outcomes of the child I manage to get my point across in these conversations. I've realised too that you must give the colleague in question an opportunity to meet with you after the initial conversation, which can come as something of a shock. I've often found that a teacher who appears to accept a decision in the first meeting will come back the next day with a different opinion. Sometimes of course you can move people on to another position within the school, so for example a head of department struggling to manage a team of people might be more suited to coordinating our programme of after school clubs.

The process of dismissing underperforming teachers is, for good reason, highly controversial. What is sometimes forgotten though is that fairness matters to teachers as much as to students. I believe that – at least privately – teachers want any poor conduct of colleagues to be tackled. Teachers want differentiation as much as children do – it makes no sense to lavish praise on all teachers equally if a few underperforming teachers have been carried along by others. It must be clear that the head means it when they tell a teacher that they've done something well, and the flipside of this is that poor performance must be tackled, not tolerated.

I should touch briefly on the risk of passing the problem of inadequate teaching onto another school by suggesting that the teacher in question seeks employment elsewhere, rather than taking formal capability procedures against them. The competitive streak in me will always prioritise the needs of my school, but professional integrity makes me reluctant to keep inadequate teachers within the profession. Two points are worth noting here though. Firstly, if I inform a teacher that I am considering capability procedures against them, then it's likely that they will choose to seek employment elsewhere. Secondly, I've already noted that working in urban schools presents unique challenges, and one doesn't need to resort to blind optimism to hope that some teachers will fare better in a less challenging school.

Challenging conversations

The role of the head encompasses occasions when staff need to be challenged about their performance. Here's how you can do it:

- Be direct, open and frank – the old adage of describing the behaviour not the person is good advice too.
- Saying how you feel – angry, disappointed, frustrated – is important; relating it back to the student experience gives it the school-wide dimension, what is best for the students is always the best reference point.

- Make sure your job descriptions are up to date. This will ensure that the teacher is totally clear of expectations and demands.

- Use your data – what is the story it tells about the teacher in question compared to other staff?

- Avoid evaluative judgements – let the teacher make those. Provide specific facts and make sure you know what you are talking about: that way the feedback is rooted in your view and is easier to accept.

- Get in the habit of giving positive feedback to your staff when it is due – postcards, notes, e-mails and verbally. It creates a buffer for the more challenging feedback.

- Never begin lesson feedback with 'so, what did you think?' This is a cop-out and it is best to start with the overall judgment and work back from there.

- Always have suggested routes for improvement: coaching, observation, a change of role. Be clear about the performance and behaviour you wish to see, attempt to provide a win-win situation.

- If it is a wider problem do not fall into the trap of admonishing the staff, or a group of staff because of a minority: pick them off as individuals.

Conversations with underperforming staff are exceptional though, and far more often I invite staff to my office to praise them and share my appreciation for their efforts. Indeed, one of the challenges of leading a young, talented, motivated team of teachers is that such teachers are ambitious, and satisfying their ambitions has become one of my biggest challenges. It helps that we always seek to promote internally. This is another principle espoused by Jim Collins in *Good to Great*. In his study of successful CEOs he reveals that the vast majority came from within the organisation (obviously I'm glad that Ark didn't follow this principle in 2008 when seeking a new head for Burlington Danes). Since then all of my appointments to the strategic leadership team (and there have been several due to members of SLT gaining promotions elsewhere) have been internal. I also retain excellent teachers by finding roles for them, occasionally adapting the departmental structure if it enables me to retain a colleague who I would otherwise lose. Jim Collins talks about getting the right people on the bus, and then getting everyone in the right seat. It's not an exact science, and anyone involved in HR would acknowledge that mistakes can be made, but when I look around the staff room each morning I see a team of incredible talent, and I'm reassured that when we do lose teachers to other schools it's invariably because they've secured a significant promotion.

This chapter in a tweet: Your success will depend on your ability to recruit, retain, motivate and develop excellent teachers.

Lesson 4:
Let teachers plan, teach and mark

'Be yourself. Trust in your personality.
Transfer your energy.'

In the course of a school year nearly 50,000 lessons will be taught at a large secondary school like Burlington Danes. Each of these lessons will need to be carefully planned and skilfully delivered. The work done in the lesson will then need to be assessed, or at least monitored. This chapter focuses on what headteachers can do to enable teachers to focus on the three fundamentals of their job: plan, teach and mark.

Let's pause for a minute to consider a typical day for a classroom teacher (bear in mind that this list omits the multitude of emails that will be pinging into a teacher's desktop throughout the day, along with the additional commitments such as uploading test scores, writing reports, departmental meetings, running clubs, attending parents' evenings and other school events).

8.15: Staff briefing.

8.30: Line-up with tutor group, then tutor time for 25 minutes.

9.00: Period 1, 10L.

9.55: Period 2, 8A.

10.50-11.10: Break.

11.10-12.05: Free period – planning and preparation.

12.05-13.00: Period 4: 7B.

13.00-13.50: Lunch. Possibly on duty or running a club, detention or intervention class.

13.50-15.30: Periods 5 and 6, Double lesson with sixth form class.

15.30-15.40: Registration: spellings and times tables.

16.00: Two or three times a week there will be a meeting, club, or intervention class after school, or 'prep time' if the teacher is a Year 7 tutor.

17.00: Marking, planning and preparation.

The intensity of such a day is impossible to convey on paper. Each group arrives at your room with its own unique energy and dynamism. Maybe 8A have just come over from a high-octane drama class, perhaps two key players in Year 10L had an argument on WhatsApp on their way to school. Yet in every lesson the teacher must assert themselves over the class, establish calm and control, then deliver an engaging lesson tailored to the personal needs of the students. Any failure to comply requires follow-up: a detention, a phone call home, a meeting with parents, not to mention the pages of students' work generated every lesson which require marking. Yes, teachers do receive generous holiday allowances. But during term time I can't think of many other lines of work, perhaps only the medical profession, where the daily pressures are so intense. My teachers are typically young, outgoing types, full of energy and vim, but I know for a fact that few of them find the time or the energy to socialise during the week, such is the frenzy of an average day. And unlike our friends in other professions, teachers don't have the luxury of being able to 'go slow' for a day, to pop out for a coffee, or perhaps arrange a mid-morning meeting with a client off site. They must summon the energy to command their lessons every day. By the end of the week my staff have very little left to give, and it pains me to see them trudge through the school gates on a Friday with a bag full of weekend marking (though I'm reassured to see most of them stop for a quick drink in the pub opposite school on their way). The job of a classroom teacher presents a truly herculean challenge and it's one faced by thousands of teachers up and down the country every day.

The role of school leaders is to create the culture and the systems which allow teachers to focus on their classroom craft. This starts with ensuring that students find their way to class in an orderly and timely manner, and that's where we meet one of the heroes of Burlington Danes: a giant Jamaican by the name of Tony Rumble. For many students and parents Mr Rumble is the most visible member of staff at the school. He was a parent of a boy at Sacred Heart, my previous school, where his sister worked in the office. As I got to know him I was impressed with his kind heart, confidence and stature, so when I was appointed at Burlington Danes I prised him away from a career with the Royal Mail to join me as the school's first behaviour manager. If you drive down Wood Lane in the morning between 8.25am and 8.55am you'll see him on the gate come wind, rain or shine welcoming students and taking the names of any latecomers. He's become a cult figure, popular yet respected by students and loved by parents, some of whom have been known to bring him cakes and other goodies.

During the day Mr Rumble patrols the corridors, urging students into lessons and supporting teachers with any behaviour issues. Tony also oversees the Step room, which is our holding room for students who have disrupted the learning of others. It's a temporary intervention which allows us to take students out of circulation for a short period of time. Typically a day in the Step room will culminate in the head of year meeting with parents and the student being on monitoring report the following day. It's another string to Mr Rumble's bow, and he's invaluable after school when he starts the daily detention and then clears the playground once darkness descends. He's a good example of the team effort required to keep the school functioning, and a reminder that you don't have to be a fully qualified teacher to be a positive influence on young people, a point emphasised by the impact of peripatetic music teachers, rugby coaches and professional authors, all of whom come to Burlington Danes to share their passion and skills with the students. Mr Rumble received the Ark School Hero Award in 2011 – a worthy accolade for one of my proudest appointments.

Corridor behaviour

There are behaviour hotspots in every school. Controlling student conduct in class is a relative breeze compared to unmonitored behaviour on the corridor. So how can corridor behaviour be improved?

- Form a positive behaviour working party that is a mix of staff and older students: identify the exact problem.

- Walk the school with the team, mapping precisely where and when there are bottlenecks. Involve the timetabler; it is useful for them to know the difficulties that can be created by having all of Year 9 on the top floor changing lessons at once!

- Launch a corridor code – put signs everywhere so there is no doubt of your expectations, advertise it in newsletters, assemblies and use the students from the positive behaviour team. Be really clear about the type of student behaviour that is desired. Consider display – make it dynamic, visual and informative.
- Supervise the hotspots by using SLT and insist all staff have 'one foot in and one foot out' (of their rooms) at the start and end of all lessons. Make departments responsible for some areas of the school. Break the problem down into single issues and focus on them one by one: punctuality, shouting, keeping to the left *etc.*

When it comes to corridor presence, Tony is well supported by my leadership team. Senior leaders spend hours each day on duty and on walkabout, and we're all out at designated points on the corridor on the strike of the bell to supervise the transition to the next period. Sometimes I worry about the extent to which we rely on supervision of behaviour, rather than self-regulation from students. I'm impressed by schools where students willingly walk with calm alacrity from one lesson to another, and intrigued by schools where students march in line, sometimes even reading books in silence – a model borrowed from a chain of charter schools in America. I've grappled with a more regimented approach to transition at Burlington Danes but our long corridors, large student body and sprawling site aren't conducive to silent transitions. so we settle for an insistence on calm, quick transition, supervised by SLT and teachers, who we ask to meet and greet their students on the corridor outside their room. SLT sweep up stragglers and take their names, adding them to the daily detention list if they fail to beat the late bell which chimes five minutes after the first bell. Members of the SLT, along with heads of year, are armed with walkie-talkies. They're a legacy of the previous regime and I've never been entirely comfortable with them, fearing that they create a reactive culture where senior leaders are forever on alert for the next call-out. My team seems to like them though, so for the moment they survive.

Once students are in class we need to ensure that they stay there. I'm not sure where they get this from but young people have a tendency to regard an ice pack as something of a panacea for a multitude of aches and pains. I remember seeing queues of students at reception after lunch waiting for their daily dose of ice! I quickly put a stop to this by insisting that students should only be out of lessons with a note from their teacher, and we're quick to challenge any wandering students during lessons. The same applies to toilet breaks. Teachers are unable to leave their lessons to go to the loo so we enforce the same rule with students, except in the case of medical needs of course. It reinforces the point that lesson time is sacrosanct.

Getting consistency right

Consistency is the key to becoming a successful school, be it 'singing from the same hymn sheet' or working together as a team.

There is a place for short-term 'drives' in schools such as homing in on punctuality one week, and homework or uniform a few weeks down the line. Assemblies, newsletters, and display screens are well suited to these short-term initiatives. But the best schools manage to maintain a constant vigilance towards the key priorities, and in doing so make prompt punctuality, completion of homework and impeccable uniform the norm.

Students need things to be dependable and routine as the majority do not possess the level of initiative or self control that most adults enjoy when things go wrong. They need consistency in equality, fairness, justice and access.

How can we encourage consistency in schools? In part the answer lies with effective teachers who ensure consistency in their classrooms through regularly applied routines.

Routines refer to specific behaviours and activities that are taught in order to provide smooth, uninterrupted class operation. When carefully taught, routines can save large amounts of time during the year. If students know exactly what is expected of them in a variety of situations, the time saved can be spent teaching rather than organising or reprimanding. Staff need to have shared routines that students expect to be applied every lesson. If all staff stick with them it is easier for everyone in the academy.

So, devise routines for:

- corridor behaviour
- lunch queue behaviour
- lining up outside
- entering the classroom
- waiting behind desks
- what should be on your desk
- taking the register
- distributing materials

- clearing up materials
- asking for help
- transition between activities or tasks
- presenting work in exercise books
- what to do when you've finished your task
- what to do when you're late
- using certain equipment
- group work
- answering questions
- handing in work
- leaving the classroom

With clear *shared* routines in place students know exactly what to do at the start of lessons. They know exactly what they have to do at the end of the lesson and they have a clear procedure to follow for every transition or activity throughout the academy day. Handing in work, what to do when you've finished work, how to behave during group-work, practical work, field work and so on can all be 'automatic' through thoroughly explained and well-practiced routines. It makes for easier teaching!

Outstanding teachers apply scores of routines to their work. That is why students get so much done in their lessons and leave their lesson with a sense of achievement.

Additionally, it may seem pedantic, but formats for academy documentation: lesson plans, schemes of work, letters home (always in Century Gothic font) mirror the expectation at whole academy level, *ie* a high degree of professionalism.

Teaching – the transfer of knowledge and skills from one person to another – is perhaps the most fundamental of all human activities. It's been practised since the dawn of time, mostly within the family unit. In more recent times it's a process that's been professionalised and outsourced in most countries (though the rise of home schooling in America suggests that these trends are not irreversible). This professionalisation has triggered intense scrutiny of the process of teaching, with academics pondering whether it qualifies as an art, a science, a craft or a vocation. So it is by returning to the essence of the task – that transfer of knowledge and skill from one to another – that we spot both the simplicity and complexity of the task of teaching. Simple because it's as old as the hills and it's intrinsic to survival, much as baby seals acquire the art of swimming by riding on their mother's back. Complex because personality cannot be detached from the transaction. The teacher brings his or her own web of understandings to the table, quite different to the patchwork of emotions, experiences and knowhow of his subjects.

This discord between teacher and student can be particularly stark in the complex urban schools where I've worked for the last four decades. We have a diverse staff body at Burlington Danes, but the reality is that teachers are mainly white, university educated and British-born, which puts them at odds with the background of most of our students. Such differences needn't be significant of course, but teachers must always win the trust of their students, a process which becomes a little more complex when common ground between them is so scarce. Teachers are thought to be *Guardian*-reading left-of-centre liberals, and while the reality is obviously more complex than the perception, it's no surprise that teaching attracts people with compassion, empathy and affinity for others – which might be said to fit with the *Guardian*-reading caricature mentioned above. Strangely enough these liberal tendencies can complicate the task of teaching. Liberalism is based on the rights of individuals, but it's a mistake to think of schools as truly liberal institutions. Of course we respect the rights of all students, and good schools engage parents and students through the PTA and Student Voice, but we're also trying to affect change, to take students from one place of learning and understanding to another. The illiberal element of this process emerges from the fact that people don't always want to be changed. The law stipulates that young people attend school until the age of 17, but that doesn't mean that they truly value or respect the education which they are compelled to receive. Thus we try to bring students along with us, to appeal to hearts and minds and goad them into enjoying their lessons and linking their current progress with their future prospects. However sometimes this consent is elusive and we must compel (but not, of course, coerce) students to comply with our expectations. I've seen several classroom teachers whose good intentions and bonhomie are ill-suited to the task of affecting change in young people. The best teachers possess the charm and compassion to cajole students into action, but they store in reserve the grit required to assert their will over non-compliant students. I think in politics they call it the iron fist in the velvet glove. To be sure, I want my teachers to have a pretty thick velvet glove, but an iron core does no harm.

Lessons are the heartbeat of a school, and the success or failure of a school will ultimately depend on the activity within our classrooms. If a school is a piece of music then an assembly can be the rousing chorus, but the lessons are the verses; sometimes humdrum, sometimes stirring, yet without them the whole piece collapses. Professor Dylan Wiliam has long argued that the biggest gaps in quality in education are not between schools but between different classrooms in the same school (www.dylanwiliam.org): 'In Canada, variability at the classroom level is at least four times that at school level'. The implication for policy makers is that efforts should be focused on improving the quality of provision within classrooms, rather than pursuing whole school reform: 'An effective school is a school full of effective classrooms'. Figures provided by the Sutton Trust suggest that the difference between a weak teacher and good teacher can be as much as one year of progress per year, with a weak teacher securing 0.5 years of progress in a year compared to 1.5 years gained by a more competent teacher. I focused on classroom delivery on arrival at Burlington Danes by preaching the simple maxim that teachers should plan, teach and mark.

Outstanding lessons

Whole books have and will be written on classroom craft and pedagogy. I can only give some brief reflections here. In my view the key mark of an outstanding lesson is that all pupils have made progress. Indeed, nearly all outstanding lessons are brilliant in their planning.

Common features of outstanding lessons that I have observed are:

- Teaching is stimulating, enthusiastic and consistently challenging.

- Teachers have an expert knowledge of their subject, how to teach it and how students learn best within their subject.

- Teachers have a passion for what they are teaching.

- Relationships in the classroom are warm and positive.

- Activities and demands are matched sensitively to students needs.

- Well-directed teaching assistants strongly support learning.

- An outstanding teacher gives glimpses of outstanding in most of his or her lessons. They are not outstanding all of the time.

- All learners make exceptionally good progress – *ie* above expectation – against well-crafted learning objectives. Indeed, objectives of the lesson are what pilots the lesson to outstanding. In feedback to staff I often begin with them: they are the route map and the foundation. In weak lessons they are nearly always poorly worded.

There is also a student development dimension that is sometimes overlooked about outstanding teaching:

- Students are keen to come to lessons; they become fiercely loyal and passionate about the subject and often take it into the sixth form and beyond.

- Students are enthusiastic, keen to work hard and want to impress the teacher whom they like. Students feel that they are making great progress compared to other subjects.

- A two-way street is operating: relationships are very good.

- Students do not want to stop working at the end of the lesson. If the teacher is for any reason absent they are truly disappointed and even feel betrayed.

- Students take the initiative and readily accept responsibilities.

- Students are helpful, considerate and consistently behave well.

Here's some tips I've shared with staff to make their lessons outstanding:

- read the latest texts and critical theories around your subject

- get to know the students as well as possible and make contact with their parent/carers

- encourage cooperation among students through group tasks and inventive seating plans

- smile, laugh, cajole

- encourage active learning

- mark work regularly and thoroughly

- ensure the time to be spent on the task is clear

- communicate high expectations by doing all of the above relentlessly

- monitor the learning: are students making progress?

I've been a head for nearly ten years now and in that time I must have opened the door to thousands of lessons. You become good at gaining a snapshot impression of the quality of learning that you encounter. On a simple level you look out for students chewing gum, drinks and bags on desks, children slumped in their seats – basic classroom norms which inexperienced teachers might overlook. More importantly, you look out for a clear sense of purpose: are the students engaged, involved and attentive? Do they know not just what they are doing but why they are doing it? Can they place today's lesson in the context of the broader unit they are studying? Are the students' books well presented, and is the classroom bright, clean and tidy? I want the atmosphere to be focused and positive, with a tangible sense of urgency and pace. You also become adept at gauging a teacher's control over their class, often conveyed by tone of voice, body language and the physical position they occupy in their learning space. It's not easy to command a classroom while hunched over your desk. It's a wonderful privilege to roam the school, perhaps with guests in tow, opening up classroom doors and catching a glimpse of the alchemy at work within.

Routines in the classroom

The best way to ensure settled behaviour is to stick to your routines and practice them regularly so students fully understand how to conduct themselves in your classroom. The checklist below might seem prescriptive, but routines and rituals provide a sense of security. Just as families have routines such as takeaway on a Friday or church on Sunday – schools should provide students with the structure and security of familiar routines.

In the spirit of Atul Gawande's *The Checklist Manifesto* (2010), *ie* getting the simple things right, we have a teacher routine checklist:

THE BURLINGTON DANES ACADEMY CHECKLIST		Yes/No
Have you...? Lesson by lesson		☑
Before the lesson	Planned a lesson with challenge for all students	☐
	Set objectives where all students can meet or exceed their targets and show progress	☐
	Marked your books diagnostically in accordance with BDA policy	☐
	An up-to-date seating plan	☐
	Manned your area outside the corridor and greeted students at the door ('one foot in and one foot out')	☐
At the beginning of the lesson	Ensured equipment is out on the desk including planner and pencil case	☐
	Displayed the homework on the first slide for students to copy into their homework planners	☐
	Engaged students with a starter of c.5 minutes which is relevant and engaging	☐
	Checked all students have copied down the title, date and learning objective	☐

	Taken the register in the first 10 minutes of the lesson	☐
During the lesson	Ensured that students know their targets and what they need to do to be on or above target	☐
	Used targeted questioning /whole group responses to check students are on or above target	☐
	Given out merits	☐
Plenary	Checked students' learning through a meaningful plenary	☐
	Checked students have met the objectives and thus made progress before the end of the lesson	☐
	Asked students to stand by their desks at the end of the lesson in silence	☐
At the end of the lesson	Dismissed students row by row on the bell	☐
	Returned to the corridor to ensure a smooth transition ('one foot in and one foot out')	☐

A key theme of this book is that you can't detach the personality of the headteacher from the personality of the school. The same applies in the classroom. Developing an effective classroom persona is an enthralling challenge for anyone entering the profession. It takes years to perfect, and after working in schools for decades I still struggle to put my finger on what distinguishes an effective teacher from a more limited one. This matters because even the most finely tuned lesson plan is only as strong as the authority with which it's delivered. Some years ago when the Conservative party was in the doldrums it was said that focus groups liked their policies until they were told that they were Conservative policies. It's the same in the classroom, the activities delivered are indelibly stamped by the personality of the teacher, and will rise or fall on the strength of this personality. Psychologists call it the 'halo effect'.

Perhaps 'persona' is preferable to 'personality' because it is the way that a teacher comes across to his students which matters most, and you never really know how people are going to react to the presence of 25 teenagers until they are confronted with this day in, day out, for a sustained period of time. I remember one teacher who joined us through Teach First. From the moment we met her we made contingency plans for her departure, such was our concern about her based on the scatty and casual manner which she presented to staff during her induction week. Yet when she met her classes in September she filled the room with warmth, charm and creativity, and three years on she remains a valuable member of our team. Young people tend to be pretty fair and astute judges of character, so they warmed to her caring manner from the start.

To say that young people are fair judges of character is quite a different thing to saying that they are respectful of authority. One doesn't have to indulge in nostalgia to recognise that in previous generations the compliance of children at schools was the norm. Yes, personality still mattered, but in most schools teachers didn't have to actively win over their charges. Who knows why? Perhaps levels of trust were higher, maybe the grip of religion encouraged allegiance to authority. No doubt the fact that people lived in smaller communities meant that there were fewer strangers, and therefore higher levels of mutual trust. You would be more likely to comply with your English teacher if there was even a slight chance that he or she would be standing next to your own parents at church on Sunday. I'm exaggerating the simplicity of pre-modern Britain, but the fact is that today, teachers can no longer rely on the complicity of young people. It must be earned, and I see this every year when new teachers strive to assert themselves over their new classes. I've used the phrase 'assert themselves' repeatedly and I think it captures the challenge. The numbers game is stacked against the teacher – in theory 25 children should be able to dictate the dynamics of a classroom, not the lone teacher. So the personality of the teacher must fill the room, must be bigger than the collective personality of 25 young people. The good news is that they want you to take control. The bad news is that plenty of them will be ready to steal the show if you fail to take command.

So how can a teacher assert herself over her class? In short, it's by identifying her unique strengths and playing up to them for all they're worth. This chimes with the advice that the editor of *The Economist*, Geoffrey Crowther, used to give to his journalists in the 1950s: 'simplify, then exaggerate'. Successful teachers focus on the most compelling part of their personality, then drench their class in the stuff. I don't mean to say that all teachers have to be bursting with charisma. Their unique selling point, to use marketing speak, could be being a disciplinarian, a story teller, a great motivator, an expert in their field, a meticulous planner or a compassionate mentor. Others gain status by proving their value to the school community through taking a football team or helping backstage at the school musical. One or two even manage to succeed through being 'down with the kids', though it's not a method I would recommend, primarily because for most of us this wouldn't be very authentic.

Authenticity is paramount. Jonathan Smith captures this in his book *The Learning Game*, in which he advises teachers: 'Be yourself. Trust in your personality. Transfer your energy' (p. 40). He goes on to describe teachers performing at their best: 'they look as if they belong. They look as if they are there by right. That's the look. When I am ready I will begin. That is their body language. I am made for this stage. This is my chosen ground. I know I can perform' (p. 42). This resonates with the observations of Peter Hyman, whose book *1 Out of 10* describes leaving Number 10 Downing Street, where he was a speech writer for Tony Blair, and training as a teacher in a school in Islington: 'I haven't begun to master all the secrets of teaching yet, but I'm now picking up on what gives one teacher authority and another less of it. The key ingredient is certainty: the absolute certainty in the tone of voice that what is being said is going to happen; certainty that you know your subject and have planned meticulously for the hour ahead' (2005, p. 371). The trouble is that this certainty is difficult, if not impossible, to fake.

This was brought home to me at one school where a drama teacher couldn't control his classes despite being a highly competent professional actor. I wanted to say to him 'if you're that good at acting, can't you take on the role of an authoritative teacher?' The fact is that the persona of the teacher has to be authentic and consistent, as this passage from the behaviour management expert Bill Rogers suggests: 'When a teacher's manner, body language, posture and communication appear confident and authoritative, and when such confidence is further maintained in both teaching and management, students are likely to co-operate with the teacher's leadership' (2011, p. 89). I've heard it said that in the current climate of rigour and accountability the role of teaching has become a purely technical one: 'The teacher's role has been reduced to that of a process worker' (Smith, 2002). In my experience a teacher who approaches the job as a technical drill will struggle to win over his class; personality can never be separated from the challenge of teaching.

Behaviour for learning

Around the middle of the year is the time to re-establish your principles and command your learning space. Here's how:

1.   If you mark thoroughly, clearly and with consistency most students will commit themselves to working for you. Focus on planning your lessons and marking their work.

2.   Cherish the heart. Students love praise, seeing their work on the wall, being star of the week, positive phone calls home *etc*. Getting to know the parents really helps.

3.   Only accept the best work and create a drafting culture in your classroom. Observations at BDA demonstrate that the key factor that underpins student behaviour is motivation. With high levels of motivation comes pride – with pride comes effort. Always follow-up homework immediately – that way it will always be done.

4.   Relentlessly follow the academy systems with the utmost rigour. Seating plans, awareness of data. Progress against well crafted objectives. Try the direct simplicity of 'active listening': a very precise instruction to classes (stop talking, pens down, eye contact to speaker *etc*).

5.   Ask for support. There are several staff who can help you, all of whom have benefitted from support themselves in the past.

Casting our minds back to when we were at school is likely to confirm the importance of a teacher's personality. At my sixth form grammar school I was blessed with some excellent teachers. My English teacher Miss Pritchard inspired me to love literature through her passion for the topic. Similarly, my teacher of American history would pepper her lessons with personal experiences, such as vivid descriptions of walking through Harlem as a middle class white woman at the height of the civil rights movement. There's a fine line between a useful personal testimony and a time-wasting ego-trip, but I encourage teachers to give something of themselves in the classroom. A six-period day can be an arduous slog for the students otherwise. Of course it's much easier for a teacher to convey a personal connection to his lessons if he is teaching something he's passionate about, another reason why the subject department is such a vital unit within the school. My own most memorable lessons involved exploring the rich layers of my favourite plays, such as *Hamlet* and *Othello*.

Much has been done to classify the features of an outstanding lesson, but it's the palpable buzz of enjoyment and engagement that's hard to describe, hard to deliver, and wonderful to experience as an observer.

The psychologist Mihaly Csikszentmihalyi captures this buzz in his groundbreaking theory of flow, in which he argues that people are at their best when absorbed in activities pitched just beyond their current level of ability. He champions that feeling of being in the zone: 'In Flow, one is so immersed in an activity that nothing else seems to matter'. Applying this to schools he argues that 'enjoyment appears at the boundary between boredom and anxiety', so it's the job of teachers to create opportunities for flow – for genuine engagement and enjoyment with learning for its own sake – in the classroom. The application of his theory to education concludes with the view that 'the value of school does not depend on its prestige, or its ability to train students to face up to the necessities of life, but rather on the degree of the enjoyment of lifelong learning it can transmit' (1990, p. 181). Howard Gardner advocates using flow to teach children: motivating them from inside rather than by threat or promise of reward: 'you learn at your best when you have something you care about and you can get pleasure from being engaged in' (1995, p. 191).

What pupils want: group work

Ask any student what they like about their lessons and I bet most will say 'group work'. It reminds me of the Henry Ford quip, "If I had asked people what they wanted, they would have requested faster horses". Group work is no panacea, but there is a time and a place for it. It is an excellent means by which to cultivate independent learning. There are pitfalls though: it must be structured and managed, with roles within the group clearly delineated. The key issue is that the skills of group work are not necessarily understood by our students and they need to be explicitly taught and critically evaluated in a consistent way across the academy just like, for instance, essay writing, and reading.

At its best, group projects provide opportunities for teaching skills such as:

- organisation
- negotiation
- delegation
- team work
- co-operation
- leadership
- explanation
- following others and accepting authority

Students love working together and teaching one another (proven to be the most effective way to learn) and group work is useful for encouraging social interaction for isolated and less confident (*eg* EAL or SEN) students. I have seen it well done at BDA in geography when role play was used to demonstrate how pupils would cope with the aftermath of a volcanic eruption, with groups assuming roles *eg* the army, emergency services and medics. As students do not wish to let each other down it provides a more contributory style of learning and can even reduce the workload of both the students and staff. Indeed, putting students into groups (*eg* for mentoring) can often be a highly effective way of channelling the competitive spirit. Is individual mentoring, carried out all over the country, an effective way of preparing pupils for exams?

Group work requires agreed rules, a planning checklist which would include: the nature of the task, group composition, roles within groups, timings, outcomes and assessment opportunities. Expectations require drafting and would include the fact that any student will be prepared to work with any member of the group. Working within an environment of tolerance and taking account of the opinions of others is made explicit.

Observed good practice includes:

- discouraging anonymity by limiting the size of groups
- sharing the final products of the group work with the entire class and inviting critique, with listening to one another a given
- allowing in-class time for group meetings and planning: it really supports independent learning
- designing formative assessment on both the work itself and the group work
- allowing for the time required to make groups work
- assigning students to groups rather than allowing them to self-select
- encouraging discussions within groups as a tool to foster creativity
- varying the outcomes of group work; flip charts, three salient points, a *precis* of a piece of evidence, poster presentations, discussion, ideas, brainstorms *etc*
- individual follow-up assessments that make the group work more worthy in the eyes of our students
- making effective group interaction and co-operation criteria in grading the outcomes or awarding merits

At Burlington Danes we're blessed with some extremely talented teachers who could thrive in whatever they set their mind on. Former head of humanities Ms Stone previously led trekking expeditions to some of the remotest spots on the planet, including the Gobi desert and the Himalayas. Her geography lessons are infused with the passion and knowledge developed on these trips, while her classroom feels more like a geography lab, complete with maps, globes, photographs, posters, and an extensive back catalogue of geographical journals and books. Maths teacher Mr Gidaropoulous frequently tells staff that maths is the most beautiful and creative subject in the curriculum and most of the students in his care end up agreeing. Vice principal Mr Fairbairn would have continued working for an engineering firm if he hadn't been lured into teaching a year after graduating from Cambridge. He discovered the joy of teaching while offering tutoring to a family friend in his evenings after spending the day designing bridges and buildings. Head of maths faculty Mr Magezi fills his room with the strength of character developed while growing up in apartheid in South Africa. He's been at the school for 15 years and only recently received a letter from a former student thanking him for changing his direction in life. Mr Magezi had spotted this boy shoplifting on a Saturday morning. On the following Monday Mr Magezi called in the boy's parents and through the support he offered enabled the student to excel in his GCSEs and progress to university to study medicine. The letter was written on completion of his medical studies. The final lines read, 'I hope this letter finds you and your family well, for you have been an important person in changing the course of my life. That's it, thank you for doing more than your job for it was what I needed. I have been aiming to write this letter for a long time but for some reason had not. I hope even though you do not remember me this letter may serve as some encouragement for the times when teaching seems hard and futile'.

I've been privileged to walk into some enthralling lessons in my career, lessons which take students on a journey of discovery, which fizz with the energy, apprehension and excitement of learning something new. They tap into the prior knowledge of the students, before entering that sweet spot of unchartered cognitive territory just beyond the students' existing skill level: that 'boundary between boredom and anxiety' described by Csikszentmihalyi. The final part of the lesson – the plenary – takes students back to their starting point and encourages them to reflect on the significance of the knowledge and skills acquired in the preceding period. Let me describe a few lessons which have hit these lofty heights.

A few years ago I remember a brilliant geography lesson delivered at Burlington Danes by Ms Stone, who is now an assistant principal. The lesson happened to be with a Year 9 class of low-ability students who sometimes struggled to focus. Here they were all involved as they worked in teams on designing a town. Some students were given the role of providing the ideas, others had to consider finances, yet more had to evaluate the impact of various proposals on different groups of people. Through the quality of their contributions the students achieved levels way beyond their targets, though they hardly realised this, such was their focus on the task at hand. Ms Stone is a great example of a teacher who manages behaviour through the quality of her lessons, with tasks carefully pitched at the skills and interest of the students.

Head of chemistry Ms Stanger commanded her classes through her knowledge and passion for the subject. There was simply no space for mischief such was the zest that she pumped into her room. Back at Sacred Heart I fondly recall a slightly older female teacher who maintained at all times an impeccably polite manner with the students. "I'm absolutely astounded that you're chewing gum in here," she would whisper. I also remember an incredibly sarcastic maths teacher who won the students over with his cynical wit. These last two examples remind us that the most effective teachers have developed a compelling classroom persona that puts the students at ease and serves as a catalyst for learning. Recalling these talented teachers and inspiring lessons fills me with as much excitement as a movie buff recalling the first time she saw her favourite film, or a bookworm waxing lyrical about reading her favourite novel for the first time. My only regret is that unlike a great book or a memorable film, these wonderful lessons have never been captured and will never be replicated. These are precious moments: classrooms buzzing with the progress of engaged students under the tutelage of masterful teachers.

Teaching is learning

Teaching and learning: two sides of the same coin. At Burlington Danes, teaching and learning is embedded in these principles:

1. All can achieve whatever the background
2. Teachers must have high expectations
3. Teachers determine the pace of lessons

4. The main determinants of achievement (challenge, pace, motivation, assessment) are the bedrock of our strategies; we aspire to promote reasoning, problem solving, evaluation and the formulation of hypotheses and to promote students' thinking about the way they have learned

5. All must know their targets and how to reach the next level

6. Students must have the opportunity to develop higher level skills and the most able must be challenged

7. Students in the bottom 20% must be motivated and challenged.

8. In spite of setting, differentiation matters

9. Progress must be made every lesson

10. Homework enables further progress

One of the most insightful books on teaching in recent years has been *Leverage Leadership* (2012) by Paul Bambrick-Santoyo. Bambrick-Santoyo rightly reminds us that our duty as school leaders is to create a culture in which our teachers can improve their practice. *Leverage Leadership* reminds school leaders to focus on teaching and learning, not operational issues, and proposes a system of teacher observation based on continual improvement rather than snapshot judgements. Bambrick-Santoyo suggests that most heads spend half their time on admin and only 6% on improving the quality of classroom instruction. At Burlington Danes we've used some of the ideas from *Leverage Leadership* to create a voluntary system of coaching and peer observations between our teachers, in which teachers receive frequent short observations focused on one particular issue. I know the system is working when staff conversations about dealing with challenging behaviour are replaced by conversations about improving their classroom practice.

It's worth pausing to consider the impact that the internet could have on teaching, or rather *is* having. The power of the internet of course is that it enables interaction between teacher and student without the students needing to be physically in front of the teacher. That's a pretty fundamental change. Since the dawn of formal education, the key constraint faced by teachers has been the limited amount of time that they spend with each class each week. Through the internet, teachers can post key resources online, or place video tutorials on their blogs. One of our Maths teachers has a blog (www.mrgmaths.

com) which contains video explanations leading students through all of the questions that have appeared in past papers over the last five years. Other teachers are using Twitter as a means of generating student feedback and to encourage students to relate their learning to current affairs. All schools now have a Virtual Learning Environment (VLE) which enables teachers to post resources on the school's intranet, and also enables students to submit work online. There are those who wonder whether the proliferation of online lessons will render the classroom teacher obsolete. Khan Academy, for example, whose motto is *'Learn almost anything, for free'* provides a rapidly growing collection of pithy instructional videos online that cover topics as wide ranging as 'Leonardo's *Mona Lisa*' to computer science theory, it's an interesting prospect. The vast majority of school lessons involve some form of teacher instruction, traditionally the delivery of information by the teacher at the front of the class. This particular method of pedagogy is well suited to the internet, where it's quite likely that another teacher has recorded her explanation of exactly the same concept that you're trying to convey, except they've used snazzier graphics and enjoyed the benefit of multiple takes. It makes good sense then for teachers to browse YouTube and other sites for such nuggets.

The founder of Wikipedia, Jimmy Wales, predicts that boring university lecturers will be the first victims of online education, recalling his own days at university:

> I was taking an advanced calculus class and my instructor was reputed to be a fabulous researcher, but he barely spoke English. He was a very boring and bad teacher and I was absolutely lost and in despair. So I went to the campus tutoring centre and they had Betamax tapes of a professor who had won teaching awards. Basically I sat with those tapes and took class there. But I still had to go to the other one and sat there and wanted to kill myself. I thought at that time, in the future, why wouldn't you have the most entertaining professor, the one with the proven track record of getting knowledge into people's heads? We're still not quite there. In university you're still likely to be in a large lecture hall with a very boring professor, and everyone knows it's not working very well. It's not even the best use of that professor's time or the audience (BBC News interview, 1 May 2013).

But teacher only instruction comprises a small fraction of classroom activity. In any half-decent lesson the students are active participants, shaping the focus of their inquiry and reaching their own conclusions. Even if a teacher is standing at the front delivering instruction he's going to be tuned in to the response of his audience, gauging their understanding and pre-empting their questions. He'll know what the students struggled with last time and where he needs to get them before the end of the lesson. He'll know that he'll lose the focus of the boy on the front row unless he asks him a question within the first five minutes. He'll know that on a Tuesday they arrive straight from dance, so they're likely to be animated and excitable, so he might start the lesson with a short dictation, or a moment of reflection; but on a Friday afternoon they need an injection of energy, so he might start the lesson by playing a recent pop song and asking students to relate the focus of the lesson to the words of the song (choose the song carefully!). They say that teaching is a bit like acting, but in truth it's more like being a film director. You refine your narrative, set the stage, and call the shots, but ultimately your success depends on your ability to bring out the best in those who sit before you, front and centre.

Skills and attitudes alongside learning

How teaching has changed in the past 40 years. The textbook, for example, is no longer the framework or scaffold on which to hang pupils' learning. Now answers to any task are readily available on the internet – therefore teachers need to devise tasks that are 'Google-proof', relating it to their own experiences or previous learning mitigates against this. So instead of asking 'explain the causes of the First World War', ask 'how does what we have learned today explain how the First World War started?'

Pupils today need to know more, learn more, work harder and for sustained periods of time. Concentration skills, resilience, grit and independence are attributes which must be developed and nurtured.

At BDA we talk of 'stretch and challenge': the point in the lesson when your brain is going to hurt. Learning is about difficulty: real learning takes you from ignorance to enlightenment, and to progress from ignorance to enlightenment you need, in my view, emotional intelligence and skills such as those listed above.

Earlier in this chapter we discussed Dylan Wiliam's view that the biggest improvements to be made in education are within classrooms rather than within schools: 'An effective school is a school full of effective classrooms.' So what can a headteacher do to facilitate the kind of lessons we've discussed here? Ideally, we recruit talented, dedicated teachers and let them get on with it. This chimes with the findings of a recent McKinsey report which suggests that schools can 'prescribe adequacy, but greatness must be unleashed' ('How the world's most improved school systems keep getting better', 29 November 2010): *ie* a top down approach can ensure certain minimum standards, but truly outstanding schools cannot be generated according to formula. Daniel Pink, bestselling author of *Drive: The Surprising Truth About What Motivates Us*, makes a similar point when he describes teaching as an 'heuristic', rather than 'algorithmic' task: there is no set formula – 'routine work can be outsourced or automated; artistic, empathic, non-routine work generally cannot'. Pink continues, 'the implications for motivation are vast. Researchers … have found that external rewards and punishments – both carrots and sticks – can work nicely for algorithmic tasks. But they can be devastating for heuristic ones' (p. 30). Instead of external rewards, Pink suggests that teachers and employers should seek to cultivate 'autonomy, mastery, purpose' in order to unleash human potential. Headteachers can do this by creating an overarching purpose for the school, giving teachers the autonomy to stamp their mark on their classes, and providing opportunities for teacher development through shining a light on the great practice taking place around the school. Similarly, our best teachers create a sense of purpose in their class, giving students responsibility for their own progress while providing insightful personalised tuition to enable them to develop mastery.

I want to explain in more detail how we give teachers autonomy in the classroom. Some routines are followed by all teachers in every lesson. These core routines include the way that students enter the class, take their seats and record homework. We also expect teachers to assess students in a consistent manner. Consistency is these areas provides stability and creates positive norms and rituals. Beyond these rituals, I give teachers flexibility to plan, teach and mark in their own style. Last week while walking around the school I found a Year 8 English class energetically acting out a scene from *Othello* – books, tables and chairs had been moved out of the way – and when I tried to pop into a Year 10 RE class I found an empty classroom, only to be told that the teacher had taken the students out onto the field to teach the design argument for the existence of God, aided by the bright spring sunshine and the buds, blossom and flowers that were beginning to emerge from their winter hibernation. So beyond consisting of a beginning, middle and end, incorporating engaging resources and challenging activities, there's no specific format that I expect all teachers to follow. I welcome the fact that Ofsted have loosened their fixation with a particular lesson format, emphasising instead the twin pillars of progress and engagement.

In 2011 I chaired a review of Teachers' Standards in England, which culminated in a report recommending the introduction of a new Master Teacher Standard to recognise our very best teachers. We also created a new framework of Teachers' Standards which is already being used to measure all teachers, from trainees to seasoned practitioners. Our brief was to replace the existing patchwork of 74 standards and 100+ pages of guidance with clear and concise standards which were rooted in classroom practice. I was blessed with a wonderful committee of 12 people with a rich variety of educational experience, from classroom teachers to university professors. We asked ourselves what kind of teacher we would want to teach our own children and devised eight over-arching principles. These principles, and the sub-points which unpick them, are intended to be minimum expectations, pinning down the most fundamental elements of classroom practice. I'm very pleased with them and I'm glad that their clarity is enabling headteachers to champion and promote high standards within their classrooms.

Teachers' Standards (2011)

1. Set high expectations which inspire, motivate and challenge pupils
2. Promote good progress and outcomes by pupils
3. Demonstrate good subject and curriculum knowledge
4. Plan and teach well structured lessons
5. Adapt teaching to respond to the strengths and needs of all pupils
6. Make accurate and productive use of assessment
7. Manage behaviour effectively to ensure a good and safe learning environment
8. Fulfil wider professional responsibilities

In this chapter I've attempted to analyse the classroom experience, and consider the complex variables which muddy the waters of what in theory is a pretty simple endeavour that consists of transferring knowledge and skills from teacher to student. We've seen that a teacher can't detach his personality from this process. Indeed, when a teacher is given her timetable at the start of the year she knows that she'll be developing a relationship with each class. Like any relationship, it will have its ups and downs, and the opening lessons of the year are crucial in terms of setting expectations and creating a positive working environment. Teachers must strike a balance at the start of the year between setting expectations and teaching the curriculum. Dive straight into the curriculum and you've missed the opportunity to lay down high expectations at a time when students are usually very compliant. But focus too much on rules, regulations and behaviour, and it can be difficult to gain the momentum and satisfaction provided by working through the programme of study.

This establishment phase at the start of the year becomes second nature to experienced teachers, but it poses a serious challenge to new recruits. Every September I see new teachers gradually expanding their domain. They start by hovering around the desk, taking comfort from their central position at the front of the class. Soon they show their growing confidence by striding around the room, crouching to meet students at their level, standing tall to emit confidence and authority. Before long the teacher's domain will include the area outside their class, and the most confident teachers will soon be bossing their whole corridor, stamping their authority on a patch of school turf. If it sounds tribal and primitive, that's a reflection of the nature of teaching; it's an intrinsically human endeavour, fundamentally rooted in the complexities of the human experience.

There's been some discussion in recent years of whether the requirements for a good lesson, and indeed a good teacher, are different in a school serving deprived communities compared to those serving more affluent ones. One academic puts it like this: 'The characteristics of urban schools make likely the necessity of employing a radically different approach from that successfully employed in preparing teachers for schools with students from middle- and upper-class settings' (Tobin, 2001, p. 942). The emergence of Teach First and Future Leaders, programmes created to train and develop teachers and leaders in the specific context of challenging schools, makes this a pertinent issue. My view is that teaching and leading in a challenging school compared with teaching and leading in a more affluent context is a different challenge by degree, rather than kind. Simply put, in an affluent school, where teachers face compliant students with a firm grasp of numeracy and literacy, the teacher does not need to draw on the range and depth of powers as a teacher in a challenging school, where students don't necessarily want to learn, and where their prior schooling or home life might not have equipped them with the tools needed to excel in the classroom. In these contexts, teachers and leaders must work harder, and be more creative, engaging and rigorous than they would need to be in a more stable school. This matters, because there is a temptation to think that tough schools need disciplinarians, and that there's no place for more cerebral teachers in the urban environment. But it would be wrong if schools in more deprived areas were full of sergeant-majors, or at the other end of the spectrum, quasi youth workers. All teachers would benefit from being intellectually competent, with decent subject knowledge, sharp communication, empathy, wit, and energy. But in some schools, where student compliance is a given, a teacher without these attributes won't be exposed so easily. In challenging schools there's no hiding place, so it's all the more vital that teachers possess this rare mix of skills and characteristics. And the wonderful thing about teaching is that these characteristics are intensely human and natural.

This chapter in a tweet: Teachers face a monumental challenge; the role of the head is to allow them to thrive in the classroom.

Lesson 5:
Create a culture of transparency and accountability

'It's true that all students are ranked from 1-180.'

In 2011 Transport for London opened up its travel data, making live journey information available to travel apps and web developers. As a result, the users of this data – commuters – can easily access live information about journey times, line closures and signal failures. Commuters gain ownership of the data that matters to them, empowering them to make decisions about their journey across the capital. In a small patch of West London I've tried to open up data at Burlington Danes, enabling students to own the data that matters most to them: their academic progress. It's a surprisingly controversial topic, but this chapter argues that using data to shine a light on student progress should be the most natural thing in any school, and that in the 21st century schools have a duty to create a culture of transparency and accountability.

Starting out: Getting the data right – and what do we do with it?

'...data only becomes effective if it stimulates questions about the actual learning that is taking place and how it can be developed further.' (Kirkup *et al*, 2005 p. 157)

We use data to:

* create benchmarks which identify the potential of the student

* group students by ability

* accurately inform the level of our teaching and assessment

* inform students and parents of their current levels of ability: make that knowledge part of the school culture

- set individual targets for achievement
- identify progress by comparing the outcomes of subject assessment and benchmarking by 'tracking' individual students
- periodically rank students in public by ability
- identify teachers who add value and share that good practice, support middle leaders through raising levels of accountability
- analyse our own individual performance, and that of the subject, in early September; and at calendared points thereafter
- target intervention immediately where a mismatch between potential and progress is identified. Look at borderline students, involve parents and, if necessary, governors
- celebrate progress and achievement

The first step of the journey towards a culture of accountability and transparency is to record and publicise the progress of students. It seems obvious, but there are plenty of schools, and school systems (some very good ones, *eg* Finland) where recording the progress of students isn't the norm. There are plenty of arguments made against assessing students frequently, many of which have their merits. It's argued that testing places unnecessary pressure on young people, and that it encourages teachers to teach to the test. These are potential pitfalls, but they can be easily guarded against. Of course a balance must be struck between tuition and testing: between feeding the pig and weighing the pig, to use that common analogy. Our solution to this is to map out an assessment calendar for the year ahead in the same way that we map out our term dates and key events. So all year groups are assessed once every term in each of their subjects – that's three formal assessment points in the course of the year. As for teachers teaching to the test, this argument fails on two counts. Firstly, if a test is rigorous and well devised then preparing students to pass it is perfectly consistent with the kind of balanced and rounded learning that we all want to see in the classroom. Secondly, I believe that young people want to do well, and frankly I think they can cope with three assessment periods per year. I would argue that it's more stressful for young people to be confronted with life-defining tests at the age of 11, 16 and 18 (as has often been the case in the past) than to be tested frequently throughout their school life. Our approach helps to normalise testing, which I believe brings the best out of students.

The Power of Assessment

At Burlington Danes Academy we:

1. Assess regularly

Each core subject area will carry out a summative assessment six times a year for each pupil. Foundation subjects assess three times a year. These assessment opportunities are in the academy calendar. Each teacher is required to give each pupil a grade, which is then entered into the school database. In truth, assessment has been a critical factor in driving up achievement, as data is forensically analysed.

Pupils should be well-informed beforehand of what is required to achieve each level. Revision guides for the test must be written and distributed.

2. Use rank orders

Through the rank ordering system, the academy aims to maintain a regular and rigorous assessment and tracking process which allows targeted interventions effectively.

We also intend to raise motivation amongst pupils through the transparency of the system, and create a competitive spirit.

Staff prepare pupils for the introduction of the rank-ordering system through a series of assemblies on the importance of assessment, ensuring that pupils know the purpose of the rank order, and how it would work in practice.

Rank orders are the key determinant in terms of which class a pupil is placed in. Pupils are assessed once every half-term in core subjects, and once a term in foundation subjects. Data is recorded in the form of percentages or scores, rather than National Curriculum levels, in order to increase accuracy.

Every half-term, vice principal Mr Wilson crunches this data to put the pupils in rank order of their academic ability within each year group. English, maths and science have a double-weighting to ensure that the rank order is focused on core subjects.

Pupils in Years 10-13 are also given a predictive grade by each teacher, ensuring the accuracy of these grades is vitally important and is done by a member of the SLT comparing predictive data on each child across all subjects.

The rank orders are displayed around the academy. In addition, pupils receive a sticky label summarising their achievement, while parents and carers receive a written report. On the day they are posted, pupils are very excited: some elated, others crushed with disappointment. We often say that this process mirrors public exams and to hold on to the feeling as a reminder of how you either want, or don't want, to feel.

On an annual basis, the rank order is used to stream pupils into different classes. We group all students in all years by ability as far as we can. The lower-ability classes have around 10-15 pupils and are supported by teaching assistants and the special educational needs coordinator (SENCO). We seek to improve from the bottom-up by allocating some of our best teachers to these low-ability classes. Intervention is also planned on the basis of the rank order and with particular emphasis in Year 11: in this year students are divided into key intervention groups based on their progress towards their target grades.

3. Set targets

Each pupil works towards personal targets for each of their subjects. These are in their planner on a sticker provided. It is *essential* that all pupils know their current 'working at' grade and their predicted grades.

Predicted grades are drawn up from a triangulation of three pieces of information:

1. A range of personal information and teacher knowledge of the pupil
2. Baseline assessment (ideally Key Stage 2 results)
3. The academy's own assessment, particularly in Year 7/Year 9

Teachers only alter targets upwards in liaison with the SLT lead on assessment. Our predicted grades are predicated on the top 50% of students in the top 25% of schools nationally, *ie* students entering the school at or above Level 4B are given:

1. A Key Stage 3 target of six sub-levels above their base grade on entry to Key Stage 3
2. A Key Stage 4 target of 12 sub-levels above their base grade on entry to Key Stage 3

The fact is that pupil progress is the most basic currency in a school - it's the whole point of a school's existence. So not knowing the rate of student progress is like a football team not knowing whether it's winning or losing in a game or a plumber not checking that the water runs after connecting a house to the mains supply. Quite frankly I think that those people who criticise the proliferation of testing in schools are simply on the wrong side of the argument. Take this quote from Christine Blower, general secretary, of the National Union of Teachers, speaking in 2013: "The hoops that young children will have to jump through, such as the Year One phonics check and the Year Six spelling, grammar and punctuation tests, will leave many children feeling a failure" ('Teachers call for boycott of primary school literacy tests', *The Daily Telegraph*, 1 April 2013). I can't read that quote without wanting to add the phrase 'if they fail' to the end of it. Surely this is low expectations of the worst kind if we equate a culture of testing with a culture of failure? Students can and will succeed if we prepare them properly. But beyond this, I feel that concerns about testing fail to recognise that transparency, accountability and feedback have become key elements of modern society.

Let me explain. When you phone a call centre these days you're often informed how long your waiting time will be, and after the call you're often given a chance to offer feedback on the quality of the experience, sometimes via a separate text message. Mobile phone operators reveal their monthly percentage of dropped calls, and factories feature wall displays which reveal to the workers the current rate of production. I was on a flight recently and soon after landing I received a text message from the airline asking me for feedback on the in-flight entertainment. In cars, dashboards give drivers feedback on everything from fuel efficiency to imminent traffic. Some dashboards even recommend to the driver that he should take a break, based on sensors which pick up signs of fatigue. Thousands of us book hotels and holidays on the basis of internet reviews.

These cases reveal the extent to which transparency, accountability and feedback have become the norm in modern society, but let's not presume that this openness only extends to consumer choice. In fact, it's in public services that some of the most radical reforms have taken place. In Brazil, public servants' salaries are posted online, a move which revealed some shocking abuses of the system: 'there were 168 public employees in São Paulo's auditing court who received monthly salaries of at least $12,000, and sometimes as much as $25,000 — more than the mayor of the city, Brazil's largest, was earning' ('Brazil, where a judge made $361,500 in a month, fumes over pay', *New York Times,* 10 February 2013). In Britain politicians' expenses are also available on the internet, while in France government ministers have recently been compelled to reveal their personal wealth. NHS heart surgery success rates are now published online, leading to a 50% improvement in survival rates, one of the highest in Europe ('Transparency in the NHS...', *The Guardian*, 12 March 2013). Even public toilets inform users when they were last cleaned, sometimes also showing a countdown to the next scheduled service. Why does this matter? In short, a desire from consumers and taxpayers to gain value for money is now matched by the technological capacity to put real time data into the hands of the public. As school leaders we can choose to bury our heads in the sand, providing infrequent and opaque data to students and parents. Or we can embrace this desire for information and feedback and use it to drive student progress by frequently placing relevant, accurate, meaningful data into the hands of the students, empowering them to manage their own progress. Of course 'pupil progress' is about character and spiritual development as well as academic development, but I'm confident that we can provide this too, and it's not difficult to check whether schools are 'exam factories' or whether they do in fact nurture rounded personal growth.

Accountability

If I could sum up leadership in one word it would be 'accountability'. High stakes data at the end of KS4 and post-16, Ofsted, governors, HMI, the academy sponsors, the local authority, RaiseOnline and many more stakeholders call the head to account at different points throughout the academic year. Coping with accountability, indeed living with it, is the very essence of leadership.

We forget that accountability is not about 'catching you out' but is intrinsically linked to school improvement. You should be driven by what pupils learn (and not just academically) in the classroom, driven by outcomes and not the process.

At its most basic, however, schools are uncertain what they are accountable for. Is it excellent academic performance? Character development? Both? Or simply progress, not outcomes? And should that progress be contextualised? Set this discussion up with your governing body.

Prioritise improvement on the basis of evidence: what's going well, what needs to improve? Make sure the buck stops with one person, not several. Define what you want to achieve: this won't always be in the improvement plan. The improvement agenda should drive all meetings. What are the critical success factors? What do you hope to achieve? What does your evidence for school improvement look like?

Data needs to make sense to parents. This is why National Curriculum levels have never really worked; it means nothing to parents to say that "your child is a 5c in geography". If the data makes sense to parents then it empowers them to take control. If you hide the truth from parents you patronise them. It's got to be clear, transparent and understandable. It's a good thing that the government has scrapped levels; it's just a pity that a system hasn't been established to replace them.

So what of those countries where student performance is hidden? Burlington Danes was featured in a Norwegian school leadership journal recently (Skolederen, January 2012) and since then we've hosted several visits from Norwegian policy makers and teachers. I was astonished when one group of teachers told me that in their school in Norway they do assess the students but only to ensure an even spread of students from each ability range in all of their classes. Students are never told their actual results! Similarly in *Finnish Lessons* (2011), a study of schools in Finland, Sahlberg reveals that testing is reduced to a 'necessary minimum' and that 'responsibility and trust' (of teachers) are prioritised ahead of accountability. Other revelations within the book might explain the success of the Finnish system more than this absence of testing. For example, teaching is a prestigious and over-subscribed profession in Finland. Finnish schools are small and teachers have plenty of free periods; a Masters is required to teach; there is practically no working class in the country; and theirs is a small and cohesive population. Ultimately it's difficult to argue with the Finnish system when their outcomes are so impressive, but we don't have that luxury in this country. I think it's perfectly natural that after a term of teaching the students and the teacher want to know how much progress has been made.

Once a schedule of testing has been established the challenge is to get the wealth of data that emerges from it into the right hands. That starts with the students. It's amazing that Norwegian school students are denied access to their own performance data. We want our youngsters to own their data, so we publish lists of student performance in each year group, sticking these to the walls and windows around the school a week or so after the assessment period has closed. We attach a weighting to the core subjects, so success in English, maths and science counts for more than success in ICT. These rank orders have attracted praise and criticism in abundance. They require some explanation. Beyond the age of 14 it's impossible to create a rank order of students in a year group from 1-180 because they choose different pathways. So at Key Stage 4 we don't seek to compare the small number of students taking vocational courses with those on the standard academic route. Similarly, at sixth form there are so many different units, modules and courses being taken that we don't attempt to rank students against their peers. Instead, for Key Stages 4 and 5 we publish the progression of students in relation to their target grades and (at sixth form) in relation to the points required to gain their first choice university place. This means that students benefit from the public display of their progress, but it's a more personalised approach that reflects the needs of individual students.

At Key Stage 3 we continue with the rank orders that have become something of a hallmark of the Burlington Danes experience. It's true that all students (with the exception of a small minority with severe learning difficulties) are ranked from 1-180. It's true that these rank orders are publicly displayed around the school. And it's true that unveiling the rank orders triggers tears of joy and despair in similar measure, and that their position in the rank order will determine the class they find themselves in. I'm often asked if I think this method of assessment is rather brutal, and here's my response.

Firstly, I'm reassured that the rank orders invariably reflect the effort that students make in class and therefore provide a strong incentive for students to work hard. This is especially true as we work through the school, and the impact of arbitrary factors such as month of birth gradually fades (I mentioned earlier that in our current Year 7 cohort, our top two sets contained 24% September-October birthdays whereas our bottom two sets contained 8%. In our current Year 11 cohort the figures are 23% and 21%, indicating that the impact of age fades as we go through the school). Secondly, it's vital that we provide frequent opportunities for students to improve, so that someone who moves down a set due to complacency can correct his ways and move back up in a few months. Teachers can't just tell students that they 'must try harder': we need to give specific feedback which enables pupils to tackle the elements of the curriculum that they find most challenging. Thirdly, it's vital that the tests on which the rank orders are based are challenging, robust, and accurately marked. So before a school introduces rank orders it needs to work with departments to develop expertise in preparing, marking and moderating decent tests. Finally, it's essential that no matter which class students are placed in they are able to make good progress. We do this by ensuring that all of our teachers are highly competent and by reducing numbers and increasing support in the lower sets. So whereas our top sets contain 30 students, our lower sets contain fewer than 20, and benefit from teaching assistants, so that progress in these classes can be accelerated. We created these smaller sets by moving from six classes per cohort to seven. So although I don't shout about rank orders from the rooftops, and there are other features of Burlington Danes which I think are more impressive, I make no apologies for publishing the performance of students at all levels of the school.

Setting by ability

Setting and streaming by ability is controversial, and I'm aware that many studies have suggested that setting only helps the most able students. I would question whether these studies included true urban comprehensives where the spread in ability is so vast that a teacher of a mixed ability Year 8 class would have to cater for students who cannot write legibly and in full sentences with students who could tackle GCSE questions. There may be some schools where the top sets get the best teachers, but it doesn't have to be like this, and I have complete faith that whatever set students find themselves in at Burlington Danes they will have a teacher who will enable them to make significant progress.

My message to all teachers is that they should always teach for the next set up, so a teacher of set two pitches the lesson as if to a top set class. This compares favourably to my experience of mixed ability teaching, which often involves pitching to the middle. Setting by ability fits with our transparent and honest approach to student attainment and is supported by regular opportunities for students to demonstrate the progress they have made and move up to the next set.

When you speak to students at the school you realise that the vast majority of them relish the clear feedback provided by rank orders. Countless times in my career I've seen teachers pretend to students and their parents that they are making good progress in order to bring the child onside and avoid conflict. Quite frankly it's immoral and patronising to deny students awareness of how they are actually progressing. If learning really is as important as schools claim, then hiding this information from students makes no sense, for if a student doesn't know where they are in their learning then it's difficult for them to improve. Rank orders have now become the norm at Burlington Danes, so it's easy to forget their initial impact, and the role they played in turning the school around. I'm reminded of a former student, Quddus, who spoke alongside me at the Conservative party conference in 2011. Quddus, who's now studying engineering at Bristol University, maintains that the introduction of rank orders transformed the school, because being frequently reminded of your progress empowers you to do something about it. The public nature of the rank orders gives huge value to the currency of academic attainment. I've mentioned elsewhere that schools deal in various currencies, with students potentially gaining 'value' from sporting prowess, popularity, physical strength and knowing the right people. By displaying academic performance so publicly we're shoring up the currency of learning, awarding status to classroom progress and therefore devaluing some of the more ignoble currencies otherwise in circulation.

Psychology provides an insight into the power of rank orders. Psychologists have long held that we judge ourselves in relation to others, rather than in absolute terms. So in tests, respondents have revealed that they would rather earn £50,000 in a company where the average salary was £40,000 than £60,000 in a company where the average salary was £70,000. This helps to explain why rank orders have such power: they reveal the progress that individual students are making in relation to their peers, rather than against an abstract benchmark. If we tell a 13-year-old that they are working at 5a in English, 5b in science and 5c in maths we're unlikely to generate a strong emotional response. But if we say to the same child that they are in the top 25% of the year group, but at the last assessment point they were in the top 20%, meaning eight students have overtaken them, then the student is more likely to be motivated to improve. Of course, the student can check the names of the eight students who have overtaken him, making the experience all the more tangible. I introduced rank orders in my time as executive principal at another Ark academy, and there too the impact was compelling. Ironically, I was sceptical of rank orders when my husband introduced them at Sacred Heart School. He had used them as head of PE at a large boys' school in South London, but when he piloted rank orders at Sacred Heart I was concerned that they were a rather blunt tool, and I shared the misgivings noted and tackled above. I've since been converted to rank orders and the power of the public display of student achievement. They played a crucial part in the transformation of Burlington Danes, and they still remain a vital element of the school experience.

One of the benefits of students possessing their own performance data is that it helps create a 'bottom-up' desire to do well. I've already alluded to the fact that in challenging schools there's a risk that all of the pressure on students is imposed on them from the top. Informing students of their performance seeks to generate interest and enthusiasm for excellence at the grass roots of the school, amongst students themselves. This desire to make progress is then transferred upwards from students onto their teachers, creating a powerful mutual interest between students, teachers and the school. Students know their target grades, they know their current grades, and most importantly they know what they need to do to improve. Teaching never has and never will be a numbers game, but if tests are properly written and promptly marked they can help us place valuable data into the hands of those who can do most about it: the students.

The data will be crunched by several other stakeholders before it's consigned to the archives. Heads of department will scrutinise trends across their subject. If it's an exam group they'll enter the data onto a spreadsheet which will project likely grades based on current progress, accounting for the relative weighting of various components of the course. Meanwhile, heads of year will look for trends across the year group, looking out for any variations based on gender, ethnicity, age or deprivation (as indicated by free school meal status). Our SEN department will look for the progress of students with specific learning needs, while senior management provide a final layer of tracking and quality control. The data needs to be laser-like in its precision, enabling colleagues to make informed inferences when they pore over the figures.

My vice principal Mr Fairbairn took student scrutiny to a new level last year when he worked with the head of Year 11 to create a Venn diagram showing the progress of all students in the year group. Adapting the idea from a course he attended, the Venn diagram provided an overview of the cohort by showing their projected progress in different areas. So one circle of the Venn was for maths, another one for English, and the third one for '3 others' *ie* the three other GCSEs which will make up the vital package of 5A*-C grades including English and maths. If a student's name was in a circle, that meant that they were currently not on course to gain a C in that subject. The beauty of the diagram was that it occupied a wall in the staff room, meaning that every day all of our teachers would see it. If a maths teacher noticed one of his students in the maths circle then the teacher would know that the child's performance in maths was worse than his or her progress in other subjects, encouraging the teacher to offer personalised support and encouragement for the student. If a student was in several of the Venn circles then the head of year would intervene with the student and parents, perhaps by placing them on a monitoring report and insisting that they attend Saturday intervention classes. The Venn diagram works alongside our previous approach for Year 11 which involves students being placed in colour-coded categories according to their targets and their current progress. This means that we can target students on the crucial C/D borderline while offering a separate layer of support for those who might be working at a C grade but who should be gaining A and A* grades. So whereas in the old days we might just let classroom teachers get on with doing their best with their classes, we now have heads of year tying the data together and leading appropriate intervention for students falling below target, regardless of how high or low their targets are.

In building a positive, can-do staff culture I'm seeking rigour rather than ruthlessness – a distinction made by Jim Collins in *Good to Great*. It's easy for heads to be ruthless with staff, and to apply pressure at the merest hint of incompetence or failure. Our August results are normally an opportunity to celebrate, but every year there are classes, and sometimes whole departments, which have underperformed. We apply rigour in the sense that these shortcomings are not hidden. On their first day back, staff receive information about their residual performance, which shows how students performed in their class compared with students' other classes. So if a student gains an A in your class, but mostly Bs overall, and if this trend is repeated across your class, then you will receive a positive residual. Residuals provide valuable information because they account for the varying attainment of students, focusing instead on relative attainment in your class against their other subjects. This data enables us to look through our seven maths classes in Year 11, for example, and identify successes and failures, regardless of which ability set we are looking at. So the rigour is there, but we're not ruthless. I meet with all heads of department in September of each year which provides a chance for mitigating factors, such as inexperienced teachers, or shifting grade boundaries, to be explained. More importantly, these meetings give heads of department a chance to explain what they are doing to ensure that the results improve the following year. Even good teachers, and good heads of department, can have disappointing sets of results, and it's imperative that professionals in any field are given the chance to put things right.

The other way in which we shine a light on teachers' performance is through lesson observations. The NUT says this about observations:

> Over burdensome observation will not help any teacher. What it will certainly do is increase stress levels and workload. No other profession

would accept this level of scrutiny and mistrust. Teaching is about getting the very best from every learner in every lesson. It isn't about 'performing for observers' (NUT press release, 7 April 2012).

Of course teachers shouldn't 'perform for observers' but this argument seems to presume that 'getting the best from every learner' and securing a favourable lesson observation are two different things. Yet when senior staff observe colleagues they're looking for progress and engagement, as specified in Ofsted's lesson observation criteria. Take some of the Ofsted descriptors for an outstanding lesson (Department for Education, 2014):

- Excellent subject knowledge is applied consistently to challenge and inspire.
- Students make exceptional progress.
- Teacher and student questioning drives assessment in the lesson and results in outstanding progress.
- Students are highly considerate and very supportive of one another.
- The learning environment is stimulating and challenges the students.

Not even head of Ofsted Sir Michael Wilshaw expects every lesson to be outstanding but it's difficult to argue that the criteria above are at odds with what a dedicated teacher would be seeking to achieve even when no-one is looking. So we make no apologies for looking. This is often done casually, as part of our hourly walkabouts. Beyond this, every teacher in the school can expect three formal observations in a year, usually from their head of department or the member of SLT who line manages their faculty. If a lesson is judged 'inadequate', which is rare, then a follow-up observation will be arranged within three weeks. It's only after several 'inadequate' lessons that capability procedures will be taken against teachers. Yet again, I feel that unions, by insisting that observations be limited to three per year, have done their members a disservice. The unions claim to be defending the autonomy and integrity of teachers, but If teachers are only observed a few times a year it raises the stakes of these observations, encouraging teachers to 'put on a show' and the observer (usually a member of SLT) to reach a judgement on the quality of the lesson. This can easily result in a perverse game where the teacher second-guesses what the observer wants to see, and in schools which follow this high stakes model of observation you'll often hear teachers say things like "I'm being observed by the deputy head, I know she favours kinaesthetic learning so I'll make sure my lesson is active". The preference for kinaesthetic learning could just as well be a preference for group work, pace, extended writing, oracy or silence. The tragedy is that observing a teacher deliver a lesson should be the most natural thing that happens in a school, a springboard for rich conversations which sharpen a teacher's awareness of what's working in their class. Yet in too many schools these observations have been reduced to nerve-jangling high stakes performances in which teachers try to show management what they think management want to see.

This chapter in a tweet: Student progress is the key currency in a school so we need to make this as free and open as possible.

Lesson 6:
Treat students as individuals and provide personalised intervention

'Is there anything about this child which prevents us from helping them?'

We started this book with the quote from Nietzsche that, "In large states public education will always be mediocre, for the same reason that in large kitchens the cooking is usually bad". This captures what we're fighting against in public education. For any public service it's all too easy to provide a one-size-fits-all approach. Perversely, until recently English schools have been encouraged to do this by the league table system, which has revealed how many students gain five or more A*-C grades, thus giving a C grade the same value as an A* grade. Plenty of schools have therefore focused their energies on the C/D borderline students, ignoring those who are significantly below or above this benchmark. So the onus is on the prudent headteacher to build a culture and create systems which are deft enough to meet the needs of individual learners. This chapter will explore the personalised intervention that all good schools should seek to provide.

At the start of a chapter on intervention it's worth recognising that middle class parents are assessing, monitoring and intervening from birth. This becomes particularly pronounced in the latter years of primary school when many parents get twitchy about their child's progress and employ private tutors, often in preparation for admission exams at selective secondary schools. It's another example of the fact that middle and upper class children are less dependent on high quality public education than their poorer peers. As leaders of challenging schools it's our job to ensure that students from deprived backgrounds receive the personalised intervention that more affluent children receive as a matter of course.

The role of the tutor

Being a tutor at BDA is a critical role. The tutor's main tasks are:

- establishing and maintaining cohesive and supportive relationships between students
- establishing and maintaining the academy's Christian ethos and standards
- liaising between students, colleagues, parents and external agencies
- monitoring progress and facilitating learning
- supporting and advocating for your tutor group

Roles include:

- registration, messages/notices/Today PowerPoint
- act of collective worship
- rewards: *eg* commendations/merits
- report writing and parents' evenings
- monitoring progress/academic reviews and tutoring
- monitoring attendance
- delivering Personal Social Health and Citizenship Education (PSHCE)
- learning in form time, especially literacy initiatives and supporting reading
- sanctions: *eg* behaviour management/attendance/punctuality
- awareness of abuse: *eg* physical, psychological, sexual
- enforcing school policies: *eg* uniform
- encouraging extra-curricular activities: trips, clubs, reward form parties
- checking the student planner
- year council/school council
- line-up, attending assemblies
- supporting students' endeavours *eg* concerts, events, productions
- an awareness of adolescence and child psychology

Creating a culture of personalised support starts with ensuring that all students are known and cared for, and that each student has an adult that they can talk to. For most students, this will be their tutor. Such is the status of our heads of year that tutors can sometimes be overlooked, but they're the first point of contact for students and parents and a good tutor can have a significant impact on a child. A good tutor takes ownership for youngsters in his care. He'll ask to see students' planners to check that homework is being recorded, and he'll monitor the performance of his class using the daybook (because most of our classes, including our tutor groups, are the same for all lessons, one member of the class takes a daybook to each lesson for the teacher to complete, so at the end of the day the daybook gives the tutor a quick summary of the conduct of the class throughout the day). Tutors also use the school database to track merits and demerits gained each day by selected students. It's comforting for a child to return to their tutor base at the end of the day and be met by a tutor who already knows what kind of day they've had. The role of a tutor can easily be overlooked by a busy teacher. Whereas lessons have to be prepared for, tutor time is less structured, which could lead to preparation being neglected. But professional people take pride in whatever role you give them, and our tutor time is invariably a rich period of reflection and discussion. As a headteacher I pay close attention to the level of pride that tutors take in their students. Such care might not show up in the league tables, and it might not be down as a performance management target, but a tutor who takes ownership of his tutor group is a teacher who I'll be keen to have on my team.

The Burlington Danes Academy checklist for form tutors		
	Have you…?	**Yes/No ☑**
At line-up – supporting your DoL	Directed your form quickly into their correct spot and in register order	☐
	Taken the paper register on assembly days and handed to DoL	☐
	Checked indoor uniform – made a note to phone parents	☐
	Checked outdoor clothing – confiscated non-uniform coats/scarves/hats	☐
	Walked up and down your line to ensure all your form are standing in silence and listening to announcements	☐
When walking to your form class	Ensured all students are walking in silence in a crocodile	☐

During tutor time	Checked all students have their planners on desk (signed and homework)	☐
	Held Collective Worship	☐
	Taken the register	☐
	Completed the registration activity – definitions & spellings/ timetables/current affairs/silent reading	☐
	Discussed Today PowerPoint – made notes in diary	☐
	Collected absence notes	☐
	Given any other notices	☐
	Held a positive learning discussion/set the tone for learning – as they leave for period one	☐
	Checked your form tutors de-merits and merits using eportal	☐
Throughout periods 1 to 6	Visited difficult lessons (if free) especially where demerits have happened	☐
	Checked all planners are on desk – open at the correct page	☐
During pm registration	Ensured that correct HW has been filled in – consequence and copy in	☐
	Taken the register	☐
	Checked the daybook – congratulations for commendations	☐
	Fill in daybook charts – stamps	☐
	Negative daybook mentions – checked they have a demerit and sanction by teacher giving demerit	☐
	Checked detention list and shown to students	☐
	Walked SLT students to two-hour detentions	☐
	Dismissed quietly – chairs under and row by row	☐

Once we're confident that all students are known and supported as individuals, we can begin developing intervention programmes which respond to the needs of individual students. Perhaps the feature of our personalised intervention which gives me most pride is what we call assertive mentoring. This involves every student in Year 11 and Year 13 (the final year of their secondary and sixth form education respectively) being mentored by a senior member of staff. Once a month the students' classroom teachers will predict final grades based on current progress, allowing a monthly discussion between the mentor and the student in which any shortfalls between targets and predictions are discussed, with plans put in place to close the gap. I personally mentor six students in Year 11 and four in Year 13. The beauty of this system is that it's focused entirely on the performance of individual students. Their target grades are based on prior attainment while their predicted grades are personalised projections completed just a few days previously by their individual class teachers. Thus if a student who should be gaining ten A* grades is predicted A and B grades this will be flagged up and we can respond with the same urgency as we would for a student falling short of the national C/D borderline benchmark. The fact that the predictions and meetings occur on a monthly basis throughout the year allows for a prompt response. At worst, assertive mentoring ensures that students and teachers are aware of the progress of individual students on a regular basis – no bad thing in itself. At best, it leads to specific and tailored intervention, with the mentor acting as an advocate for the student, perhaps by discussing issues with teachers or with home, and implementing plans for improvement. During the meeting students receive a sticker from their mentor which they stick into their planner. Again, intervention is about getting the right data into the right hands.

Assertive mentoring

Every six weeks Year 11 and Year 13 students are 'assertively mentored' at BDA. This is one of the strategic ways we track and monitor every student in the run up to exams. The concept came from a course attended by one of the SLT. I often think of it as a little like running a GP health check appointment.

Assertive mentoring is rooted solely in data: predicted data and actual data from end of term assessments. Consequently it is very professional; focused and business-like. The meetings involve disseminating the latest set of predicted results, noting changes and asking what the barriers to learning are. Mentors (all senior colleagues) do their utmost to help students overcome these barriers by networking with colleagues, supporting with coursework, visiting mentees in lessons and facilitating with revision. There is a three day 'window' for all meetings to be held: this minimises potential disruption to the school day. Each round of assertive mentoring is supported by department meetings that interrogate data and 'drill down' to ensure that all students are on target. Mentors track each meeting and we report back to one another in the next SLT meeting.

Assertive mentoring meetings are so much more effective (as, more importantly, are the outcomes for teachers in terms of moving the students forward in their subjects) if information is passed on to the mentor to discuss with the students.

Subject teachers provide mentors with information such as:

- upcoming examinations/assessments/pieces of coursework

- concerns relating to classwork, homework, attitude, preparation for assessments, completion of coursework, missed deadline, underachieved in end of term assessment *etc*

- interventions that you have put in place but mentees have failed to attend/failed to respond to

- any major successes; things that have worked well with students who were below target and are now on target.

If the Venn diagrams and colour-coded spreadsheets are towards the cutting edge of student intervention, then running extra classes after school, on Saturdays and in holidays must count as more rudimentary ways of accelerating student progress. I'm sometimes a little sceptical of running extra classes, fearing that it creates a dependency culture, rather than students trusting themselves to be able to revise and learn on their own, at home or at the library. Part of me thinks that a maths teacher should make optimal use of the 200 or so hours she has with her students in the course of the year rather than call them in beyond school hours. A recent staff consultation exercise revealed concerns amongst our teachers that our intervention culture had evolved to a point where it placed undue pressure on teachers to devote their own time to ensure student success. Whether in a lesson or in the school as a whole it's always interesting to question who is working harder, the teachers or the students, and I share the unease of my staff if they feel that they are absorbing all the pressure of student achievement, rather than sharing this with the students. It would be disheartening to think that our improved exam results in recent years were simply down to teachers putting in overtime, rather than students acquiring a deeper set of skills and a richer learning experience. Following this staff consultation we've begun rolling back some of our intervention strategies, returning intervention to its rightful role of targeted additional support to raise achievement in a specific area, rather than being 'more of the same' of what happens in class. We've done this by working with heads of department to assess their curriculum delivery, ensuring for example that Year 10 is treated with the same pace and urgency as Year 11, thus freeing up lesson time in Year 11 to focus on exam preparation, rather than doing this beyond school hours. We're also working hard to increase the rigour of our Key Stage 3 curriculum so that success at Key Stage 4 is less dependent on intensive remedial work at the end of the course. Finally, we're developing revision skills with students so that they understand how they can prepare for exams, rather than feeling that they are reliant on their teachers.

Outstanding results – by design, not accident. Intervention, assessment and graft

At BDA there are many GCSE intervention strategies that are deployed to ensure that pupils do well.

1. Learning

- **Coursework/controlled assessment:** Pupils and parents are provided with clear criteria about what is expected to gain at least a C grade.

- **Exam preparation:** All courses being completed in good time, allowing teachers to deliver focused revision and exam practice. Students know how to tackle each type of question.

- **Identifying key skills/ideas needed for at least grade C:** Teachers scour mark schemes and examiners' reports to identify the difference between each grade point.

- **Booster lessons:** Focused intervention sessions on Saturdays, in the holidays and after school.

- **Pupil mentoring:** All students in key year groups are mentored by a member of staff.

2. Data analysis and target groups

Year 11 last year were divided into five groups. Students received tailored support based on the group they are in and are rewarded when they progress to the next group.

- **Light Green:** Confident will achieve five A*-C (inc. English and maths) at target grades

- **Dark Green:** Confident will achieve five A*-C (inc. English and maths) BUT under target grades

- **Purple:** Confident will achieve five A*-C (NOT including English and maths)

- **Red:** Underachieving – may not achieve five A*-C (inc. English and maths)

- **Orange:** Hard working – can achieve five A*-C (inc. English and maths)

- **Pink:** Will achieve English and maths but not three others

3. Increasing accountability of all involved

- **SLT:** Rigorous line management of departments to ensure accuracy of prediction and timely completion of courses.
- **Parents:** Informed through evening meetings, handbooks, revision guidance, reporting, greatly escalated contact through phone calls, letters home, texts, emails and so on.
- **Pupils:** Motivated through the rank order being publicly displayed.
- **Heads of faculty:** Lead the intervention programme for their department, ensure consistency between teachers and classes.
- **Subject teacher:** Keep students on track through high quality lessons; track progress through rigorous assessment.

4. The short-term 'aggregation of marginal gains'

- This may involve free breakfast on the day of the exams; last-minute revision seminars, cram timetables, free water: anything relatively minor that supports pupils to do better.

Of course, it is the classroom that makes the most significant and important difference. Plan, teach, mark; outstanding teaching will get outstanding results!

But for all my misgivings I can't deny the popularity of after-hours classes, and they form a key pillar of our intervention programme. I allow teachers to claim payment for the extra lessons they teach at weekends and in the holidays as long as they can justify their purpose and ensure that students attend. By and large they turn out in their droves, especially during Easter, May half term, and summer Saturdays in the run-up to end of year exams. The fact that these are focused revision sessions, perhaps on a particular topic which specific students need to improve on, gives them a sense of purpose which standard timetabled lessons might not always possess, so on the whole I'm proud of our after-school intervention.

The worst part of being a head is making the decision to permanently exclude a student from the school community. Such is the gravity of the situation that it's a decision I make rarely, but in each of my five years at Burlington Danes I have permanently excluded one or two students. Such a measure really is a last resort. Before the head gets involved the student will have received demerits, Friday detentions, Saturday detentions, fixed term exclusions and plenty of letters home. They will also have received support from their tutor and their head of year, and will have been placed on monitoring report for a sustained period of time. The only exception to this is when a student commits one single misdeed of great severity, such as bringing in drugs or a weapon, or setting off fireworks at school – a potential annual menace that fortunately hasn't troubled us for a few years now. I always seek to keep students in school, and make the most of less severe options such as a 'managed move'. This is when parents agree for their child to be transferred to another school in the area. Heads make these arrangements on a reciprocal basis, and sometimes a fresh start works. Such moves aren't always possible though, and don't always have the support of parents, leaving the head to bite the bullet and weigh up the needs of an individual against the interests of the whole organisation.

It can be an impossibly tough call to make, easily clouded by the fact that as a head you tend to see students at their best when they're calmly explaining things to you in your office. You have to remind yourself of the disruption caused to other learners that has resulted in the child sitting in there. Similarly, the process of weighing up an exclusion often gives you exposure to the background of the child, which is rarely the loving, stable, reasoned home that we would wish for our children. I repeatedly ask myself 'Is there anything about this child that prevents us from helping them?' Added to these anxieties is an awareness of the grim prospects for anyone excluded from secondary school. In our borough this normally means students serving the rest of their schooling at the local Pupil Referral Unit (PRU). PRUs are managed by dedicated, committed staff, but the concentration of troubled youths demoralised by their experiences of school rarely makes for the corrective rehabilitation that's required. Excluded children often visit us months, even years after their exclusion, perhaps waiting for friends or siblings at the school gate. Their attitude on these occasions does little to change my concerns about the prospects of students excluded from school. So it's with a heavy heart that I occasionally make this decision. As I write this I can picture the scene as I explain my decision, often with child and parents crying in front of me, begging to keep them in school. I always try to hand an olive branch to these vulnerable students, but sometimes I have to resolutely prioritise the needs of the whole community. Each time I'm left with a painful sense of failure.

Fortunately, for every one student that we've excluded there are ten that we've saved. One student was with us from Year 7 through to Year 11 and then stayed on when we opened our sixth form in 2009. He was very bright but didn't want to conform to the school's expectations, and half way through the first year of sixth form he found himself excluded by the head of sixth form for failing to meet basic expectations such as conforming with the dress code and being respectful towards teachers. On hearing of his exclusion the student came to my office to see me. He literally begged to stay, and we both recognised that there was very little chance of him completing his education if we said goodbye to him. The teachers who actually taught the boy, rather than those who encountered him on the corridors or led his year group, spoke highly of him and were distraught at the prospect of his departure. So I over-ruled the head of sixth form and allowed him to stay, and I'm pleased to say that he's now at a good university studying philosophy. I mentioned earlier that we enforce a rigid code of conduct in some areas, such as punctuality, but when it comes to life-changing decisions about denying a student access to the school you have to consider mitigating circumstances. This student had a tricky home life and ultimately I'm glad that I prioritised his needs ahead of the sixth form code of conduct, which the head of sixth form felt was being undermined. It's an example of the tough decisions you face as headteacher, balancing the needs of the students with those of the school.

Another student that I recall vividly is a girl who had difficulty managing her anger throughout her time with us. I remember being called up to a corridor on one occasion because she was refusing to leave the building after her latest outburst of anger and aggression. Outside of school she was getting in trouble with the police, and on one occasion was arrested for striking a police officer. The girl was charged for the crime and eventually returned to school wearing an electronic tag on her ankle. We supported this student through encouragement and frequent contact. She would regularly check in with me to let me know how long she had gone without any flare-ups. She shot up the rank order and ultimately acquired a very respectable set of GCSEs. Ironically she also joined the police cadets which at that time would meet at our school two evenings per week which seemed to give her a sense of belonging and pride. In my office I have a picture of this student standing with the judge who presided over her case in the Youth Offending court. The photo was taken after the girl had successfully completed the terms of her community order and the beaming smiles of the girl and the judge make for a touching picture.

A third and final success story involves a transformation so dramatic that it could be from a Hollywood move. I'll let the *Daily Mail* take up Arthur's story:

> "I had no interest in school. I was in Year 10 and I knew the teachers expected me to fail all my GCSEs. I didn't care. I played truant most of the time, and when I did turn up at school I would disrupt lessons just for the fun of it. Some teachers tried to tell me that I had a good brain – but I didn't care. I had no pride, no ambition and no sense that my life was worth anything."

> But in June 2008 two things happened. First, Arthur was arrested by police in possession of drugs and a court date was set. Shortly after, his drug suppliers came looking for their money. When Arthur could not pay them, they wreaked a terrible revenge – lying in wait for the boy at the school gates. Arthur says: "As I walked out of school, about 12 men jumped on me. They were all aged around 18, and I remember thinking "This is it, I'm going to die", as they knocked me to the ground. I was kicked unconscious, and I vaguely remember lying in someone's arms, before waking up in hospital." ('How Arthur went from drug dealer to head boy (with a little help from a very inspiring headmistress)', *The Daily Mail*, 6 May 2010).

Arthur was in Year 10 at the time and I was reluctant to allow him to return to school after he'd brought such trouble to the school gates. I met with Arthur and his mother in the week after the attack and he promised me that he would change, that he couldn't bear to cause pain for his mother again and that he was determined to focus on his studies. I allowed him to return on the condition that I would personally mentor him. Arthur was true to his word and his turnaround culminated in Arthur being made head boy once he had progressed to our sixth form.

What these three success stories have in common is that in each case the young person showed the will to improve and to replace damaging behaviour patterns with more positive ones. As a school we played our part by looking at each case individually, and by giving the students a chance when the rulebook would probably say we should have closed the door on them. Just as important, individual teachers showed faith in these young people and took time out of their busy schedules to offer individual support and encouragement. You rarely see the fruits of your labour as a teacher, not least when it comes to the stuff that exams don't reveal, like character and conduct. But any school that recruits teachers who genuinely care, and which treats young people as individuals with the potential to improve, can be sure that it's having a transformational impact on children, and it's the job of the head to create these conditions.

In his book *School Blues,* Daniel Pennac, a teacher in France, recalls his own experience of being rescued by persistent teachers: 'The teachers who rescued me … they were grown-ups confronted with teenagers at risk. They recognised this as a matter of urgency. They took the plunge. They failed. They dived in again, day after day, again and again … They pulled me out in the end. And plenty of others too. They literally fished us out. We owe them our lives' (p. 27). Pennac was rescued by teachers who nurtured his love for literature, and after 40 years of teaching I know of no better way of aiding a child's development than by helping that child find something they love, something they are good at. We do this in several ways. We encourage teachers to share their passion for their subjects. We provide a wide range of extra-curricular activities – if the next Andy Murray arrives at Burlington Danes he won't be lacking access to a tennis court or tuition. Finally we encourage teachers to look out for latent talents in our students. So a teacher whose lessons are being disrupted by the boy on the back row drumming his desk will inform the boy of the time and location of our weekly samba drumming club! It sounds simplistic, but the confidence, self-respect and self-discipline that children get from finding a positive outlet for their energies quickly spreads to their other endeavours.

This chapter in a tweet: No matter how big the school is, we must be agile enough to respond to the individual needs of every student.

Lesson 7:
Create clear systems and structures

'You can't talk to me – I'm a Danes student and you're in Burlington.'

On his first day at Burlington Danes my senior vice principal, Michael Ribton, confronted a boy in the corridor. The child had dropped litter. "You can't talk to me", said the boy, "I'm a Danes student and you're in Burlington". The divide that the boy referred to was the legacy of a small school model which had been imposed on the school when it became an academy. Under this model the school was split into four small schools. Year 7 was the first of these, Years 8 and 9 were divided into Burlington and Danes, leaving Key Stage 4 as a separate small school. It was a model which worked well on paper but caused utter confusion in practice; confusion which students like the boy above eagerly exploited. The organisational structure of the whole academy was opaque. It seemed that heads of year focused on teaching and learning while 'directors of learning' dealt with behaviour. Meanwhile, heads of small school acted as pseudo-headteachers of an entity which had no actual significance. These confused layers of bureaucracy were caused by leaders adding new systems without removing the existing structures. The result was predictably chaotic, and I was left with no choice but to demolish these structures, shatter these systems, and build a coherent organisational framework from the bottom up.

At the top of the school structure, at least in theory, is my strategic leadership team. I say 'in theory' because I believe in servant leadership, and I'm heavily reliant on my SLT to carry out duties and support the numerous evening events which litter the school calendar. It's quite typical for a member of SLT to do two hours of duty every day – 20 minutes on the gate before school, the same at break, 50 minutes at lunch then half an hour on the gate at the end of the day as we encourage students to disperse quickly and calmly. That's two hours every day, and on top of that they'll probably do at least one period of walkabout in a day, and possibly a cover lesson. My five assistant principals teach approximately 40% of the time, while my four vice principals teach between eight and 11 hours per week, giving them even more time for whole school support. In doing these duties my SLT relieve the burden on teachers: most teachers just do one 20 minute duty per week. Extra-curricular events also cast a heavy burden on the SLT. Concerts, musicals, options evenings, drama productions, prizegivings, open evenings and parents' evenings take place throughout the year, but fall with particular frequency towards the end of terms, especially just before Christmas and the summer recess. Take the Christmas concert which took place just a week before I write this. It was a freezing cold evening and with over 100 students performing to a sellout Potter Theatre it was up to my SLT (along with some student helpers) to supervise the gates, check tickets, manage the green room and serve refreshments. It's no wonder they sometimes remind me that the S in SLT stands for strategic. They accept though that the challenge of running a school is 99% operational, so they serve willingly. The SLT at Burlington Danes have become really close over the years, not least due to the amount of time we spend together. We huddle into my office at 7.45 every morning to go through the day ahead before moving onto the staff briefing. They're used to me calling, emailing and texting them at evenings and weekends. I can be demanding but they know I appreciate their efforts, and I take great pride when I see them gain promotions elsewhere.

When appointing someone to my senior team I'm often seeking to retain a key member of staff who would otherwise be looking for a job elsewhere. Opportunities in education have never been so plentiful; nor have young teachers ever been so ambitious! I guess that's the price we pay for attracting top graduates into teaching. Beyond this pragmatic concern, it's vital that every member of SLT has the respect of other members of staff, and of course they need a strong presence with the students. They also need to be outstanding classroom practitioners. It's a truism that as teachers move up the ranks they spend less time in the classroom, but teaching and learning remains the bread and butter task for everyone involved in the school, so it's imperative that my leadership team can cut it in the classroom. Honesty and integrity are also paramount at this level. Conversations we have at SLT meetings must remain confidential, even when two members of my current team are married to colleagues at other levels of the organisation. We have a two-hour SLT meeting once a week, and a daily SLT briefing before school, but throughout the week I have many private conversations with members of my senior team. These conversations enable me to manage each senior leader individually, tailoring my approach to their specific characteristics. It goes without saying that some people respond best to praise, others to encouragement, others to criticism, while others simply need to know that you recognise and value the work they are doing. I try to ensure that everyone on my senior team feels valued, and just like a teacher with his class of students, it's my job to bring the best out of those in my senior team. I like to give members of SLT a large degree of autonomy in the work they do. Each senior leader is responsible for key areas, so for example one of my vice principals takes control of teaching and learning, curriculum planning and staff development. Giving autonomy to my senior leaders is vital because once you have autonomy you become responsible for outcomes. I also have a knack for keeping a close eye on the minutiae of school life which helps in keeping my senior team honest and active.

How Burlington Danes works – a 500-word summary

The headteacher creates a culture of high expectations and applies this to students (supported by parents) and staff. Students are expected to attend on time every day in exemplary uniform. If they are more than a few seconds late they will be detained for one hour on the same day. If they do not wear the correct uniform they will be sent home. Once in class pupils are expected to be polite and studious, and complete their homework before the next lesson. Failure to complete homework results in a centrally managed detention – we run this each day.

Teachers are expected to plan challenging, engaging lessons; to manage their classes with professionalism and pride; to cultivate a passion for their subject within their students; to set meaningful homework and to mark students' work regularly, providing feedback which helps the students to improve. Teachers tweak their approach depending on the understanding of their students, and they differentiate their tasks for students who find them easier and for those who find them more difficult.

Data is employed throughout the school to shine a light on performance. Students who fail to meet their target grades are monitored and given extra support. The same applies to teachers whose classes fail to make expected progress. With students and teachers the monitoring and support is based on the premise that everyone can and will succeed.

We equip students to thrive in the exam hall. We do this by holding regular formal assessments in every subject, at every year in the school. The results of these assessments enable us to group students according to attainment. With such a diverse intake, we believe that this is the best way of meeting the needs of our students. There is frequent opportunity for movement between sets, and classes towards the bottom of the attainment spectrum are smaller and benefit from the support of teaching assistants. For our key exam groups (Years 11, 12 and 13) we provide personal mentoring and offer intervention classes after school, during holidays and at weekends.

The whole child is nurtured through a culture of love and support, and a comprehensive programme of trips, clubs and special events. Our house system provides support and boosts morale. Our tutor groups provide daily contact with the same teacher and an opportunity to discuss current affairs and develop awareness of citizenship and personal health. Regular assemblies provide a sense of belonging. Special events throughout the year, such as Charity Week and our Cross Curricular Project, provide students with the skills and confidence to understand and enrich the world beyond the school gates.

All of the above places an enormous strain on staff, so we seek to recruit teachers who are keen to impact the lives of students. We foster a strong sense of team amongst our staff, as demonstrated by our daily staff briefing, which commences with a moment of reflection led by a different member of staff each day. A proactive leadership team works tirelessly to ensure that the various cogs in the organisation are aligned. We constantly strive to improve.

There's a popular theory in organisational management known as 'the rule of 150'. Again it was the writer Malcolm Gladwell who helped make this theory popular when he described it in his bestselling book *The Tipping Point*. The rule of 150 suggests that organisations are at their most vital when composed of 150 people or less. According to Gladwell, '150 is the maximum number of people with whom we can have a genuinely social relationship'. He cites prehistoric communities, religious organisations and the traditional size of army units as evidence for this, and gives examples of modern corporations who flourish by following the rule of 150, such as the Gore Company (makers of GoreTex products) who multiply into separate organisations when they reach this size. Gladwell argues 'that personal loyalties don't count for much when the size of the group is above 150, and peer pressure begins to break down'. He then applies this theory to schools: 'If we want to, say, develop schools in disadvantaged communities that can successfully counteract the poisonous atmosphere of their surrounding neighbourhoods, this tells us that we're probably better off building lots of little schools than one or two big ones'. In short, 'Crossing the 150 line is a small change that can make a big difference' (2000, p. 183).

Sure enough the rule of 150 has found favour amongst educators in recent years. In America, the Small Schools Movement promotes the perceived benefits of more intimate learning communities, a model which has chimed with the rapid growth of Charter Schools. Charter Schools – self-governing community schools – are conceived from scratch mainly in deprived American communities and often save on start-up costs by taking over existing building such as empty office blocks or disused community buildings. As such, the rule of 150 fits them well. Here in England many of the hundreds of free schools in the pipeline will seek to provide a more personalised learning environment by limiting their intake, while several Ark schools are based on the small school model. One of these, the impressive Globe Academy in South London, says on its website (www.arkglobeacademy.org): 'The small school model offers a distinct advantage for students and their education. In a small school each student is known as an individual. Students have an education tailored to his/her need, has achievement tracked and intervention strategies implemented if required. The small school model allows all students and parents/carers to know the staff well; it offers security and a family feeling.'

On my arrival at Burlington Danes the school was following a hybrid approach, with Key Stage 3 divided into two schools (of approximately 150) called Burlington and Danes. I soon changed this, replacing the small school model with a more traditional year group structure, coupled with traditional academic departments by subject. My reasoning was that for a school structure to be effective it has to reflect (a) the school site/facilities; and (b) the size of the student body. Given the site we have at Burlington Danes, combined with a student body of 800 (now 1,150) and a staff body of 110 (now 150, with 95 teachers) it seemed arbitrary to divide the school into separate 'camps' (there was never actually a physical divide). A student in Year 8 might be in the Burlington School rather than the Danes School, but his lessons would still be all over the sprawling site (it's difficult to uproot specialist rooms such as science labs and art studios) and his break and lunch times would involve mixing with students in other 'schools', thus breaking some of the perceived benefits of an intimate small school where everyone knows everyone. The effect on teachers of trying to break an existing staff body into four separate schools is even more disorientating. A maths teacher, previously part of a united department, is suddenly a 'Burlington School maths teacher' or a 'Danes School maths teacher'. This presents timetabling headaches and disrupts the *esprit de corps* that we seek to cultivate in our academic departments. Small schools often resolve these timetabling issues by having one teacher deliver several subjects, so a teacher of history might teach geography and religious studies alongside her main subject, a solution at odds with the high level of academic scholarship that we seek to promote. So I decided that the small school model didn't fit the needs of Burlington Danes. It's probably an example of the fact that the tail shouldn't wag the dog when it comes to school structure, and another reminder that schools must fit the contextual challenges in which they operate, rather than stick rigidly to a prescribed formula.

There are two layers to the traditional school structure which I restored to Burlington Danes soon after my arrival: one academic, the other pastoral. The academic structure is based on departments and faculties. Each department is led by a head of department. The department then sits within a larger faculty, overseen by a head of faculty. For example, the history department sits within the humanities faculty. Each member of my senior team will line manage one faculty, creating a two-way channel of support and accountability. The pastoral layer is based on year groups. We have seven form groups in each year group, each led by a tutor. The seven groups are led by a head of year, and again I have one member of the senior team to oversee each of the three key stages. The cross-hatched approach enables us to ensure rigour and accountability in both of the key challenges that are faced by schools: academic tuition in a context of personalised pastoral support.

This traditional model encourages departments to become hotbeds of excellence and specialism in the delivery of its particular curriculum. It's strange to think that on any given day there are several hundreds of teachers across the country teaching a biology lesson on reproduction, yet they're probably all using custom made resources and their own preferred method of delivery. Perhaps more alarming is the fact that even within the same school teachers can be left to fend for themselves rather than collaborate with departmental colleagues. So as well as establishing a staff room we also have departmental bases, fostering collaboration and support within departments. I encourage teachers to be themselves in the classroom, and to adapt lessons to their own style, but there is so much to be gained through collaboration and it's impressive to do a learning walk of seven Year 8 English lessons and see all classes deconstructing the same passage from *Macbeth*, for example. There are clear benefits for students receiving a consistent diet across classes given the frequent opportunities for progression from one class to another. 'Scholarship' has become something of a buzzword in urban education in recent years, with schools vying for the claim of being 'scholarly' – developing a love of learning and serious academic study. This stems from teachers being rooted in their departments: experts in their field championing their subject. Stroll through Burlington Danes and you'll get a different feel from each corridor, with some departments proudly displaying the names of students who have gone on to study their subject at university.

Strategic planning

'With a clever strategy, each action is self-reinforcing. Each action creates more options that are mutually beneficial. Each victory is not just for today but for tomorrow.' Max McKeown, *The Strategy Book* (2012).

Middle leadership is the engine room of the school. Again, taking the spirit of Atul Gawande's 'The Checklist Manifesto' (2010), we devised the critical things that heads of department need to do.

The Burlington Danes Academy checklist for middle leaders

	Have you...?	Yes/No ☑
Winter term	Analysed GCSE results by teacher and student groups	☐
	Reviewed your SIP	☐
	Closed last year's performance management and opened this year's performance management for your staff	☐
	Held at least four learning walks per half term (throughout the year)	☐
	Monitored display, marking, homework, merits & demerits, underperformance of staff(throughout the year)	☐
	Planned your lesson observation programme	☐
	Ensured main examinations for EVERY year have a revision guide submitted to head of Small school	☐
	Analysed GCSE results by teacher and student groups	☐

Spring term	Planned revision/intervention programmes/written all revision guides	☐
	Reviewed and rewritten your SIP once AIP is released	☐
	Held midyear review of performance management documents	☐
Summer term	Organised cram revision	☐
	Organised your timetabling and staffing for following year	☐
	Reviewed your schemes of work	☐
	Reviewed your department handbook	☐
	Ordered your resources for the following year	☐

It's tough: I remember reading Alan W. Kennedy's *The Alpha Strategies, Understanding Strategy, Risk, and Values in Any Organization* in which he states, 'If every day at work feels like a Friday, then you are doing what you were meant to do' (2013). I guess that's a noble utopia to aim at but the relentlessness nature of teaching means that for most of us Friday is particularly sweet and well-earned.

The role of the head of department is therefore a critical one. He or she serves as the face of the department and is expected to promote it with passion at our open evenings and prizegiving events. More prosaically, the head of department is responsible for the quality of teaching and learning within the team they lead. This involves creating a relevant curriculum, developing engaging resources, writing rigorous exam papers and mark schemes, as well as supporting staff in their classroom delivery: a challenge all the more pertinent if developing trainee teachers, such as those from Teach First. Departmental meetings are scheduled throughout the year, approximately once every three weeks, allowing heads of department to share ideas and foster collaboration. The head of department will also spend plenty of time in the lessons of her team, offering developmental coaching and guidance. It's a tremendous task, and one that I've entrusted to some relatively inexperienced colleagues. Our heads of history, English, languages, vocational, maths and science are all in their twenties, indicative of the vitality of our staff, and the opportunities available to ambitious, talented teachers in urban schools. It fits perfectly with the headstrong model that I expect all of our heads of department to lead their subjects with passion and purpose, and you can count on heads of department to come in on results day in August to see how their department performed against their targets, and against other subjects.

Leading from the middle: what are the competencies middle leaders need to demonstrate?

When visited by Ofsted my middle leaders described themselves as 'the engine room of the school'. I really like that. They do the planning, model great teaching in their department and strategically plan ahead through rigorous self-evaluation. Many have mastered the art of the quick win: providing biscuits and tea and coffee in the department office; starting meetings with a teaching tip led by a member of the team, department newsletters freeing up valuable meeting time for strategic items only (and making meetings shorter and sharper).

Investors in People is a worthwhile exercise: it requires you to identify all the competencies that are required at each level of the organisation, thus making a progressional pathway transparent to all staff.

We jointly defined ours to be:

* to totally support and implement the academy's vision, in word and speech, giving clear direction to colleagues

* develop staff in their team professionally in the academy's expectations

* inspire and praise others to further the success of the academy

* challenge and motivate colleagues whenever relevant

* plan effectively

* self-evaluate, knowing their weaknesses and strengths, to further inform planning

* fully understand the national agenda and in particular Ofsted expectations

* respond with integrity to colleagues concerns

* meet deadlines

* model great teaching

* be a professional role model to all colleagues throughout the academy

* have a heightened sense of financial 'acumen'; adhering to best value

* be driven by a student – focused raising achievement agenda

* achieve positive residuals/agreed performance measures in examination results of their class

* achieve positive residuals/agreed performance measures in examination results of their department, or at the very least have evidence of the extensive qualitative work undertaken to achieve that aim

* minimise negativity amongst colleagues, actively pursuing collegiality, have a calm authority within the team they lead setting high expectations, seeking solutions to issues and not being overly negative. Enthusiasm and joy are important to all of us

- have a whole academy point of view when making judgements
- lead on performance management
- lead on induction of new colleagues
- identify professional development needs
- demonstrate the analytical, interpersonal and organisational skills which unite teams
- have a profound ability to 'multi-task' and keep 'live' a number of issues simultaneously
- interpret data, evaluate it and act upon it

There has been a recent trend for schools to adopt a vertical tutor group model, so that all tutor groups contain students from all year groups, typically from Year 7 through to Year 11. It's not a model I would advocate because it involves disbanding the most natural of and fundamental of school entities: the year group. Students in the same year arrive at school together in September of Year 7, they go through rites of passage together – residential trips, Year 9 options, GCSE exams, the school prom – before leaving together at the end of Year 11 or Year 13. A year group therefore takes on a life of its own, which a strong head of year will nurture and shape as they progress through the school. There are so many obstacles to creating a fraternal ethos in a school and I feel that getting rid of year groups makes the challenge even harder.

One of the most basic structures of school life is the length and composition of the school day. Given the intensity of lesson time it's paramount that we give our students a decent break at lunch, and it fits with our traditional academic model that we give students a proper midday break of fifty minutes. This might sound obvious but there are schools which have replaced their lunch hour with two short breaks of equal length. One of my assistant principals joined us from a school in Croydon where students had one break of 20 minutes at 11am and another one at 1pm. School finished at 2.30pm. The rationale from the (then) headteacher was that most of the fights and serious incidents erupted at lunchtime so they might as well squeeze the school day and reduce the free time available for disruption to occur. It's a hopelessly short-sited way of dealing with behavioural problems, and you wonder how many additional issues were created in the local community by the fact that 1000 young people were released from school in the early part of the afternoon each day.

The challenge of feeding 1,150 young people and 100 teachers in 50 minutes is formidable. It's made more complicated at Burlington Danes by the fact that the canteen was built for Burlington School for girls, a school less than half the size of the current student body. It's a cramped space that requires meticulous management from my senior team each day. Vice principal Ms Downey keeps an orderly queue outside the canteen, Mr Fairbairn calls students through in batches while also distributing plastic cups for the jugs of squash on the tables. Meanwhile, our finance director Mr Maeers manages proceedings at the food service area where students pay for their meal before joining friends in family-style tables. A similar scene is played out in the Burlington Atrium, where associate vice principals Ms Morris and Mr Magezi man the tiller. It's perhaps ironic that our most experienced and highly paid staff manage the canteen each day (the rest of the senior team will be on duty at other key points throughout the school) but such is the operational challenge of feeding everyone in a calm and orderly manner that I think it is justified.

Soon after I arrived at Burlington Danes we took ownership of the canteen from the local council. Under the original academy agreement we bought into a small number of local authority services, of which catering was one, but it fits with my view of a school as a family body that I wanted control over our food provision, and we've now managed our own catering for four years. Our students are not required to purchase food in our canteen – we provide picnic tables and indoor areas for those with packed lunches. I'm pleased to say that our payment system is based on scanning students' fingers so at the point of sale there is no embarrassment for students on free school meals. I'm envious of smaller schools where they have more space to enjoy family style dining at lunchtime. Our Ark neighbours King Solomon Academy, for example, have a wonderful lunchtime arrangement where students and staff sit in small clusters and serve each other at their tables before clearing up and leaving together. Alas our lunchtimes are more frenetic but they provide an important opportunity for play and relaxation during an intense day of learning.

As I close my reflection on the minutiae of the school day it's worth pausing to consider the recent trend in education for an extended day. From Kipp Charter Schools in America to our very own Ark Academies, it seems that a longer than average day is now *de rigueur* for any school hoping to make progress with students from low income backgrounds.

The appeal of an extended day is obvious: it simply allows more contact time between teachers and students, providing more of a chance for low-income schools to close the achievement gap. At Burlington Danes the school day begins at 8.30am and finishes at 3.50pm, with a daily selection of after school clubs. We also allow students to use our sports facilities after school, and stay on to study in the library and in our dedicated homework room. Yet is a longer day the smartest solution to closing the achievement gap? My natural instinct to maximise the learning opportunities within the confines of the standard school day before we seek to lengthen it. I'm always wary of solutions which simply involve throwing more time at the problem, like the inexperienced teacher who struggles to control his lessons so stays up all night refining his lesson plans, only to find that his fatigue gives him even less impact in the classroom. I would encourage schools to look closely at what's working within their existing school day before extending it: at which points in the day do students make the most progress? Is the length of lessons optimal for rich learning? How many minutes of the average lesson are wasted with admin/arrival/departure? If students aren't making much progress in the existing six lessons then pinning hopes on a seventh lesson seems rather optimistic.

A chapter on school structure would be incomplete without discussion of that most basic unit of school life: the size of a class. Conventional wisdom would have it that the smaller the class, the better, as this allows greater contact between students and teacher, enabling the teacher to respond to the personal needs of each students. It's difficult to argue with these benefits in principle, but it's worth considering the purpose of the lesson being delivered. For example, before big exams we sometimes take whole year groups to the hall for something resembling an approach known as 'spaced learning', which involves embedding knowledge through visual stimuli and repetition, interspersed with regular breaks. For this type of activity it doesn't matter whether the teacher is presenting to five students or 105, as long as each student has a good view of the screen and is able to hear the teacher. No interaction takes place between teacher and students. Clearly this is a very specific type of activity, but it leads one to question whether the traditional arrangement of one teacher and 20-30 students is always ideal. Reducing the size of classes is an extremely expensive measure to take, and there is some recent evidence ('Smart Class-Size Policies for Lean Times', Southern Regional Education Board, 2012) to suggest that a bigger class with a better teacher makes more progress than a smaller class with an inferior teacher, especially beyond primary level. We've invested heavily to reduce our class sizes – our top sets have 30 students but our lower sets have 20, and in our sixth form the average class size is just 10 – but I'm open to flexibility in this area. This flexibility was tested recently when we found ourselves without a geography teacher just six weeks into the new school year. We requisitioned a big classroom and merged our two Year 10 geography classes into one class of 50, taken by our exceptional head of geography. Ms Stone was supported by teaching assistants and when I visited her classes I was impressed by the progress students were making. It was a temporary measure taken for just over a month but it suggested to me that 30 needn't be the magic number when it comes to class size.

The benefits of being in an academy chain

Local Authorities are often, in my view, blighted by (in no particular order):

- poor leadership
- lack of funding
- low expectations
- staff intransigence and militancy
- poor outcomes

Academy chains offer both challenge and support that perhaps may exist in some local authorities but certainly does not exist in all.

Academy chains are a relatively recent addition to the educational landscape. Academies have turned around failing state schools, granting an opportunity for reinvention and freedom for school leaders. Finance plays an important part in this; a chain can pool monies and deploy to needier areas if needs be. This type of flexibility simply does not exist at local authority level. Human resource management can be similarly deployed; developing, coaching and nurturing a talent pool ready to support and lead schools as they join the group. Additionally, chains are especially well suited to executive headship: a strengthening of leadership at a local level. They have different models of governance that sharpen school leadership. Promoting a 'brand' also matters: a strong social mission, for example, rallies staff behind the cause, as does the chain's ethos and values. In sum, I guess it's the 'quality assurance' aspect that is so strong and clearly defined that sets chains apart from local authorities.

Good sponsors challenge and inspire their academies to do better.

So far I've outlined the school structure as it appears to me, the headteacher, looking down at the organisation below me. But of course accountability flows both ways, and when I look up I see two very important bodies which hold me to account: our board of governors and Ark. Let me start with Ark, and there's an irony here because it's frequently said that becoming an academy gives schools more autonomy, yet for me it was quite the opposite. By the time I left Sacred Heart we were well established as a successful South London school, and because of this the London Borough of Southwark were very hands-off with us, pretty much allowing me, as Head, to get on with things as I saw fit. So moving to an Ark academy meant getting used to the scrutiny that Ark applies to its schools. This should not be taken as a criticism: quite the opposite. The best thing about working with Ark is the aspirational culture which is engrained in the DNA of the organisation and flows through all the work that they do. Ark targets apply to every child at every Ark school, and they're based on students in Key Stage 3 making six sub-levels of progress during the whole key stage (eight sub-levels in maths). This well exceeds national expectations, which suggest nine sub-levels across Key Stages 3 and 4. These aspirational targets have a huge impact and ensure that conversations about how well the school is doing are firmly rooted in student data. New teachers joining us from other schools sometimes get a shock when, for example, they notice the level of scrutiny applied to Year 8 English levels at the end of the first half term. In other schools attainment at Year 8, and sometimes the whole of Key Stage 3, passes under the radar.

One of the other advantages of being an Ark Academy is that it enables us to tap into the contacts that exist both within the organisation and beyond. Ark was established by successful financiers with strong connections in the world of business, media and entertainment. I love networking on behalf of the school – I think it's part of the role of the head – and the pool of contacts associated with Ark has enabled me to bring several VIPs to Burlington Danes from Premier League footballers and chairmen to Hollywood stars, the Mayor of London and even the Prime Minister. The students take huge pride from these visits and we've been able to extend our relationship with a few of these VIPs into tangible partnerships involving university bursaries and work experience opportunities. Ark's support is tailored to the needs of the organisation, so in my first few months I received plenty of HR support for example, but over time we haven't had to call on them so much and the focal point of our relationship with Ark is now the half termly monitoring visits which provide a regular health check for the academy. I would be lying if I denied that there is tension at times between head office decisions and my own preferences, for example when central office has chosen an IT provider on behalf of all their academies, but when it comes to the important issues I enjoy a close relationship with ARK and I value the scrutiny and high expectations that they impose on us.

Ark schools

Ark is an education charity operating a network of schools dedicated to closing the achievement gap. In the UK, Ark operates 31 academies, educating 17, 000 young people, across Birmingham, Hastings, London and Portsmouth. Each Ark school has its own ethos and character but they all share the same mission: to give every child the very best start so that, when the time comes, they are able to go on to university or the career of their choice.

Originally set up in 2002 by philanthropists from the financial sector, Ark delivers high social returns on charitable activity, leveraging intellectual, financial and political investment. Ark picks the best people to run its operations, or partners with those charities which it feels are doing a good job. Funding decisions are made by the board only after months of due diligence – a forensic study to ensure the investment will pay off. Funding is maintained only if key targets are met..

Burlington Danes was the first Ark school, opened in 2004. A belief pervades Ark's work that every child can reach their potential given the right encouragement, teaching and support. This 'no excuses' culture pervades the way the academy operates and underpins our work. They support and train governors, lead on CPD, monitor our data and undertake an 'Ofsted style' monitoring visit (sometimes unannounced) every term. Ark supports us through HR work, managing press and publicity and intervene only when the direction of the school appears to have taken a wrong turn..

Like all good leaders they create energy and capacity. Ark's expectations of us are demanding: the Ark Target-Setting Process has expectations derived from national pupil achievement data for the top 50% of schools based on actual average progress made by the fastest progressing quintile. The expectation is that ALL pupils reach a minimum expected level of achievement at key points: a level 5b in English and level 6c mathematics at the end of Key Stage 3 and a grade C GCSE in English and mathematics by the age of 16..

My analysis of our governing body must start with our chair of governors Lord Stanley Fink, who has been a true friend to Burlington Danes since he committed £2 million of his own money when the school converted to academy status in 2006. As I write these lines I've just received a text from Stanley offering a day out to 12 of our students at the House of Lords as a prize for a forthcoming essay competition, and such gestures have become commonplace throughout Stanley's association with the school. For a man once described as the 'godfather' of the hedge fund industry Stanley possesses an impressive knowledge of urban education, and has a natural feel for what it takes to succeed. Stanley is the son of a grocer whose own chances were transformed when he won a scholarship at Manchester Grammar School. In a speech at one of our prizegiving ceremonies he hinted at the motives behind his philanthropy: "Those lucky enough to make it to the top have a duty to send the elevator down to those below." I'm extremely grateful for Stanley's support over the years and in spite of his deep pockets and extensive list of contacts, it's his guidance and encouragement that I've come to value most.

As for the rest of the governing body, again I've had to learn to deal with a more muscular team than I was used to at Sacred Heart, where the governing body was drawn largely from the school community, with parents, teachers and neighbours of the school all contributing. While the Burlington Danes governing body also contains these elements, they are sprinkled amongst managers and leaders from a range of sectors who are keen to examine the workings of the academy at a micro level. This, of course, is exactly how it should be, and I welcome their probing questions and informed suggestions. Andrew Adonis captures the importance of strong governance when he says of academies: 'Independence therefore matters. But it is good governance plus independence, not independence alone, which is the distinctive feature of academies.' (2012, p. 123).

The foundation stone on which our school structures rests is accountability. They say sunlight is the best disinfectant and the over-riding aim of our school structure is to shine a light on the workings of every aspect of the organisation. So my PA manages the office staff, and the finance manager oversees the canteen team, while our pastoral and academic provision is tracked by the systems described above. That said, and this is vital, we must guard against the risk of issues being passed up and down chains of command, rather than being dealt with head on. I remind my SLT at the start of every year that if they encounter an issue, they should deal with it. Not only is it unfair on heads of year if senior staff pass issues onto them, but it also undermines the credibility of that senior leader. So if an assistant principal spots a student vandalising school property I expect her to lead the follow-up until completion, which usually involves meeting with parents and setting an appropriate sanction. It's a principle which is fundamental at all levels of the school. We strive to create robust and comprehensive behaviour management systems so that we can support all teachers in a systematic and consistent way, but the reality is that schools work when teachers take responsibility for their lessons and assert themselves over the children in front of them. If they call for support from the senior team we'll back them to the hilt, and we're happy to provide a calming word in the ear of students, or offer a brief cooling-off period in a different class. But within a few days the timetable will direct that student back towards the same teacher. Perhaps by that point the teacher in question has phoned home, or sought out the child in a corridor, maybe caught them doing something good in a different class, or simply tweaked the seating plan to suit the particular needs of the child. No school structure can be as strong as a group of determined teachers who take responsibility for what happens within the four walls of their classroom.

This chapter in a tweet: Schools are complicated enough without murky systems and structures: keep things simple.

Lesson 8:
Cultivate a bullet-proof culture and ethos

'May love and respect dwell here among us every day.'

The values of the street can easily become the values of the school. To turn this culture on its head, to create a positive learning culture in which all students can thrive, requires clarity, persistence and constant vigilance. A good school smothers students in a positive ethos, banishing fear and replacing it with love, warmth and compassion. Ethos matters because young people absorb more from their peers than from their teachers, so once a positive ethos is established it will serve as an invisible hand, regulating behaviour and promoting cohesion. The challenge of creating this ethos starts with high-quality assemblies.

Throughout human history people have gathered together at regular times in regular settings to engage in fellowship, celebrate success, reflect on recent events and share information. Humans love sharing stories. At schools around the world these ritualised ceremonies are known as assemblies, and they're a vital part of the school day. Everyone has memories of their own school assemblies. Perhaps we recall them as drab, humdrum affairs. Yet, properly done, a school assembly can pump fresh oxygen into the arteries of the school. I like them to be vibrant, life-affirming gatherings, where students and staff leave feeling more buoyant than when they arrived. I'm quite old fashioned when it comes to assemblies. I think there's something about the human psyche that allows us to absorb ourselves in a compelling narrative, and there's no better forum for this than a few hundred people gathered in unison before an engaging speaker. Visual aids and videos can be helpful, but speakers shouldn't apologise for dominating their stage and speaking from the heart about issues that matter. Just as early man congregated on the savannah to take instruction from tribal elders, there's little else which is more fundamental to a school than the provision of informative, engaging, regular assemblies.

Our Academy Prayer
Bless this academy.
May we all live happily together and may our academy be full of joy.
May each one of us learn and achieve together.
May love and respect dwell here among us everyday. Love of learning,
Love of one another, Love of life itself and love of God.
Let us remember that as many hands build a house so every student can make Burlington Danes Academy a better place.

We start our assemblies with a spiritual reflection and a prayer, usually led by the chaplain. We are a Church of England school, so it's natural that our assemblies begin with this religious element. 40% of our students are Muslim and when I speak to their parents I realise that most of them actively appreciate our Christian ethos for the values and stability it promotes. So I make no apology for our Christian culture, and it's imperative that students respect it, even if they choose not to actively participate. We are unapologetically Christian but completely inclusive, and I see no tension between these two positions. On my arrival at school we wrote an 'Academy Prayer' which we speak together if the chaplain can't be with us to share a prayer of her own. We also developed a Christian Values statement.

Our Christian Values statement
At Burlington Danes Academy we teach Christian values all day long.
We teach them in mathematics by being powerful, accurate and precise.
We teach them in English by learning about the experience of others.
We teach them in science through reverence and awe.

We teach them in PE by learning to rely on one another.

We teach them in RE by learning how faith can be applied.

We teach them in languages by learning to say what we mean.

We teach them in geography by broadening our horizons.

We teach them in history by learning the lessons of the past and realising our humanity.

We teach them in dance by being expressive.

We teach them in design technology by realising our ideas.

We teach them in drama through empathy.

We teach them in music through celebration.

We teach them in economics and business studies by learning to value what we have.

We teach them in art through creativity.

We teach them in sociology by understanding why people behave as they do.

We teach them in business studies and economics through justice and equality.

We teach them in ICT by being innovative.

We teach them in government and politics through respecting ideology.

We teach them in media studies through awareness.

We teach them in health and social care through consideration, sensitivity and respect.

At Burlington Danes Academy we teach Christian values all day long.

We teach them through good manners to one another, and by truthfulness in all things.

We teach them through our house system, recognising the importance of collegiality and togetherness.

We teach each and every student to love life borne out of the relationships they have with their teachers and their school friends. Joy matters to us. We value the importance of the home and of caring and nurturing.

We teach our community by providing an education of the highest possible quality. We value each child as an individual. We encourage an understanding of the meaning and significance of the Christian faith.

We teach and practice forgiveness and reconciliation. We live, love and learn together.

We teach, and we learn, by learning to mean what we say.

Each year group has two assemblies per week. One is the SLT assembly – a formal gathering in the main hall with two years groups combined, led by a member of the senior team. The other assembly for students will be for their year group, and led by their head of year. Heads of year play a crucial role at all assemblies, leading students in, hushing them, orchestrating their departure, but it's in the year group assembly that she or he will really take the stage. For all my commitment to a strong headteacher – whose influence pervades the school – I give plenty of autonomy to teachers and heads of years to stamp their own authority on their lessons and their assemblies. If you took a tour of our year group assemblies, as I often do, you'd be treated to a range of styles and approaches. Ms Quinton might be reminding her Year 8 students of the importance of manners in a motherly, vigilant tone, while Mr Stephenson will be holding court with his Year 10 cohort, week by week imparting more of his confident, caring character.

Sometimes it feels that the task of running a school is 99% a logistical one, and the logistical challenge is never more apparent than when hundreds of students need to file into an assembly hall and then file out again 20 minutes later, hopefully having received at least a small dose of spiritual and intellectual sustenance in between. There's something eerie about waiting in an empty hall for the arrival of those first students. Tutors ensure that seats are taken swiftly, while heads of year carefully scan the faces of students as they enter for the merest hint of restlessness or mischief, promptly tackled and resolved with a word in the ear. Anticipation builds as the final students file through, and a quick nod from the head of year at the back of the hall will indicate that the SLT member in charge of proceedings can begin. This is when SLT members stake their claims for Oscars with suspense-building pauses worthy of Hollywood's finest.

There's nothing more authority-affirming than biding your time at the front of the hall, scanning the faces of those before you, once a few hundred young people have fallen silent in anticipation of your opening words. Public speaking regularly features at the top of people's lists of greatest fears, but I think the mistake people make is that they presume that other people find it easy and natural. I don't tend to believe in natural talent. Invariably when you encounter an expert in whatever field, public speaking or public health, you dig a little deeper and find that circumstances allowed them to hone their craft over many years. So most people petrified of public speaking have probably only done it a handful of times – weddings, important presentations, interviews – and therefore associate that feeling of standing in front of a crowd with the pressure of those big occasions. It's one of the blessings of teaching that addressing an audience is part and parcel of the job. In any case, compared to teaching a lesson, where the success of the endeavour is entirely dependent on the response of those before you, delivering a message to a passive audience is relatively simple, when you think about it. That said, the greatest fear of a public speaker is the outright rebellion of those before you, and the embers of this fear still glow even when you've been taking assemblies for years. So you speak with vigilance, seeking out the inattentive eye at the back, the girl on the front row looking out of the window, the teachers whispering to each other. You try to correct these with a subtle nod, a prolonged stare, or perhaps by firing a quick question to the girl transfixed by the Wood Lane traffic. When I started taking assemblies I would be worried about filling the time available, but like the pages of a newspaper, the content of an assembly always manages to fill the allocated time. In any case, the head of year is on hand to reinforce the message if your own flow of wisdom has run dry.

I mentioned above the issue of checking the 'behaviour' of teachers in assemblies. When I arrived at Burlington Danes I noticed that tutors would stand by the side of their charges, glaring at them in anticipation of trouble. I quickly challenged these low expectations and asked teachers to model the behaviour I expected of students by sitting with their classes and listening attentively to every word. There's perhaps no bigger challenge for a school than nurturing a sense of wonder in children, a sense of the incredible scope of the world around us, and that comforting realisation of our own insignificance within the grand scheme. Assemblies provide a chance to cultivate this awe and wonder and develop a powerful sense of belonging. I believe that humans have an innate desire to belong. Yes, people are driven by money, fame, power, sex, popularity, but so too, in my view, by a desire to fraternise, to lose oneself in something bigger.

In *School Blues* (2010) the French educator Daniel Pennac reflects on a career teaching students from tough neighbourhoods. He grew up as a middle class boy in rural France, but recognises that if he'd grown up at a different time in the inner city he'd have joined a gang: 'what's the attraction of gangs? Losing yourself in the belief that you're finding yourself. The illusion of identity. Anything to forget your alienation from school, to escape the contemptuous gaze of adults' (p. 20).

The power of praise

'Cherish the heart' is a phrase I have often heard used. Teachers need to be tuned in to the culture of the street and be sensitive to the vast array of needs that vulnerable children bring to the classroom.

'By providing emotional support, modeling, and other forms of scaffolding, teachers can help students use their strengths, skills, and knowledge to develop and learn' (Marlowe and Page, 1999).

Respect, as understood by all street wise pupils, is generated by building positive relationships for learning. Creating a positive climate in the classroom is a critical element in this and praise is a powerful support in the teacher's toolkit. Teachers have the right to support from SLT in maintaining a positive culture in their classes and the responsibility to seek this support when necessary.

Positive approaches to pupil and class control are well documented: sincere praise develops self-esteem in all students and promotes a positive, nurturing environment wherein students feel valued. It helps to build ties with the home as everyone loves good news. Pupils need clear boundaries and affirmation. Parents have to be involved as much as possible in their child's schooling. Students are motivated and engaged, they behave better, they talk of their own learning and consequently teachers' morale improves. We have tannoy announcements celebrating good deeds, exemplary work or great effort. We give out book tokens, certificates, 'praise postcards' (which act as a raffle ticket for end of term bike raffles), we even give out hard cash. But the greatest reward is public recognition of your progress from a teacher you respect. That is how to break the street culture.

Feeling a sense of identity with their school should never be illusory for young people. Exploring the attraction of gang culture is beyond the study of this book but Pennac's comments chime with the views of the motivational speaker Tony Robbins. He argues that there are six things we all seek in life: certainty (*eg* food, water, shelter); variety (excitement, action); significance (feeling important), love; growth; and helping others. Robbins goes on to argue that the person in the ghetto who pulls a gun on someone else is trying to achieve certainty, variety and significance in the same way that the firefighter rescuing a family is pursuing the same ends. The implication for schools and society is that unless we find positive outlets for the needs and ambitions of young people, there are plenty of less worthy means by which young people can find this release.

One of the most joyful nights of the year is our Year 11 prom which we hold at the end of June once students in Year 11 have sat their exams. I must admit I was rather shocked at the state of the prom in 2008, just two months after I arrived. It was held in the main hall, senior staff reluctantly acted as bouncers on the door refusing entry to the more raffish elements of the year group, and once inside even our most respected teachers could barely establish the order required to do the usual round of awards and speeches, not that the awards celebrated the kind of qualities that I felt should be championed. Students vied for honours such as 'best looking female' and 'most popular male'. There might even have been a category for 'most likely to end up in Wormwood Scrubs' – the prison just a few metres from our gates. Since then we've held our prom at a decent hotel, and we encourage staff to attend to set the right tone for the evening. Yet again, students respond to our heightened expectations of them and it's a date I look forward to every year.

In his seminal work *Learned Optimism* (1991), the American psychologist and educator Martin Seligman suggests that one reason for the increase in depression in society is the erosion of 'the commons' – allegiance to 'family, faith and flag'. It's a common theme amongst sociologists and was portrayed persuasively in Robert Putnam's book *Bowling Alone: The Collapse and Revival of American Community*. Before offering solutions for the restoration of collective bonds, Putnam laments the decline of social capital: 'social capital refers to connections among individuals – social networks and the norms of reciprocity and trustworthiness that arise from them' (2000, p.18). Putnam argues that the poor are especially badly hit by the decline of these social bonds, because low income groups are particularly reliant on support from the community. Schools are uniquely placed to restore some of these bonds, and we ignore this duty at our peril. Take this line from the book *Flow*, by ground-breaking professor of psychology Mihaly Csikszentmihalyi: 'The meaning of life is meaning: whatever it is, wherever it comes from, a unified purpose is what gives meaning to life' (p. 217). I don't entirely accept the post-modern relativism of this comment, but I've seen for myself the enormous opportunity that schools have to craft a sense of meaning and purpose amongst their charges. Assemblies are the breeding ground for this sense of collective purpose, just as our daily briefing serves the same function with the teachers. It's no surprise that when the hall is requisitioned for exams during May and June of each year we miss the calming effect of our assemblies.

One of my favourite recent assemblies was delivered by Michael Ribton during black history month. I will explain this in some detail as it is, in many ways, typical of the assemblies we enjoy at Burlington Danes: precisely planned, well-executed, incorporating a range of media and student involvement. Our black history month theme was 'Nelson Mandela – A Life, an Inspiration'. Michael's perfectly constructed assembly began by posing the question 'how powerful can words be?' A short video clip of a blind man fruitlessly begging in the street was shown. The man's fortunes change when a woman scribbles out his sign stating 'Hungry – please help' to 'It's a beautiful day and I can't see it'. He then continued by stating that the power of words to affect your emotions and actions are well demonstrated in science. For example, scientists have found that just hearing sentences about elderly people led research subjects to walk more slowly. In other research, individuals reading words of 'loving kindness' showed increases in self-compassion, improved mood, and reduced anxiety. Studies reveal that we place our attention toward words differently depending on our own biological or personality traits. For example, individuals with eating disorders pay greater attention to words reflecting body parts or body image than others. A Bible verse or two strengthened the point. The assembly then looked at the time Nelson Mandela spent on Robben Island, where Mandela spent 18 of his 27 prison years. Confined to a small cell, the floor his bed, a bucket for a toilet, he was forced to do hard labour in a quarry. He was allowed one visitor a year for 30 minutes. He could only write and receive one letter every six months. How important words were to this amazing man, Michael pointed out to the packed assembly hall. Can we perceive how much each and every word mattered? Robben Island became the crucible which transformed Mandela. He emerged from it the mature leader who would fight and win the great political battles that would create a new democratic South Africa. Mandela took comfort and strength in the poem *Invictus* (Michael used a clip from the movie of the same name to illustrate this) which Michael presented to each student in the form of a bookmark. A student read the poem to the assembled pupils. You could have heard a pin drop. It was a great message about the power of language, of how words can heal as well as hurt. And all delivered in a 20-minute time frame to a captivated hall.

Invictus William Ernest Henley

Out of the night that covers me,
Black as the Pit from pole to pole,
I thank whatever gods may be
For my unconquerable soul.

In the fell clutch of circumstance
I have not winced nor cried aloud.
Under the bludgeonings of chance
My head is bloody, but unbowed.

Beyond this place of wrath and tears
Looms but the Horror of the shade,
And yet the menace of the years
Finds, and shall find, me unafraid.

It matters not how strait the gate,
How charged with punishments the scroll.
I am the master of my fate:
I am the captain of my soul.

Another assembly often recalled by students was one when Andy Moore, one of my vice principals, covered the hall in litter and talked about the school environment and students' responsibility towards it. I remember reading of the headteacher who shared his New Year's resolution of learning to juggle: in the first assembly in January he showed his inability to keep the balls in the air. He brought his juggling balls back in July and wowed the audience with his new skills (the lesson of course being that practice makes perfect). I also like to see students take the stage in assemblies: it's extremely powerful for young people to listen to their peers and older students, and it provides valuable experience of public speaking for those under the spotlight.

I want to reflect in more detail on the conundrum we face at Burlington Danes of being a Church of England school with a substantial body of Muslim students. It has already been noted that our Christian ethos is embedded in the very DNA of the school. Burlington School for Girls was established to teach poor girls to "read, write and cost accounts...and instructing them knowledge of the Christian Religion..." while St Clement Danes boys school emerged from one of London's most famous churches. To this day we enjoy a close relationship with the London Diocesen Board for Schools (the educational arm of London's Anglican churches) and it was due to this deep-rooted Christian ethos that Burlington Danes was for a long time Ark's only 'faith school'. Our Church of England status sits comfortably with my own faith, but we can't ignore the fact that the community we serve has changed since the school was founded. So how do we stay true to our Christian heritage while accommodating the diverse community we serve, 40% of whom are Muslim?

Firstly, we emphasise the values of Christianity, rather than the specific application of the Christian faith. Not only are values such as love, tolerance and charity powerful drivers of harmony and cohesion, but they're also pretty universal, and certainly strike a chord with our Muslim families. Given the fact that all of our students have actively chosen to enrol at Burlington Danes we make no apologies for imbuing the school with Christian principles. Why should we be mealy mouthed about a facet of school life that has served us well and which parents actively seek? So we proudly begin every assembly with a prayer from the chaplain, we reflect on a weekly bible verse which reinforces the theme of the week, and we conduct Christmas and Easter assemblies in which we stand together to sing and pray. The truth is that not one child has opted out of an assembly, and not one parent has said they don't want their child to partake in our acts of collective worship. I sometimes wonder whether this is a result of the strong community ethos we have developed: we do everything together. On a personal level, my Christian faith remains very important to me, reminding me to see beyond the material concerns of daily life. Given the strength of my own religious commitment, the deep-rooted Christian ethos of the school and the popularity of these values amongst our students and parents, it's only natural that the Christian faith permeates the life of the school.

Being a Church of England school

My view on being a Church of England school is unless it makes the school distinctive there is no point in holding such status.

At the centre of the Christian faith stands Jesus, his teachings and his sacrifice. So it should be in the Church of England school – a place where, like in a Church, if you choose to look you can find God. This is, I think, the awe, wonder and fascination of Christianity. I am totally clear and unapologetic about this with parents on Open Evenings: your child, Christian or not, will worship alongside us.

The implication is that the values of Christianity – love, honesty, goodness, truth, grace, healing and trust – must be explicity taught.

Success of the school is all the more crucial as the Church of England school ought to be a beacon of faith in the community; an advert for the transformational power of the love of God.

To draw on *Zen and the Art of Motorcycle Maintenance* (Pirsig, 1974): 'we may not be able to define it but we all know when we see it.'

That said, we go out of our way to accommodate our Muslim students. Many of our Muslim students choose to pray at lunchtime and we gladly provide them with a prayer room in which to do this. It's a custom that began when we had a Muslim science teacher who was keen to provide a space for those who wanted to pray at lunch. He has since left us but we now entrust the keys to a student in Year 10 who opens an unused classroom every lunchtime as around 20 boys engage in their daily prayers. We also support students fasting during Ramadan by providing a separate room for them, away from the temptation of food and drink in the playground, and of course we allow time off school for students celebrating Eid. Perhaps the trickiest decision concerns serving Halal food in the canteen. It's difficult logistically to serve Halal meat alongside non-Halal meat, so as a school we've made a decision that all of our meat is Halal. I recognise that this might not be the preferred option for all of our non-Muslim parents, and we've taken one phone call of complaint in recent years, but on the whole I think it's the best option given the tricky combination of logistical and religious issues that we have to consider. Championing Christian and British values includes being tolerant of alternative practices.

About ethos

Achieving a 'positive ethos' is the aim of every head, but what does it mean? Some of your ethos is explicit and stated in policies, documents, mission statements and assemblies but much of it is implicit and subtle. It is led from the front by the headteacher and exemplified in how the school goes about its business.

In my view it is when:

- students are happy and achieve
- teachers and support staff have a profound sense of fulfilment
- students are treated fairly

- relationships between staff, students and the community are positive
- bullying is a rare occurrence
- there is a lively, creative and inclusive atmosphere forwarding a sense of identity and belonging that recognises diversity and differing abilities and needs
- teachers motivate students

So we've seen the role of ethos in a challenging school; the invisible hand that regulates behaviour and sets the conditions under which students can flourish. If the community in which the school is based provide such conditions then the school can relax, and simply let the ethos of the street permeate the school by osmosis. Such a luxury is not afforded to schools in big, complex cities, so it's up to us to erect the greenhouse, to enhance the dim rays of light offered by the outside world and protect our charges from frost, wind, rain and pests. We do this every day, through assemblies, décor, behavioural nudges and positive communication. Ethos is the feel of the school, and for those of us who work there each day it's easy to become desensitised to this feel, so we rely on the comments of those who visit us and we remind ourselves that for all our time spent with the 10% of students who struggle to comply, the bigger challenge involves nurturing fertile conditions for the remaining 90%. Ethos can't be transplanted from one school to another. It has to be true to the character of the staff and students at the school, as well as the local community and even the history of the school. My daily visits to assemblies serve as a litmus test of this ethos.

Schools like mine are sometimes accused of imitating traditional independent schools, and those making the accusation would find plenty of ammunition at Burlington Danes: blazers, Latin lessons, debating clubs, rugby coaching, rowing, outdoor pursuits. I make no apology for any of this, and in truth we've adopted such measures for their own merits rather than in blind adherence to a nostalgic view of private education. Creating a house system, as I did on my arrival at Burlington Danes, certainly raised a few eyebrows, but I cherish the impact it's had. Staff suggested the names of our six houses and we opted for the first six epistles of the New Testament: Romans, Corinthians, Galatians, Ephesians, Philippians and Colossians. Every member of the BDA community, from the youngest student to the most senior lunchtime supervisor, is allocated to a house, with each house led by a member of staff who is supported by a student house captain. The first task was for each house to nominate a role model and then design a crest. The crests now adorn the lapels of our students and teachers in the shape of a pin badge, while the role models such as Aung San Suu Kyi and Nelson Mandela provide inspiration for each house. Throughout the year, events such as a staff cook-off, alternative Olympics and topical debates contribute to a rolling tally of house points, culminating in our sports day when students dress in house colours and march into the Linford Christie Stadium under their house flag. The house system serves as an extra layer of glue bonding us together, another potential source of solidarity and belonging that I referred to earlier. I see this even in the way that a student might respond to an unknown teacher who belongs to the same house: wearing the same badge on their chest can provide a valuable point of connection between the two. There's another benefit to the house system and that's the fact that it allows me to give a position of responsibility to a young, enthusiastic teacher eager for progression. Retaining great staff is always a challenge so I'm grateful for any opportunity to meet the ambitions of industrious teachers.

A house system

In my view, all schools should have a house system. It develops a greater sense of togetherness, belonging and identity and provides opportunities for mixing students from all year groups. Through a variety of opportunities it encourages competition in sport and academic areas of academy life and allows pupils to demonstrate a responsibility, affinity and loyalty to their house. We link it to Charity Week. It is a major part of our celebration of achievement. I believe it is a powerful motivating force: appoint a member of your SLT to oversee it and drive it on behalf of the school. It encourages students to invest in the life of the school and greatly supports ethos and self-esteem.

Pupils are awarded House Points for all aspects of school life: good work, handwriting competitions, sports day, our cross-curricular project days, attendance and punctuality, charity week events and so on.

There are six houses at BDA: Romans, Corinthians, Colossians, Ephesians, Galatians and Philippians. Each have a unique symbol and colour. All houses have particular qualities and virtues rooted in the eponymous New Testament letter. Students wear their house badge on their blazer and staff have a house lanyard as well as the badge. On office or classroom doors there are posters proclaiming which house the teacher is a member of.

Every term there are at least three major house events, which result in points being awarded in rank order. The House 'league table' is published throughout the year and it all builds up of course to the end of the year to see who will win the house cup.

Assemblies provide a window into the soul of the school, so I'm always keen to bring visitors along to our school assemblies. Friends and colleagues have described to me working at schools where in the assemblies students get jeered by their peers as they leave their seats to collect awards. I can't think of anything more indicative of a failing school than this. You almost want to shut the school down at that very moment and start from scratch, such is the scale of decay when those worthy of collective praise are humiliated by the community. It's a reminder that positive, supportive cultures do not grow on their own, they must be emphatically established and constantly reinforced if they are to have any grip on the school. Like most teachers, I'm optimistic about human potential, though I use the phrase 'human potential' rather than 'human nature'. Without positive social structures individuals can easily find negative outlets for their energy, and the responsibility lies with families and schools to offer a more fulfilling alternative to the rule of the mob. At the annual Ark summit in 2011 we heard from the gifted America teacher Doug Lemov. He shared a memorable analogy of a dysfunctional school being like a bucket of crabs, where the crabs at the bottom pull down the one or two crabs which have the audacity to seek a better life beyond the bucket. A good school is a bucket of crabs in reverse, and our assemblies are invaluable in reinforcing this.

What I'm arguing here is that a school must reject the values of the street and create its own code of honour – an inversion of the world beyond the gates. One way of looking at this is by questioning which students in the school have the influence and respect of their peers. If it's simply the toughest, the biggest, the best looking or the loudest boys and girls, then we have a problem. If, on the other hand, the alpha males and females of the playground are also the students who perform well in class, and represent their school in sport and the arts, then we're on the right track. It's imperative that being successful is seen as 'cool'. I'm told that following the desegregation of schools in 1960s America some black children fared worse in mixed schools because they were accused of 'acting white' if they tried hard or did well. It's heartbreaking to think that effort and success should be ridiculed, and the effect on those high achievers is all too predictable.

The 'street' vs the school

It is often correctly said that the street should be left behind at the school gates when a pupil attends school. Uniform, correctly worn, assists this objective. Trappings such as hoodies or caps must be confiscated, tucking trousers into socks, wearing a ludicrously short tie, trousers pulled low; all and more are part of street culture that has to be stamped out. Our school serves an area of huge social deprivation and, in common with other urban schools, simply living in such an environment places young people at special risk of falling victim to aggressive behaviour, knifings, muggings, vandalism, burglary and more have engendered a despair, an alienation and a hopelessness that in turn has spawned the subculture we know as 'the street'.

Yet at the heart of this counter culture is a code of respect. Respect in the street sense is a term which means that your masculinity is recognised and that you have a certain fearlessness.

Cuss a parent? You have broken the code. Respect is a very fragile entity: it must be protected and guarded at all costs. This means who you talk to, the gang you are in, the clothes you wear and the trouble you get yourself into. All help to either earn or lose 'respect'. Violence, poor parenting, poverty, racism and endemic joblessness all contribute to hardening the street attitude.

Breaking this cycle is the job of every headteacher. Educational success that leads a student out of poverty is one such way. Developing sensitivity to oneself and others is another. I strongly believe in the value of 'cultural capital': reading, watching good films and plays, visiting museums and art galleries, exposure to poetry, music and dance: all can help lift a pupil out of the mundane and into the extraordinary.

In recent years we've been able not only to ensure that the street stops at the gate; we've proactively taken the values of the school into the local community. At the end of each day members of my senior team are strategically positioned at potential neighbourhood hotspots: outside a take-away chicken shop (which we have banned students from entering), on a busy street corner and by a congested bus stop. They serve as a visible reminder to students that the standards set within school also apply beyond the school gates. Complaints from neighbours about students loitering in nearby streets are treated with the same urgency as misdemeanours that take place in school, and the same goes for the conduct of our students on public transport. Students know that while they are wearing our uniform they are expected to meet our expectations. In doing so, we hope that our values go out with the students as they leave our gates every afternoon.

It's not uncommon for these after-school duties to be interrupted by some kind of drama. Perhaps a former student or an older brother has come to the school gate to settle a score with an old foe. Perhaps a stand-off takes place between a group of our students and some pupils from another school. We're located on a busy road and it's a sad fact that approximately once every couple of years one of our students becomes involved in a road traffic accident. News of such incidents fills headteachers with dread. I remember on one occasion a girl in Year 9 was dazed when a lorry's wing mirror clipped her head while she was waiting at a bus stop looking the other way. On another occasion a boy in Year 7 was struck by a car as he ran for his bus. Fortunately the car was travelling slowly and the boy avoided serious injury.

On one occasion I was in my office with a film crew from BBC News giving my thoughts on the latest educational policy announcement. My PA came in looking as white as a sheet and hurriedly whispered 'one of our girls has been stabbed at the bus stop; she's been taken into the dining hall; there's an ambulance on the way.' I calmly excused myself from the BBC crew and walked towards the canteen, bracing myself for the scene that I would face. I knew that all eyes would be on me and that no matter how serious the situation I had to maintain my poise and keep a calm head. By the time I arrived in the dining hall paramedics and police were already in situ. I was reassured to see the casualty sitting up and I was soon informed that the weapon had been a pair of scissors and the wound wasn't deep. I comforted the girl's mother when she arrived and saw mother and daughter onto the ambulance, relieved that the injury wasn't more serious and that we wouldn't be making the front pages. The only headline generated by this incident was deep inside the pages of a local newspaper: 'Head plays down scissor fight outside Burlington Danes Academy'.

In January 2011 it was me who required medical treatment after an incident on the gate after school. I walked onto the Wood Lane pavement to see the students off site when I tripped on an uneven paving stone. Blood immediately streamed from my nose and forehead, but I soon realised that an injury to my arm was giving me the most pain. I couldn't get up from the pavement and it wasn't long before I was surrounded by concerned students. Paramedics soon arrived and I was taken to hospital where they found that I had shattered my elbow, taking out both bones in my forearm in the process. Doctor's orders meant that I rested at home for two weeks, summoning members of my team to visit me occasionally to keep me in the loop. Needless to say the show went on at Burlington Danes in my absence.

This chapter has focused on the challenges schools face in creating a positive culture. Our seven heads of year carry more than their fair share of this burden. Just as when I started teaching in the 1970s it remains the case that most teachers at some point in their career will choose between the pastoral route and the academic route. Of course teaching rarely fits into such neat categories, and the two tasks can never truly be disentwined. There was a time a few years ago when it became popular to employ non-teachers in pastoral roles. So police officers, church wardens and counsellors dropped their batons, alms bowls and tissues to become heads of year. I have no objection to this in principle – I've previously noted the success of non-teachers such as Mr Rumble – but the head of year role is so critical that I prefer holders of the post to be men and women who have demonstrated that they can cut it in the classroom. After all, controlling a class is the bread and butter task for anyone working in a school, and possessing a reputation as a strong classroom teacher generates the capital required to be a strong head of year.

Along with young teachers on a full timetable I think that our seven heads of year have the toughest job in the academy. Every day they are ultimately responsible for the behaviour of 180 young people. Let's take an average cohort of 180. Probably two thirds of them rarely get in trouble. At the other end of the spectrum there are perhaps about five students in each year group who seriously struggle to function. These are students who in another era would have found themselves in 'special schools' or behavioural units, but now join us in mainstream schools. That leaves 55 students. We could split these in two between those who sometimes enjoy creating mischief, and those who will sometimes join the mischief given a nudge in the wrong direction. I know this analysis seems rather clumsy but I'm trying to give a sense of the potential volatility of a year group. Again, imagine if it was adults we were talking about, and you were responsible for the conduct of 180 adults each day. I lead a team of over 150 adults and I can testify that on any given day there will be a few of these who present issues that require attention – perhaps triggered by illness, fatigue, bereavement or relationship breakdown.

So it's with a sense of gravity that I appoint heads of year, for I know that they absorb more stress than anyone. It's literally energy-sapping carrying the weight of 180 youngsters each day and I'm full of admiration for the job they do. And of course it's a wonderful role for those who can cope with the stress. A head of year is the figurehead of the year group, honoured with the privilege of seeing a cohort through from the age of 11 to 16 (our heads of year move up the school with their students). Even the most austere head of year develops an extremely close bond with his charges. In fact this can be a source of conflict when a student is at risk of exclusion. Heads of year are often very defensive of their students having got to know them and their personal background more than any other teacher. It's good that students have an advocate when it comes to the tricky question of exclusion – but it's for others to make the tough decision based on the needs of the whole school.

When appointing a head of year my first requirement is for someone who is strong on discipline. If a class can sniff out a weak teacher then a year group can certainly sniff out a weak head of year, not least because a head of year can never drop their 'game face' – they must to be ready to deal with a student incident at any time of day. The second requirement is someone who is tactful and perceptive enough to deal astutely with parents. Heads of year become the face of the school to the parents with a child in that year group, therefore the head of year must be adept at liaising between teachers and parents. Again, the skills could be called upon at any time of day. We encourage parents to make appointments with staff but it's common for them to turn up at reception asking to meet with the head of year, and unless the head of year is teaching they'll tend to oblige. So I need my skilled behaviour manager to possess deft communication skills, but if we stopped there we'd have a head of year who can do little more than ensure compliance between home and school. So on top of that I want someone who has an eye for detail and the analytical skills to track the academic progress of his charges, intervening where necessary to address underachievement where it occurs. Finally, a head of year must have a fierce sense of pride and ownership of his or her year group, pride which must be transferred to their cohort. Our heads of year hate it when their year group is singled out for criticism. They fight their corner, like a patriarch defends the family name, like a chief protects the honour of the tribe. Of course they will criticise their own year group, but they don't want anybody else to. It's a vital role, being a head of year, and we've relieved one or two heads of year of their duties when things haven't worked out as planned.

One of the joys of appointing heads of year is seeing them develop their own style of leadership, a style indelibly transferred to the students under their watch. As with any leadership role, authenticity is paramount. Of course you adapt when you advance in your career – as head of English I had to be more firm than when I was a classroom teacher – but I've seen great classroom teachers make the mistake of thinking that as head of year they have to become something they are not. The key is to know your strengths and play to them. If a teacher has become successful in the classroom through being disciplined and rigorous, then such traits will serve them well as head of year. But if a teacher has cultivated a nurturing, supportive spirit in the classroom, laced with warmth and humour, then adopting an austere manner as head of year will surely fail. Such is the intensity of school life, and the frequency of human contact it presents, that being inauthentic is a cardinal sin. A head of year can't walk from their office to their classroom without issues being presented to them; whether it be a sullen girl standing outside a classroom having been sent out, or a pale boy complaining of sickness. At every corner the head of year could face a situation requiring a calm head, a quick decision, a compassionate smile, a sharp tongue, a thick skin or a blind eye. It's a true test of human spirit and it's a privilege to see a head of year revelling in the role.

So what I look for in a head of year is the confidence to be that authentic figurehead and the resilience to carry the burden of 180 sets of hopes and dreams. We're blessed with some brilliant ones at Burlington Danes. My head of Year 10, Ms Akingbule knew the names of all her students before they arrived at the start of Year 7 having learnt them over the summer using primary school photos. From the start of their time at secondary school she emphasised the importance of manners, and four years on it's still her students who are best at holding doors and minding their Ps and Qs. Head of Year 11 Mr Stephenson attended Burlington Danes as a child and still lives in the community, 15 years after leaving. This gives him huge personal capital amongst the students and he spends it well, imbuing his year group with confidence and character. Increasingly I expect my heads of year to take responsibility for the academic development of their students so that they don't feel pigeon holed as being purely pastoral. If they develop this side of their skill set they complete their head of year role after five years well placed for senior leadership. They've effectively been headteacher of their own school of 180.

As I close my thoughts on creating a positive culture and ethos it's worth recognising the power of communication. I'm loathe to call it 'public relations' because critics would rightly question whether schools need to engage in PR, but it's my view that being a headteacher means being the cheerleader for the school, proactively networking and championing the community which I lead. I said early on in this book that as far as students are concerned their school should be the best school in the world, and I believe that positive communication has a part to play in reinforcing this.

How do you make students proud of their school?

It is the job of the headteacher to make pupils believe that they are in the best school in the world for them. Here are some important pointers:

- Inclusiveness is key: a sense of achievement eradicates the notion of failure that embitters pupils.
- And so is behaviour. Drop into lessons, be on the corridors, talk to students at break and lunch: all of the SLT must have a presence.
- Positive relationships between staff and pupils: stop the shouting, smile, be interested, engage, listen. Refer to the school as a family, nurture togetherness and community spirit.
- Ensure there is a palpable focus on students, not staff: their learning comes first. Indeed, 'learning' is the focus of every conversation with students, no matter what the conversation is about. Ensure that every student knows how to improve in every subject. Communicate this to parents too.
- Team sports, debating, spelling bees and drama performances: anything that brings students together, all the better if it mixes pupils vertically (different year groups). This too can be replicated within the school: inter-tutor group competitions, houses, between year groups.
- PR: place a good news story every week with the local press office: make someone responsible for this on the senior team. Assemblies are important to the school ethos. And a vibrant Student Voice.

- Environment: ask teams of students to clean the school for a raffled reward – we have a 'green team' to do this. Have an eye for detail: don't let the environment slip; paint out graffiti; clean, sweep and tidy on a daily basis; re-carpet wherever there is more chewing gum than carpet; each holiday change the school's appearance.

- Be particular too about student appearance: it is an honour to wear the uniform; ensure it is worn properly and pupils understand that when wearing it they are ambassadors for your school. Even better if you can change it slightly at the start of your headship!

- Photographs: display pictures of students smiling and thriving all over the school – it's great for raising self-esteem. Make someone responsible for the display, and buy them a good camera.

- Tradition matters to developing an ethos: we have an 'honours boards' listing sixth formers' university destinations; they return to talk to lower school about being an undergraduate. An alumni association, that occasionally visits the school to do talks *etc*, is a great support.

- Publications: we have a bi-annual magazine called 'The Griffin': a showcase of all that has happened around the school, delivered free to pupils' homes. We also circulate Parent News on a weekly basis.

- Greet students at the gate each day, ensure that SLT are patrolling the local community for half an hour or so at the end of the day.

- Display good work.

- One-off days or special weeks: we have a cross-curricular project that is taught in vertically mixed groups by house on themes such as 'democracy', the London Olympics, ecological issues; and PE week or maths week.

- Celebrate every achievement in assemblies, over the tannoy, or morning line-up *etc*. All pupils love the fact that you know: have the PE department list the successful sports people, for example, in the morning briefing. Individual and collective success helps nurture the sense of belonging.

- Reach out as a school community: charity weeks, tea dances for senior citizens, volunteering in the neighbourhood (we have a 'social action' week), tea dances for senior citizens, collecting donations for the homeless.

- Peer mentoring helps foster a collective spirit.

When I arrived at Burlington Danes the school had a rudimentary one-page newsletter which went out to parents each week. I asked the author of the newsletter to expand it, as well as to develop the school website and to communicate more frequently with parents through letters, emails and texts. The purpose of this wasn't just about spreading information; I was seeking the positive glow that emerges from shining a light on the great things happening at school each week. Michael Ribton, my right hand man, would write the opening message of the newsletter, while on the back page a Coates Commendation would celebrate the good deeds that had come to my attention that week. Occasionally I would have to offer generic praise to the student council, or to a particular class, but more often than not I would be able to highlight a specific act of kindness that had occurred that week.

The same colleague responsible for the newsletter and the website, who soon became one of my assistant principals, was also responsible for our external relations, including increasingly frequent relations with the press. Schools aren't businesses, and I wouldn't want to invest too much time and effort into our public relations, but every organisation benefits from conveying a strong impression of itself to the world beyond. Slowly but surely we gained favourable press coverage. Our summer 2010 results made the front page of the *Fulham Chronicle* with the headline 'Former special measures school gains best ever results'. We even received positive coverage for a national award we had been shortlisted for, but missed out on: 'Burlington Danes Academy shines despite missing out on top award'. Other headlines in this popular local paper (it's distributed free to the majority of our parents) include 'Outstanding A levels (again) at Burlington Danes Academy', 'Boxing helps Burlington Danes teens gets back on right path', 'Burlington Danes Academy pupils handed special Olympic role', 'American teen hails Burlington Danes after GCSE success', 'Youngsters excel as Burlington Danes toasts opening AS Level results' and 'Burlington Danes nurture teenage prodigy heading to university after stunning GCSE results'. Such publicity creates a buzz around the school, and I relish using the line in assemblies and with parents: 'People are talking about this school, they can see what's happening here, and we know that by working together we can make this school even better'.

It's also worth cultivating some positive media coverage because you know that there will be the occasional negative story. In the interests of fairness I'm happy to share two headlines of recent years which haven't been so positive (though you might not find them on our website): 'Academy dispute over Mohican-style haircut' and, as previously mentioned, 'Head plays down scissor fight outside Burlington Danes Academy'. As word has spread about our success we've received positive coverage in *The Financial Times, The Sun, The Independent, The Evening Standard, The Daily Telegraph, The Times, The Guardian* and *The Spectator*. We've also welcomed TV crews from Al Jazeera, ITN, Sky News and the BBC, with the latter no doubt encouraged by their close proximity to us on Wood Lane. Clearly you have to have a positive story to tell before you can seek publicity, and our status has been boosted by comments made by Michael Gove, Nick Clegg, David Cameron and Ed Miliband, but I'm proud of the fact that we celebrated our achievements from the very beginning, and it helps that we answer our phones and open our doors when journalists come knocking.

Public relations

Schools are not businesses, and I would be loathe to invest too much time and energy into our public profile. That said, any self-respecting organisation must take pride in its reputation and I make no apologies for seeking to present a positive image of Burlington Danes to the world beyond. Public relations shine a light on the great things happening within the school, and in doing so generate a sense of pride amongst students and staff. One of my assistant principals oversees our public profile, receiving support from one of our teaching assistants who happens to be training to be a journalist.

Here's how we communicate with external partners:

Website

Our website (www.burlingtondanes.org) is updated at least once a week. A school's website has become the first port of call for Ofsted inspectors and it's vital that the website tells a story of what the academy is like in the present moment. Parents can easily see what's happening at school each week, while the curriculum information shows what students will be studying in all of their classes in all year groups.

Twitter

Our twitter (@ArkBDA) has proven to be a popular way for various partners to keep in contact with the school. Students make up a significant proportion of our followers, alongside plenty of teachers, parents, bloggers, community leaders and local activists. Twitter comes into its own when there's a threat of a snow day (as long as you ignore tweets from students longing for a day off) but it serves a wider purpose as a platform for announcements ('Year 9 trip to First World War battlefields has been delayed, new ETA 8.30pm') and links to stories in the press, YouTube videos, learning resources, and new stories on the school website. Of all modes of communication nothing is as immediate or as personal as Twitter, hence it's a good way for schools to communicate with interested parties.

Many of our departments also have their own twitter handles (@BDAGeography, @BDAHistory, @BDABiology) which enable students to keep track of the links and resources used in class.

Newsletter

Our weekly newsletter has been distributed to all students every Friday for six years now, while a full colour PDF version sits on our website for posterity. It provides a snapshot of the preceding five days alongside announcements for the week ahead. Heads of year are given 100 words to communicate with their year group, while the Coates Commendation recognises acts of selflessness. The weekly staff interview is a popular column.

The Griffin

This is our biannual magazine that showcases highlights from the previous six months at Burlington Danes. It's packed full of stories of trips, competitions, academic success and special events. The magazine is distributed to parents and local residents.

Prospectus

School prospectuses have lost some of their potency in recent years, thanks mainly to the internet. There's still something appealing about the formality of a school prospectus though, and we are currently in the process of producing one which will serve us for the next three years.

The press

Our location on Wood Lane, just ten minutes' walk from the BBC Media Centre, has meant that we've attracted BBC journalists and news crews seeking a quick interview with a teacher or just some playground footage for a story on the latest educational reform. We try to accommodate such requests, and in doing so we've attracted the attention of other broadcasters and publications. As a a headteacher you know that there will be the occasional bit of negative publicity, so it makes sense to gain some positive exposure if it's there for the taking. More meaningfully, we've cultivated open and honest relations with our local newspapers, who in my experience are always keen for a good news story celebrating the achievements of local young people.

At the same time that the student newsletter reached our inboxes on a Friday afternoon Michael would be emailing out the weekly staff bulletin, which he created in our first week and is still published every Friday. It's a simple, yet profoundly significant document that lists the schedule for the week ahead, along with the word of the week, theme of the week and scripture of the week, all of which rotate throughout the year. The bulletin always includes a pedagogical element, perhaps highlighting some good practice observed in class that week, or some advice from a recent Ofsted publication. We also include a 'butterflies' section in which we mention two students who staff should seek out to encourage and praise the following week (the name refers to the butterfly effect and the idea that small words of praise can have a large impact in the long run). We try to select quiet, timid students who could easily be lost in the maelstrom of an urban academy.

This chapter in a tweet: Create a positive learning culture in which all students can thrive; an inversion of the rules of the street.

Lesson 9:
Develop the whole child

'We ought to find out not who understands most, but who understands best.'

I recently contributed to a study which revealed that 'a 16-year-old today is more likely to own a smartphone than have a resident father' ('Breakthrough Britain', Centre for Social Justice, 2014, p. 10). In the face of evidence like this, the case for developing the whole child, rather than settling for a narrow set of academic outcomes, is overwhelming. The historian Benno Muller-Hill wrote an interesting article, 'The Idea Of The Final Solution And The Role Of Experts' (1994), on the academic qualifications of the 15 or so ministers and high-ranking officials who attended the 1942 Wannsee conference. The drafted document contained 16 signatures from the upper ministries of the German establishment; 16 signatories in total, of which exactly half held PhDs. Similarly, 43% of the concentration camp officers were either MDs or PhDs. Goebbels, the propaganda minister, had three PhDs. Educated, yes, but without a moral, ethical or spiritual dimension. League tables might focus on academic indicators, but no self-respecting head can ignore the challenge of developing the whole child. Therefore our pursuit of academic excellence can never be extricated from the challenge of developing responsible, mature, compassionate citizens who are able to channel their talents towards healthy, productive ends. Pupils should emerge from school with a broad, expansive education, sensitive to themselves and others. Academic qualifications alone are not enough. Schools make enough noise about educating the *whole* child and not instructing them solely to pass tests but give too little time to considering the methodology. Character development is not at the expense of an academic education: it enhances it.

> **'Ubuntu' is the quality that you seek to recruit in staff**
>
> 'Umuntu ngumuntu ngabantu'- a person is only a person through their relationships to others. (Zulu proverb)
>
> 'Ubuntu' is the essence of being human. It speaks of the fact that my humanity is caught up and is inextricably bound up in yours. I am human because I belong. It speaks about wholeness, it speaks about compassion.
>
> A person with Ubuntu is welcoming, hospitable, warm and generous and willing to share. Such people are open and available to others, willing to be vulnerable, affirming of others and do not feel threatened that others are able and good, for they have a proper self-assurance that comes from knowing that they belong in a greater whole. They know that they are diminished when others are humiliated, diminished when others are oppressed, diminished when others are treated as if they were less than who they are.

The interplay between academic and social development is complex, as any parent will know. Confidence is contagious, and if we can find one thing that children enjoy and feel good at, it won't take long for the confidence gained from this to spread to other areas of their life. I was reminded of this recently when I sat down with a 12-year-old girl who had clocked up the most demerits in the school and was at risk of exclusion due to persistently failing to meet our basic expectations such as punctuality and completion of work. Lauren had started Year 7 in our second set, but by the end of Year 8 she was languishing towards the bottom of set four, with levels pretty much identical to those she arrived with at the end of primary school. As she slumped in her chair before me, mumbling vague responses to my questions, it was clear that she lacked any kind of drive or motivation. It was left to her father, sitting beside her, to explain that at the weekends Lauren enjoyed playing football, baking cakes, and playing with her little brothers. She also took charge of technical issues in the family home, helping her siblings and parents fix glitches on their mobiles and laptops. Lauren left this side of her character at home as she moped through the gate every morning, journal at the ready to record her late detention. She explained that she often left her PE kit at home because she didn't like getting changed in front of other students. Quick fixes are illusory when it comes to changing patterns of human behaviour, but we shouldn't underestimate the potential for self-improvement once a problem has been identified and a response agreed. I asked Lauren's head of year to contact her teachers with the request that they quietly seek her out for praise and support. I also sent her from my office with a copy of our programme of after school clubs and encouraged her to join the tech club. We made an appointment with the school nurse to make a diet and exercise plan, and I spoke to her PE teacher to encourage involvement in her PE lessons. It's too early to report a transformation in Lauren, but I've no doubt that if she can sustain the willingness she expressed to participate more actively in school life then it won't be long before her effort and grades in the classroom begin to improve too.

Pupil self-esteem

In the inner city, many pupils come from home and family backgrounds which for a variety of reasons may already be creating conditions of stress and low self-esteem. Low levels of self-esteem affect pupils' willingness to get involved or take risks in the classroom.

Our job as leaders is to create classrooms wherein pupils can flourish. This is a huge topic but one which matters to me: I do not believe in heavily regimented schools where pupils are cowed into silence by militaristic staff. However:

- Pupils must feel emotionally (and physically) safe: from bullying, ridicule, 'cussing' and humiliation.
- A calm, caring atmosphere should pervade in the classroom and corridors. This will encourage pupils to try new things and in the process learn more about themselves.
- Self-identity needs to be strong (one of the many reasons we display lots of photos around the academy and the school magazine being a photo journal).
- There must be an affiliation to the teacher and subject, a real sense of belonging and fierce loyalty.
- Pupils must be made to feel competent and capable.
- There needs to be a sense of purpose – almost mission – that gives the learning meaning and direction.

Emotional intelligence is closely linked to self-esteem. The emotionally intelligent student:

- is confident – meaning that we need to build on this and find ways to help pupils succeed, not just academically but socially too
- is curious – we should explore concepts and encourage independent learning even in areas not directly linked to academy work
- has goals/targets – levels and grades, yes, but in other areas too: has your school defined what a student should be like when they leave?

- has self-control
- has a deep understanding of what happens around them
- can communicate well – not just facts and information but feelings, fears and ideas: what opportunities are there for this and what are the implications for the classroom?
- is co-operative – meaning that we need to offer opportunities to encourage interdependence as well as dependence. 'Circle time' is a valuable tool in this regard. At BDA we switched from playing football to rugby in part to provide opportunities for interdependence!

Lauren and her peers have access to more than 40 lunchtime and after school clubs. Indeed, every single teacher at Burlington Danes contributes to our co-curricular programme, either through involvement in a club or by leading an intervention session in their subject after school. The clubs range from a daily film club, which caters for up to 150 students in our theatre every lunchtime, to pursuits as diverse as samba drumming, chess, cooking, bike maintenance, film making and creative writing. It absorbs a significant slice of the school budget, and a similarly important share of our collective energy, but I take great pride in our co-curricular programme and the opportunities it offers. These clubs help to develop character, and enable us to provide opportunities that we can't offer during the normal school day. Many of our students are keen to stay at school beyond the end of the day (I recently found two Year 9 girls revising in a maths classroom at 6.45pm, just before the caretaker was due to lock-up for the day) so it makes sense that we provide a structured programme for them. After all, what we're about is turning out people for life, not just for A levels.

Introducing a broad range of clubs (and ensuring the quality of delivery) wasn't on my list of priorities when I first arrived in West London six years ago, but over time I've been able to widen my glare and treat clubs with the same rigour that we treat our academic provision. Every student in Key Stage 3 is expected to attend at least one club each week, a commitment which many of our older students willingly continue. We don't presume that our young people spend their Saturdays at swimming clubs, or gaining their badges with the scouts and guides, so we seek to provide these opportunities at school. Our efforts are sometimes thwarted by the experiences of our students. For example, our delight in being able to offer rowing on the Serpentine in Hyde Park as a Year 11 PE option quickly waned when we found that most of our students couldn't swim. Similarly, a large portion of our Duke of Edinburgh Award budget has been absorbed by rucksacks and sleeping mats, which students in more affluent communities might find in the garage of the family home.

One of my favourite clubs is our enterprise club, which has tapped into the spirit of enterprise you'll find in any playground in the country (I've often found students charging their peers to do their homework, while another student sold his mother's sandwiches to his classmates for decent profit – I never did find out whether he split the spoils of his sandwich sales with his mother). The enterprise club at Burlington Danes offers a delivery service from the local café, where two sixth form students take orders from staff each morning, pick up around 20 lunches from the café outside school, then deliver them to teachers at their usual lunchtime hangout. They charge cost price, and make a 10% margin from the discount offered by the café.

Other lunchtime activities include clubs for boxing and film. The boxing club has an interesting story behind it. A YouTube video came to our attention of a group of Year 11 students boxing on top of a local tower block. There were no ropes, barriers or head guards in place – it's a miracle that no-one was seriously hurt. Despite the obvious folly of their activities we noticed how seriously the boys were taking their new hobby – the video revealed a designated referee, a panel of judges and a timekeeper. All that was missing, I'm pleased to say, was girls dressed in bikinis parading the ring to announce the start of each round. This particular group of boys was proving hard to engage with, particularly at lunchtime when their pent-up energy needed an outlet. So on the condition that their tower-top bouts would cease we purchased a boxing ring, extended the hours of our resident boxing coach and provided lunchtime boxing lessons for these Year 11 boys. The atrium we used for this has since been turned into a designated gym, with the boxing ring still at the centre of it. It's proved incredibly popular at lunchtime and after school, particularly with our more energetic boys, while a large group of girls have also excelled in the boxing ring.

Meanwhile, throughout the winter our film club shows one movie per week in the Potter Theatre, sometimes generating crowds of more than 150. It's a quiet area where students can bring their lunch and catch their breath in the heart of the day. If it ignites a love of film in just a few of them then all the better. At lunchtime our SEN department operates a 'sanctuary' for youngsters who want a quiet place to relax, and our library provides solace and last minute homework opportunities. The table tennis tables provide a focal point for lots of our younger students, while the all-weather Astroturf pitch offers year-round football for others. For senior staff lunchtime is perhaps the most stressful time of the day; and walkie-talkies splutter with warnings of baguette shortages in the cafe and spillages in the canteen, but I'm proud of the diverse range of opportunities we provide for children every day for 50 minutes.

The type of food provided by school canteens has been the subject of much discussion since Jamie Oliver's healthy eating campaign in 2005. His efforts made a difference, and the legacy of his crusade against junk food is evident at Burlington Danes, where we only serve chips once a week and where students taking a main meal are compelled to have a portion of salad. We have no vending machines in school, meaning students are unable to purchase fizzy drinks or chocolate. Schools can only do so much though, and I've previously noted the ubiquity of Lucozade around the school, with students seemingly oblivious to the fact that each bottle contains more than half of an adult's recommended daily allowance of sugar. There are four shops selling confectionary within a few minutes' walk of the school, and the food that students eat as they walk through the gate in the morning would arouse the ire of Jamie Oliver and his pals – Pringles, Doritos, Haribo, donuts and cookies all feature on the breakfast smorgasbord for our students. There's also a fast food shop a few minutes' walk from the school gate where you can buy chicken wings and chips for £2. We prevent students going in there while we're on duty for 30 minutes after school, but beyond that they make their own choices. It's always difficult to know where to draw the line in terms of the school's influence, something I will go into more depth about later.

The notion that academic tuition is a necessary-but-not-sufficient component of education has a long history. Take the words of Montaigne, written nearly 500 years ago:

> I gladly come back to the theme of the absurdity of our education: its end has not been to make us good and wise, but learned. And it has succeeded. It has not taught us to seek virtue and to embrace wisdom:

it has impressed upon us their derivation and their etymology... We readily inquire, 'Does he know Greek or Latin?' 'Can he write poetry and prose?' But what matters most is what we put last: 'Has he become better and wiser?' We ought to find out not who understands most but who understands best. We work merely to fill the memory, leaving the understanding and the sense of right and wrongs empty.

The riots which swept across London in the summer of 2011 provided a stark reminder of the need for society (and if not schools, then who?) to provide a moral as well as academic foundation for our young people. Investigations into the riots revealed that 66% of those charged had special educational needs, compared with 21% across the population as a whole ('Reading the Riots', *The Guardian* and London School of Economics, 2011). Thirty-five per cent of the adults involved were in receipt of unemployment benefit, compared with 12% nationally. The origins of public disorder on this scale are clearly complex, and it's very difficult to separate causation from correlation; but the two figures quoted above would indicate that many of those involved had struggled to acquire the academic qualifications that would enable them to benefit from the riches available to others in London. Furthermore, 42% of the 10-17-year-olds charged were on free school meals, compared to the national figure of 16%, indicating that schools in challenging areas have a particular role to play in any attempt to prevent a repeat of that summer of disorder. But the riots were as much, if not more, indicative of moral failure as academic failure. Of the rioters themselves, 56% of them suggested that 'moral decline' was an 'important' or 'very important' cause of the riots, with 70% of them ticking the same boxes for 'greed'. Showing commendable but grim honesty, 40% of the rioters blamed 'poor parenting' (along with 86% of non-rioters surveyed) suggesting once again that we can't rely on the family to provide the moral foundation our young citizens require. Sixty-eight per cent of rioters cited boredom, and it's surely no surprise that the riots occurred exactly half way through the six-week school summer holiday, adding weight to the argument that schools should provide year round supervision. Such a solution is too simplistic. Like installing CCTV on every street corner, extending schools' opening hours in the hope of preventing disorder reduces the function of schools to one of supervision. Free time is a fundamental right of all young people, and it shouldn't be asking too much to expect them to match the right to free time with the responsibility to behave appropriately (as the vast majority of young Londoners did in the summer of 2011).

Wise words for young people and adults from a judge in New Zealand

"Always we hear the cry from teenagers 'What can we do, where can we go?' … My answer is, 'Go home, mow the lawn, wash the windows, learn to cook, build a raft, get a job, visit the sick, study your lessons, and after you've finished, read a book'.

"Your town does not owe you recreational facilities and your parents do not owe you fun. The world does not owe you a living, you owe the world something. You owe it your time, energy and talent so that no-one will be at war, in poverty or sick and lonely again."

"In other words, grow up, stop being a cry baby, get out of your dream world and develop a backbone, not a wishbone. Start behaving like a responsible person. You are important and you are needed. It's too late to sit around and wait for somebody to do something someday. Someday is now and that somebody is you…"

('Exporting to the Americans', The Northland Age, 23 August 2012)

So how can schools nourish the moral development of our young people? The answer lies not in bolting on a separate moral curriculum but in weaving moral fibre into the very fabric of the school. This starts in the classroom, where teachers speak to students with respect and courtesy, rarely raising their voice, never swearing and avoiding rude and confrontational phrases such as 'shut-up'. Teachers are sometimes justified in raising their voice, but – more often than not – shouting only serves to generate frustration and animosity. That said, I'm similarly averse to the flip-side of the shouting teacher: the teacher who comforts students with hugs and sympathy. I encourage teachers to act with professionalism and to model the characteristics we seek to nurture in our students, avoiding the stereotype of the sergeant major but leaving the counselling to the professionals.

The role of assemblies in reinforcing our efforts to develop the whole child has already been noted. Alongside our guest speaker programme these assemblies seek to broaden the horizons of our students and develop their awareness of life beyond the school gates. There's no substitute for actually leaving the school site though, and I'm incredibly proud of the frequency and range of trips that we offer throughout the school year. In recent months, Year 7 visited the New Forest for a week's camping to consolidate the relationships and skills developed in their first year of secondary education. Year 8 students went to Lille's Christmas market to develop their French skills and 60 Year 9 pupils experienced for themselves the trenches of the western front. Year 10 students also paid a visit to Jamie's Farm to experience rural life and 80 boys and girls in Year 11 recently went to Winter Wonderland in Hyde Park as a reward for exceeding our expectations regarding attendance and completion of work. Sixth form students have visited Parliament, the headquarters of Bloomberg and the Yorkshire moors, where *Wuthering Heights* is set. Fundraising is currently underway for a return visit to India, where sixth formers went last year to support Ark projects in Delhi. Despite the fundraising, most of these trips are subsidised by the school. We're lucky to have access to the trustees' fund which receives money from rents paid to property held by the school's historic trust. This enables us to make our plentiful trips affordable for students, and we're keen to ensure that all of our students benefit from our range of school journeys. A few years ago the unions were encouraging teachers to boycott school trips due to the risk of legal action should things go wrong. It's certainly a huge responsibility to take young people into the crowded carriages of the London Underground, not to mention the frenzied streets of Delhi at rush hour, but for most of our teachers the chance to attend such trips is a highlight of the job; it offers a rare chance to bond with students beyond the pressure of the classroom.

In the summer of 2013, we embarked on two days of cultural capital, where all students in Key Stage 3 were taken off timetable for two days to visit two cultural attractions in London from a selection of 12. From the British Museum to St Paul's Cathedral; Kew Gardens to Tate Modern; we hired 12 coaches for each day and subsidised the full cost of the visits for each of our 550 students in Key Stage 3. The visits were combined with an essay-writing competition, with each student choosing to write an essay on one of the two places they had visited. Cultural capital brought learning to life for our students and provided memories that they will retain for a long time, as well as giving students and staff a chance to learn together and enjoy each other's company in a different setting. I saw for myself the enthusiasm of our science teachers rub off on the students as they interacted with the exhibits in the Science Museum. Our students live in one of the world's great cultural cities, but I know from previous trips that many of our students seldom leave their post code. The cultural visits took place just before the summer holidays and I emphasised to the students that with their free London bus passes and with entrance to London museums being free, there's no reason why they couldn't engage in cultural capital of their own over the summer vacation.

Our school council provides further opportunity for student leadership and participation. Schools vary in the powers bestowed on school councils. At their worst, a school council is a rudderless talking shop for trivial grumbles, a pointless echo chamber which leads to nothing more than a noticeboard of similar complaints with no action or improvements. At the other end of the spectrum some schools seem to confer more powers to their student council than to their own staff, empowering the council to interview prospective teachers, lead training of staff and manage a hefty budget. I tend to follow something of a middle ground. Students must know that they are represented and that they have a voice in school, but we must also recognise the expertise of professional teachers and school leaders. The limits of student consultation are exposed when teachers seek end of term feedback from their students. I actively encourage the process, but enacting the requests and advice of students would result in a classroom diet comprising exclusively of group work, videos and trips. That said, carefully framed questions can yield useful insight. In a recent student council meeting we asked students to share the most powerful learning experiences they had encountered that term. Some of their reflections are copied below:

- Year 9 student recalls English lessons by Ms Pretsell because 'her lessons are interesting'. S/he advised teachers to let more children read their work to the rest of the class.
- Year 10 student recalls Ms Annan's science lesson in which they used information from memory to make display boards. S/he wants more physical work in lessons, and quizzes.
- Year 8 student recalls learning PEE (Point Evidence Explain) paragraphs with Dr O'Hear in English.
- Year 9 student recalls making clay pots in art with Ms Bell. S/he enjoyed this because it was active and creative.
- Year 8 student recalls an RE lesson with Mr Whitlock in which they studied philosophy and were encouraged to think for themselves. S/

he realised that there is no right/wrong answer. S/he would like more opportunity to share thoughts rather than write in books.

- Year 9 student recalls Ms Williamson's French lesson in which the students taught each other.
- Year 8 student recalls a maths lesson in which they played games about sequences. S/he advises teachers to ask students at the end of the lesson if they understood it.
- Year 7 student recalls making an apple crumble with Ms Ford in a food tech lesson. S/he wants lessons to be more active and physical.
- Year 10 student recalls a physics lesson with Mr Barker in which they learnt about forces. It was good because they experimented for themselves before feeding back to the group, which was better than being talked to.

This list serves as a powerful insight into the student experience, with any given day involving apple crumbles, philosophy and physics. I was similarly impressed by the feedback students gave me during a recent Saturday detention when I asked them about rewards and sanctions. Their list of the toughest sanctions confirmed the effectiveness of our current range of punishments, with students mentioning Saturday detentions and days in Step (our internal isolation room), with the risk of getting 'perm' (permanently excluded) being the most feared. The list of optimal rewards was also interesting, with several students simply wanting their list of demerits to be cleared. We therefore adapted our approach to demerits so that the cumulative tally returns to zero at the half way point in the year, wiping the slate clean for all students. One student suggested that the most motivating reward would be a day trip to Southend. At last I understood the phrase 'poverty of aspiration'.

A glance at our school calendar provides clear evidence of character development being woven into the tapestry of the school experience. Take a random week in February 2013. On the Monday morning during our PSHCE session students from Key Stages 4 and 5 gathered in the theatre to hear the latest in our Speaker Series lectures, with this one being from an Old Dane (alumnus of St Clement Danes, our predecessor school), who is now a leading practitioner of cancer research at Imperial College's Hammersmith Campus, occupying an office which overlooks our playing fields. Later in the day students in Year 9 enjoyed a workshop on personal finance led by the charity MyBnk. After school, students in Key Stage 3 competed in a West London debating league against prestigious establishments such as St Paul's and Latymer Upper School. Later in the week students in Year 11 went to the headquarters of city firm Bloomberg for careers mentoring, while undergraduates from Imperial College came to Burlington Danes to deliver one-to-one maths tutoring for pupils preparing for their Maths GCSE. During this same week sixth form students took the central line across town to the campus of SOAS (School of Oriental and African Studies) for the latest instalment of their six-part Global Matters series of workshops. Valentine's usually falls during the half term break but this year it fell during the week I'm describing. Our enterprise club tapped into the annual outpouring of amour by offering a rose-delivery service within the school. Some students received more cerebral gifts, with our head of literacy championing International Book Giving Day which involved teachers presenting students with books to read for pleasure. Returning to more traditional valentines pursuits, enterprising sixth form students cajoled gallant teachers into starring in our own version of Blind Date, an event which drew a packed crowd to the theatre on two consecutive lunchtimes. Such events might not add to our five A*-C pass rate but they provide lasting memories and create an atmosphere of positivity and cohesion between students and staff which permeates our corridors and classrooms. Believe it or not, the week described above is fairly typical for us at BDA – our weekly newsletter archive on our website is testament to this. Indeed the newsletter is a powerful tool in celebrating our extra-curricular provision. The weekly Coates Commendation champions the small acts of honesty that take place each week, from the £5 note found on the playground and handed to reception to the local resident who writes to the school thanking that student who helped them up after they stumbled on an icy morning.

If the week described above is typical, we also schedule events throughout the school year where students are encouraged to engage with the world beyond their classrooms. Our cross-curricular week takes place in July. Normal lessons are cancelled for the week and teachers work with students in small groups on specific projects (exam classes have departed by this point so we're able to tap into a healthy teacher student ratio at this time of year). In 2011 the focus on cross-curricular week was local history. Groups investigated different aspects of our local history, from immigration to the 1948 Olympics to Queens Park Rangers and the BBC. In 2012 the focus was London 2012 Olympics and the week incorporated a 'Jamaica Day' to celebrate the fact that BDA students had been selected to give the Jamaican team a guard of honour as they entered the Olympic Stadium for the opening ceremony. Students and staff dressed in the colours of the Jamaican flag and our Jamaican teachers (we have several) cooked up a BBQ in the playground at lunchtime.

Charity Week has also become a regular fixture in our annual schedule. The week is packed with activities such as sponge the teacher (teachers volunteer to allow students to throw wet sponges at them), morning marathon (students and teachers run round the Fink building before school), and a talent show. The week generates a few thousand pounds for our nominated charities. Perhaps more importantly, it galvanises the school community and encourages students to make an effort for people in less fortunate circumstances than us. It's an exhausting week but it never fails to provide lasting memories. Perhaps the highlight of our community service is our Christmas tea dance, in which students plan, prepare and deliver a Christmas party for elderly members of our local community. It's a valuable opportunity for students to gain experience of planning an event and serving others, and it does wonders for our standing amongst our senior neighbours.

Our annual tea dance has become one of several showpiece events sprinkled throughout the school calendar. Our Cultural Gala, Shakespeare for Schools performance, Christmas Concert, Spring Musical and Summer Gala (alongside other Ark academies at The Barbican) ensure that we're never far away from a memorable set-piece event that develops talent and reminds us that we are more than the sum of our parts. Inevitably such events put a strain on the school. Schools run on routine, and any change to established order poses problems. So you can imagine that a well-intentioned request from the head of performing arts for the cast of the musical to be released from lessons during the week of the performance (along with the staff who are helping with the show) will cause headaches and disagreements for heads of department who might lose teachers, teachers who might lose students, and the cover supervisor who has to find other teachers to cover the lessons of the teachers involved. Solving such logistical challenges seems to occupy at least half of the time that my SLT spend together, and the tension continues on the night of the performance, when vice principals become door staff and assistant principals practise their assertiveness by denying access to the ticketless guests who arrive to see their friends and family on stage only to find out that the performance is sold out. These stresses are soon forgotten once the show has been delivered, and I must say that our recent performances of *Guys & Dolls*, *Hairspray* and *Little Shop of Horrors* have provided some of my best memories at Burlington Danes.

In recent months we've formalised our efforts to develop and stretch the character of our students. One of my vice principals has selected a character trait for each year group to focus on (resilience, compassion, integrity) and has worked with heads of department and other stakeholders to reinforce the chosen value in assemblies and lessons for each year group. So film club recently screened *Life is Beautiful* to explore the Year 8 theme of resilience, while the same year group analysed poems on this theme in their English lessons. Students have been issued with a 'passport' which enables them to acquire stamps demonstrating progress towards their chosen values. There's a fine line to tread when seeking to enhance our 'character curriculum'. Over-regulate it and we risk turning it into a tick-box exercise which might yield some impressive policy documents for inspectors but little in the way of actual character development – 'Not everything that can be counted counts, and not everything that counts can be counted' (Einstein). On the other hand, leaving character off the curriculum risks neglecting this vital element of our provision and gives students the impression that all we care about is their academic performance. Our solution, as has been shown, has been to weave an appreciation of character and personality into our calendar, classrooms, corridors and curriculum.

The American psychologist Martin Seligman has written powerfully on the importance of soft skills and character, with this quotation capturing his views on the importance of optimism: 'success will not necessarily go to the most talented. The prize will go to the adequately talented who are also optimists' (1991, p. 191). Kipp Schools in America, rightly lauded for their incredible success in tough urban neighbourhoods, have incorporated Seligman's work into the daily diet fed to their students, focusing on 'seven highly predictive strengths: zest, grit, self-control, optimism, gratitude, social intelligence, and curiosity'. Kipp's combination of rigorous academic tuition and character development is captured in their wonderfully simple and widely cited motto '*Work hard. Be nice*'. Incidentally I've seen teachers successfully condense a long list of classroom rules into these four words. Kipp describe this double-edged challenge as the 'yin-yang that make our schools come alive' and I can't think of a better way of putting it myself. Kipp's approach to developing character features in *How Children Succeed* by Paul Tough. A key message of the book is that soft skills can be acquired later in childhood even if they've been neglected in early childhood, as long as schools proactively cultivate these skills. For Paul Tough, Dweck's growth mindset therefore applies to character as much as intelligence; he describes character as nothing more than a collection of habits: 'the traits we call virtues are no more and no less than simple habits' (2012, p. 94). Tough is impressed by the two-page questionnaire that Kipp Schools have developed to measure the soft skills of each student. The questionnaire leads to a character report card for each student which teachers discuss with students and parents at parents' evening alongside their academic report card. Some of the measures adopted by Kipp, such as students wearing sweatshirts emblazoned with the slogan 'Infinite Character' with the seven character traits listed on the back, and huge signs on the walls imploring students to 'Actively Participate' seems slightly oppressive to my English sensibilities, but I'm enthralled by the rigour which Kipp has applied to the development of character. Interestingly, Tough compares Kipp schools to Riverdale County, one of the top private schools in New York. Here too the headteacher is keen to develop the character of his students, this time because he fears that their comfortable existence will deny them a taste of failure: 'Randolph [the headteacher] wants his students to succeed, of course – it's just that he believes that in order for them to do so, they first need to learn how to fail' (2012, p. 86).

What do we want our students to be?

This relatively simple exercise to do is all too often looked over by schools but I think it is an essential part of your improvement planning. How should your pupils emerge having spent their formative years in your school?

We believe that pupils taught at Burlington Danes Academy should be:

*   **successful individuals** who work hard and enjoy learning, achieve, are scholarly and make progress, continually engaged in learning new things, capable of more than even they themselves thought possible, eager to utilise the brain to think, research, study, experiment and find results

- **confident individuals** living fulfilling lives, not dependent upon other people finding out the answers and handing them over but thriving in their 'own thinking', avid readers, culturally aware, good listeners, analytical by nature, with good comprehension skills, eager to discuss and reason

- **spiritual individuals** compassionately sensitive to the needs of others and 'self', instilled with a heightened sense of morality and with a readiness to challenge all that would constrain the human spirit, for example, poverty of aspiration, lack of self confidence and belief, moral neutrality or indifference, force, fanaticism, aggression, greed, injustice, narrowness of vision, self interest, sexism, racism and other forms of discrimination; individuals with an appreciation of the intangible – for example, beauty, truth, love, goodness, justice, order, as well as for mystery, paradox and ambiguity.

- **motivated individuals** who have a purposeful and aspirant direction in life, a love of learning, a sense of vocation and are flexible for future work needs

- **responsible individuals** who live contented, safe and healthy lives, making a positive contribution to society and who have a heightened awareness of both citizenship and charity instilled with a strong sense of community; individuals with a sophisticated understanding of the importance of courtesy, appropriate behaviour and care of others; individuals who shun bullying and work to eradicate it; individuals who care about the environment; individuals who look to the future without forgetting to enjoy the experience of today

The conclusion of this chapter is that the binary distinction between academic success and character development fails to capture the nature of the challenge faced by teachers and schools to develop the whole child. Take this line from *They Call Me Coach* (1972) the heart-warming memoirs of a legendary American high school basketball coach named John Wooden: 'Jack was so afraid of not being accepted that he made sure people had a reason not to like him'. Jack's fears will clearly have a negative impact on his own learning, and the learning of those around him, unless they are addressed. Perhaps Jack needs one-to-one counselling and professional emotional support, but it's more likely that he needs to find something that he loves, something he feels good at, and the confidence gained from this will quickly spread to other areas of his life, including his performance in class. And of course Jack is far more likely to find that hidden talent and shed his prickly skin in a school with a rich co-curricular programme and a culture steeped in appreciation of the depths of human character.

The circle of truth

The circle of truth is an established moment in the BDA calendar for Year 11 pupils, and has become an integral part of the BDA journey. It is held on the day they are sent off for what used to be called 'study leave' but is now referred to as 'the end of the formal timetable'.

The hall is cleared but for 180 seats around the edges of it. The aura of mystery is heightened by the fact that it is sprung upon the pupils without their prior knowledge.

Year 11 pupils sit in a huge circle. They are then reminded that this would be their last time together; their final opportunity to put right anything they felt ought not to be left 'undone' and a chance to state a parting message. What is said in the circle stays in the circle.

Only those in the circle can speak. Tutors contribute too, but it is the pupils themselves who come into the circle and open up in the way that only children can. Through the inevitable tears, they share their memories and stated their friendships and hopes for the future.

It is always a revealing, moving and emotional event. By the end of the meeting many boys and girls are in tears. It is a priceless sight to witness huge, supposedly streetwise boys shaking and trembling with emotion, overwhelmed by the emotion of the importance of the particular moment in time.

It reminds me that we deal with children: no matter how they want to be perceived, they are not yet adults, not yet the 'finished article'. The academy has clearly brought them together, shaped them, taught them, prepared them for adulthood.

Afterwards they sign each others shirts; ironically most if not all students are usually in school the next day as we run an intensive cram timetable.

I am humbled to think of the influence and effect we have over their lives.

This extract from Pennac's enchanting account of teaching in deprived communities in France, *School Blues*, captures the importance of schools reaching out to every child within their care:

> To all those who attribute today's youth gangs to the phenomenon of the banlieues, I say: Yes, you're right, unemployment, yes, marginalized communities, yes, ethnic ghettoization, yes, the tyranny of designer brands, yes, one-parent families, yes, the growth of a parallel economy and trafficking of every kind, yes, yes, yes … But let's not underestimate the one thing we can do something about, which goes back to the dawn of pedagogical time: the loneliness, the shame, of the student who doesn't understand, lost in a world where everyone else does (2010, p. 26-27).

This chapter in a tweet: Regardless of league tables and inspections, headteachers have a moral duty to develop the whole child.

Lesson 10:
Schools don't operate
in a vacuum

'Government must cajole, nurture and energise the school system with the same care, and the same regard for long-term improvement, as a good headteacher applies to her school.'

In the previous chapter I shared my view that headteachers must be willing to set their own priorities for the success of their school, rather than being slaves to the shifting sands of government policy. In recent years schools have been judged solely on narrow academic indicators. Yet good headteachers, driven by a sense of social duty, have continued to develop the whole child. This chapter will explore in more detail the relationship between schools and policy makers. It is my belief that successful school leaders keep track of policy developments and academic research in the field of education, yet it will always be the responsibility of the headteacher to tailor any policies and innovations to the needs of their school. As head at Burlington Danes I've worked hard to ensure that we are agile and informed so that we can respond quickly to government directives. One way in which we stay in touch with educational policy and innovations is through a weekly summary of relevant articles and blog posts, which one member of our SLT emails to the rest of the senior team each week. At the same time, I've tried to ensure that we possess enough integrity to prioritise the needs of our students rather than act as a faceless delivery unit of centrally prescribed educational policy. One example of this is the introduction of the English Baccalaureate. This basket of five traditional qualifications was introduced to confer more prestige to conventional academic subjects, such as history and languages. League tables would reveal how many students in each school gained the English

Baccalaureate, thus encouraging schools to re-focus on these traditional subjects. This served us well, since even when no-one was looking we built a traditional, academic curriculum, shunning the temptation to churn our students through easier but less valuable qualifications. The introduction of the English Baccalaureate was one government initiative which worked in our favour, but the underlying message is that the prudent headteacher focuses on the best interests of her students rather than fickle government policy.

Autonomy and accountability have been the twin engines powering education reform in recent years. The theory behind the autonomy-accountability dichotomy is that autonomy gives schools the opportunity to innovate, unleashing creativity and drive in schools free from centrally imposed constraints such as national pay scales and rigid curricula. The other side of this coin is that clear and robust lines of accountability keep schools honest, drawing attention to the schools which use their autonomy to improve the outcomes for their students, and exposing the failure of schools where underachievement remains entrenched. Given the importance of what we do as gatekeepers of the next generation, I wholly accept the accountability to which we are subjected, and as this book has revealed, I'm keen to make use of the autonomy offered to heads to tailor their schools to fit their local context.

Let's start by explaining why accountability matters. I recently checked the website of a South London secondary school and was surprised to see this claim on their home page: 'This year 92% of our students gained 5+ A*-C grades'. My surprise was caused by the fact that I knew this school was under pressure having missed the government's floor target of 40% of students gaining five 'good' GCSEs at A*-C – *ie* five GCSEs including English and maths. As a headteacher in a similar school it didn't take me long to realise that this school had published its figure without English and maths (92%) while hiding its figure with English and maths (36%). We can presume that such a discrepancy is caused by students taking plenty of GCSE 'equivalent' exams which, shamefully, are often much easier and therefore far less valuable to the students who gain them. The travesty of this situation is that local parents who don't understand the education system might be fooled into thinking that this is a high-achieving school. They might know that the national average is 59% (including English and maths) so when they see the 92%

figure staring back at them from the school's homepage they could easily conclude that this school is over-achieving. You can only imagine the shock they get when it gradually dawns on them that in fact almost two thirds of students at this school left after five years without a decent set of qualifications. This might sound harsh, and I hope that proposals to restore vocational qualifications to their former value are delivered, but at the moment a 16-year-old who leaves school without five A*-C including English and maths has no chance of moving on to A levels and no chance of going to a good university. So two thirds of young people from this deprived South London neighbourhood will have been failed by the education system, and missed out on their chance of a golden ticket to future prosperity – a stark reality at odds with the shameless triumphalism of the school's home page.

There are still those who doubt whether schools and teachers should be held to account at all. They argue that measuring schools conflicts with the values of education, and that schools and teachers should be trusted to act in the best interests of their charges, rather than forced to pursue a narrow set of outcomes. These views were captured by an unlikely source: the Hollywood star Matt Damon, who delivered a passionate speech at a teachers' rally in Washington DC on July 30, 2011. It's worth quoting in full:

"I had incredible teachers. As I look at my life today, the things I value most about myself – my imagination, my love of acting, my passion for writing, my love of learning, my curiosity – all come from how I was parented and taught.

"And none of these qualities that I've just mentioned – none of these qualities that I prize so deeply, that have brought me so much joy, that have brought me so much professional success – none of these qualities that make me who I am ... can be tested.

"I said before that I had incredible teachers. And that's true. But it's more than that. My teachers were empowered to teach me. Their time wasn't taken up with a bunch of test prep – this silly drill and kill nonsense that any serious person knows doesn't promote real learning. No, my teachers were free to approach me and every other kid in that classroom like an individual puzzle. They took so much care in figuring out who we were and how to best make the lessons resonate with each of us. They were empowered to unlock our potential. They were allowed to be teachers.

195

"Now don't get me wrong. I did have a brush with standardized tests at one point. I remember because my mom went to the principal's office and said, 'My kid ain't taking that. It's stupid, it won't tell you anything and it'll just make him nervous.' That was in the '70s when you could talk like that.

"I shudder to think that these tests are being used today to control where funding goes.

"I don't know where I would be today if my teachers' job security was based on how I performed on some standardized test. If their very survival as teachers was based on whether I actually fell in love with the process of learning but rather if I could fill in the right bubble on a test. If they had to spend most of their time desperately drilling us and less time encouraging creativity and original ideas; less time knowing who we were, seeing our strengths and helping us realise our talents.

"I honestly don't know where I'd be today if that was the type of education I had. I sure as hell wouldn't be here. I do know that.

"This has been a horrible decade for teachers. I can't imagine how demoralized you must feel. But I came here today to deliver an important message to you: As I get older, I appreciate more and more the teachers that I had growing up. And I'm not alone. There are millions of people just like me."

So the next time you're feeling down, or exhausted, or unappreciated, or at the end of your rope; the next time you turn on the TV and see yourself called 'overpaid'; the next time you encounter some simple-minded, punitive policy that's been driven into your life by some corporate reformer who has literally never taught anyone anything ... Please know that there are millions of us behind you. You have an army of regular people standing right behind you, and our appreciation for what you do is so deeply felt. We love you, we thank you and we will always have your back.

It's an appealing argument, but it's deeply flawed in several ways. Firstly, it's based on the misconception that schools must choose to do one or the other – to coach students to pass tests *or* nurture them to develop their true talents. I hope this book has demonstrated that it's perfectly possible, in fact essential, for schools to do both. Secondly, Damon presents a caricatured picture of standardised tests, suggesting that they simply require students to fill in the 'right bubble'. A standardised test is simply a test given in the same conditions to all takers – it doesn't have to be multiple choice, or narrowly constrained to prescribed outcomes. Take this question from a GCSE biology paper (Edexcel): 'Mitosis and meiosis are types of cell division. Compare these two types of cell division (6 marks)'. Here's one from an RE paper (also Edexcel): 'Explain how the argument from design may lead to belief in God (8 marks)'. I'm not arguing that these questions are particularly tough – a bit of revision and a clear head in the exam hall should suffice for both of them – but they prove that standardised testing needn't mean formulaic testing. This antipathy towards tests, towards a measurable 'end product', seems to be at odds with most of life's pursuits, where the end product is important. I'm sure that while Matt Damon is filming his latest movie he receives encouragement and support, and I've no doubt he's given time and freedom to adapt his instructions – his scripts and character notes – to his own style and preferences, but ultimately he's expected to deliver a faultless performance in front of the camera. Would Damon prefer to work in an environment where months of practice and tuition fail to yield an end product, or where the praise he receives for his spellbinding performance in *Good Will Hunting* is the same as the response to his box office flop and critically slammed *The Rainmaker*? Of course not, and I think it's equally appropriate that after studying maths for five years students are given the chance to demonstrate their progress, and check their aptitude against their peers. My experience is that teachers and students alike enjoy working towards something, and that the desire to perform well in end of year tests injects lessons with purpose and precision throughout the year. It is possible to enjoy the journey as well as the destination.

As a middle class child, Matt Damon would have been monitored and assessed from birth. Parents would have checked that cognitive development, teeth, first steps and first words all emerged at the correct time. If at any time this constant assessment was to find flaw then the parents would have had the means to seek professional support. Many students from deprived backgrounds lack this early intervention and unless we use appropriate testing and assessment once they're at school then they will continue to fall behind their more affluent

197

peers. Anti-testing rhetoric is therefore patronising and damaging to the disadvantaged. It is understandable that there is antipathy towards testing in some liberal quarters, but it's absurd that teachers' unions and some headteachers, particularly primary heads, have joined the calls to cut down on testing. They do their pupils a grave injustice which may never be put right. Accountability brings credibility to the profession. Thankfully, the days when teachers were viewed as glorified babysitters who could not be held to account for their work are long gone.

Perhaps there's been a generational shift when it comes to teachers wanting to demonstrate success with their students. More than 25% of the teachers at Burlington Danes are from the Teach First programme, where high-flying graduates actively choose to work in challenging schools. Teach First has an explicit social purpose, captured here on its website: 'How much you achieve in life should not be determined by how much your parents earn. Yet in the UK, it too often is' (www.teachfirst.org.uk). Teach First participants have explicitly bought into this social mission and therefore want to demonstrate progress in closing the achievement gap. Similarly, we have several teachers who have joined us from other professions, mainly through the Schools Direct training programme. These ambitious lawyers, bankers and engineers didn't switch careers for an easy life – mostly they were fed up with the fruits of their labour ending up on a corporate balance sheet. They want a more fulfilling career, but they are still driven and determined to succeed. The fact that teaching, through standardised tests and league tables, now exposes classroom success, is therefore a reason to join the profession. If we simply let teachers and schools get on with their jobs, with no scrutiny or accountability, no focus on the end product, we would lose hundreds of ambitious, talented teachers keen to make a demonstrable impact.

My final criticism with Matt Damon's well-intentioned speech is that he mistakenly assumes that what worked for him in the suburbs of Cambridge, Massachusetts, would work for a child on the wrong side of the tracks in South Boston (ironically his debut movie *Good Will Hunting* touched on underachievement and lack of opportunity in 'Southie'). A quick glance at Damon's Wikipedia page suggests that he is the son of successful, well-educated parents: a stockbroker and a professor of education. He attended public (state) schools in Cambridge – a city known for being liberal and affluent and home to two of the world's finest universities, Harvard and

MIT. His primary school was Cambridge Alternative School; he then attended Cambridge Rindge and Latin School. At the risk of judging someone I've never met, I get the impression that Damon would most likely have thrived in any school. His mother could go to the school to protest against assessment safe in the knowledge that her son would gain proficiency in reading and writing, with or without standardised testing. Matt Damon's life chances – educated parents, affluent community – were such that his default path was one of success. He would have to have swum against the tide to end up long-term unemployed, on the streets or in prison. Yet in many communities the default route for young people is a bleak picture of unemployment and crime. These communities need schools which swim against the tide of underachievement and it's difficult to do that if achievement isn't being monitored.

For these reasons I passionately believe in schools being held to account, not least when I recall the days before league tables when schools rose and fell on the basis of reputation, history and hearsay. The need for accountability is especially pressing for schools in deprived communities where cycles of failure and low expectation can easily become entrenched. In schools populated by more affluent children some of this accountability can be provided by parents. Teachers who fail to set homework, or who fall behind in their marking, will quickly be brought into line by a letter, email or phone call from a concerned parent to the student's tutor or the headteacher's PA. In private schools this accountability is provided by the fact that a perceived drop in standards will affect student admissions, and thus the financial viability of the school. Schools in deprived communities, lacking this financial imperative, and often lacking engaged parents, have been left for too long to wallow in failure. Robust lines of accountability and transparency offer a much-needed remedy to this.

Perhaps at this point I should qualify my comment on the engagement of parents in low-income communities. Wherever I have taught, I have found parents to be ambitious for their offspring and desperate for schools to deliver on the democratic right of a good, accessible school for all. As such, I've found parents to be extremely supportive of my attempts to raise standards and lead highly successful schools. Yet this support tends to be of the passive, arm's-length kind, compared to the proactive support offered by more affluent parents. Here's an example from Burlington Danes. Recently, our PTA recently held a parents' forum, where parents were invited to the school to meet with myself and a panel of key staff. They were free to ask any questions about school policy. Yet, despite weeks of publicity, we only attracted a handful of parents. The following day we held Year 10 parents evening, where, as usual, we reached our target of 90% attendance. This captures the passive support we receive from our parents. They're passionately interested in the progress of their children, hence the 90% turnout at parents' evening, but when it comes to school policy and direction they're happy to trust us to make the right decisions in the best interests of their children. In many ways this is a good thing, but democratic institutions require informed and educated citizens to keep them in check, and this accountability does not always emerge automatically.

In primary schools, parental engagement comes with the territory: parents drop their children off at 8.30am and collect them at 3.30pm. Secondary schools need to replicate this level of parental engagement, for if you lose the support of parents, then you then lose the child. According to maths educator Jo Boaler: 'Researchers [have] found that when mothers told their daughters "I was no good at math in school" their daughter's achievement immediately went down' ('Changing the Conversation about Girls and STEM', The White House, 2014). We can apply this argument to parental influence as a whole: if parents give the impression to their children that they struggled themselves when they were at school, or that school is pointless, then this will quickly have an impact on the child. I saw a clip of the dog trainer Mary Woodhouse recently which illustrates this point. A dog owner had approached Woodhouse because her dog wouldn't travel on trains with her. Woodhouse asked the woman 'are you scared of travelling by train?' The woman replied 'yes', and Woodhouse explained that the woman was transferring her own anxiety of train travel onto her dog. Perhaps schools can do more to ease the anxiety of children by winning the hearts and minds of parents.

Questions that parents should ask – but often don't – at parents evenings

Parents evenings: like every school in the land, we have debated their merit, toyed with different models (academic review days, appointments, parent assemblies) but it always comes down to what the customer wants. Every teacher ought to have a marked set of exercise books in front of them. If you can get every parent in, what should they be asking? Here's what I would suggest:

- What is my child's present rate of attainment? What is their target grade/level? What exactly do they need to do to reach the next level: may I see an example? Can you show me in their current workbook?

- Is my child making progress at the right rate? What are the things my child does well? What do they need more help with? What can I do to help?

- How much homework should my child be doing? How can I help? Are they up to date with homework completion? Could you talk me through the homework set so that I can match them to my child's planner? May I see their marks?

- Does my child have any special aptitudes or abilities? How can I help with that?

- Is my child happy at school? How do you know they are happy? What do they most enjoy doing? Who do they talk to if they are not happy?

- Do they get on well with other children? Do they get on well with adults? What can I do to encourage them to get on with other people? How well are they behaving?

- Is my child up to date with any coursework? What percentage contribution to the overall exam is coursework/controlled assessment? How can I support?

- Is my child well organised: planner, revision, keeping on track *etc.* How can I support?

- Is my child an independent learner? What can I do to progress this further? What independent tasks would support their learning?

- What does my child do if they do not understand a piece of work? Who do they talk to? Is there after-school support?

- How is my child progressing compared to peers in the school and beyond?

Thus, accountability plays a particularly powerful role in schools in challenging areas. These schools have to proactively challenge the expected outcomes for the young people who pass through them, and I believe that a robust system of accountability plays a strong part in this. Like many teachers, my experience of schools that I work in is different to the experience of schools that I've sent my own children to, not because I've sent my children to private school but because I live in a predominantly middle class suburban community, whereas I've chosen to work in a predominantly low-income urban community. This is indicative of the social stratification that blights so many education systems. It's problematic if students from low-income backgrounds are clustered together. This point is powerfully made by academics Butler and Webber in a 2007 study:

Thus children from poor neighbourhoods are often doubly disadvantaged. First, they live in neighbourhoods where it is not expected that they will do well. Then they attend schools where they are surrounded by other pupils with below-average expectations. Likewise, those middle class children who attend predominantly middle class schools enjoy the double benefit of home advantage reinforced by a school peer group with high aspirations' (Butler and Webber, 2007 p. 1243).

Such stratification poses many problems for those concerned about social justice. Perhaps the biggest one is the danger that without middle class stakeholders, schools in low income areas are neglected, as appeared to be the case in the 1980s and 1990s. Since then, high-poverty schools have been the focus of considerable scrutiny. This creates the possibility of another problem though, that of a two-tier education policy with some schools being perceived to serve low income families, and other schools catering for more affluent children. Burlington Danes is surrounded by affluent streets, but few of these parents choose to send their children to us. When I talk to them they question whether their child will be stretched, and whether our aspirations are sufficiently high. Thankfully our results at the top end, the calibre of our teachers and the university destinations of our sixth form students enable me to make a strong case that we can provide challenge at all levels of the ability range. That said, I admit that our rigorous approach – one hour same-day detentions if students are one minute late; lining up in silence in the playground at the start of the day – might deter those who favour a more relaxed and child-centred approach to education. In his 2008 memoirs Tony Blair suggests that traditional public services don't work for a small minority of dysfunctional families who require 'gripping and seizing' by the state, but such an interventionist approach doesn't sit well in liberal middle class circles. This tension is captured in this extract from *The Economist*, in which that newspaper's resident political commentator 'Bagehot' takes a visit to the South London primary school led by Greg Martin, famed for his tough love approach and exceptional results:

I met Mr Martin at a seminar on school discipline and pupil behaviour last month, organised by aides to the education secretary Michael Gove. Something Mr Martin said at that seminar stayed with me. He said that some of his young pupils, who come from some of the poorest households in London, were being raised in such unstructured, chaotic homes that before they could learn any formal skills, they needed to be taught something simpler and yet vital: how to access education. In concrete terms, that means taking his intake of three-year-olds and teaching them how to sit still, how to listen, how to walk calmly, how to eat in a canteen, even to dress themselves. In more philosophical terms, they needed to learn that they were constantly making choices, some of them good and some bad, and that both sorts of choices had consequences. At Durand, lessons all begin the same way, all classrooms follow the same basic design, with a blackboard on which is written the date and the objectives for that lesson. Children wear a uniform, and must wear it correctly. They are taught to walk along school corridors in hushed crocodiles, and to avoid shouting or yelling in the canteen. Voices are never raised, rules are applied consistently and swiftly. The aim is a calm, secure working environment that tells children they have left their home lives and come somewhere different: school, where they come to learn. ('What happens when you set good head teachers free', *The Economist*, 27 October 2011).

So what can be done to avoid a two-tier education system, where (to exaggerate slightly) middle class children learn through play and creativity in loosely structured schools while their lower-income peers are drilled into success in regimented, disciplined environments? A good starting point would be to have socially diverse neighbourhoods, something that local authorities have recently pursued by insisting that new housing developments contain a prescribed proportion of 'affordable housing'. That said, it's already been noted that the community around Burlington Danes is in fact quite diverse, yet over the years the school lost the support of its well-heeled constituents, and we're still working hard to win this back. Admissions codes clearly have a role to play here, and I think there should be more scrutiny and transparency when it comes to the social composition of schools. This would encourage schools to ensure that their own social composition reflects that of the neighbourhood in which they are based. Ofsted, for example, might deny the 'outstanding' tag to schools with a large discrepancy between their own deprivation indicators and the indicators of their neighbourhood. Fair banding, where schools take an equal number of students from different ability ranges, is fine in principle but it should be administered outside the schools in order to remove the temptation for schools to covertly select particular students.

I mentioned earlier that we've worked hard to win the support of our middle class neighbours, but crucially we haven't tweaked our admissions code to make it any easier for middle class students to gain a place with us. As a Church of England School we could easily have exercised our right to select some of our pupils on the basis of religious faith – a loophole that hundreds of schools use to handpick affluent students. Yet we continue to forfeit this right, admitting students instead on the basis of siblings already enrolled with us and the distance, as the crow flies, from their front door to our school gates. We're proud that this makes us a truly local community school. It's frustrating to see other schools manipulate their intake, but my social conscience – and that of my governors and of Ark – remains steadfast.

When it comes to admissions, too many schools play lip service to their fair admissions policy while employing underhand tactics to ensure that they recruit brighter applicants. Proving allegiance to a religious faith serves as a handy social filter, as does reserving a certain number of places for students with a particular aptitude for the school's 'specialist subject'. This becomes rather absurd when schools have a specialism for business or enterprise, as if budding entrepreneurs can be identified at the age of ten. A more covert way of doctoring the admissions policy in favour of the more able is through admissions exams and fair banding. This is when all applicants sit an exam and the school then randomly selects students from each quintile of ability as measured by the exam. In theory, this ensures that the school has a balanced cohort of students from across the ability range. In reality, some schools set extremely challenging tests which over-fill the lower end, so 60% of applicants might find themselves in the bottom quintile. In doing so, the school has made it much more difficult for students of low and average ability to gain a place. It's no surprise that where schools operate such measures there is no redress for parents: they can't ask to see the exam paper once it's been marked. If schools want to carry out 'fair banding' this should be nationally administered and tests should be centrally marked. If schools want to cherry pick students it should only be students from deprived backgrounds. We talk about parental choice and market forces in education but in reality this choice only works when schools have spare capacity. Yet good schools are invariably oversubscribed, leaving hopeful parents in the hands of the gods, or subject to the covert admissions tricks mentioned here.

Beyond the admissions code, funding arrangements can serve as a powerful tool in correcting the disadvantages faced by children from low income backgrounds. The situation in America, where school funding is derived from property taxes, meaning that schools in rich areas have more money than those in poor areas, is clearly an affront to anyone with an interest in social justice. The pupil premium, introduced in England in 2011, is a huge step in the right direction. It provides schools with an extra £900 per year for every student in receipt of free school meals (or who has been in receipt of them at any point in the last six years). At Burlington Danes this equates to nearly 70% of our students, so it provides us with a significant fund to invest in raising the achievement of low income students, which we do through subsidised trips, extra classes, small-group tuition and subsidised resources for students on free school meals. This extra payment (an additional 15% of the funding that schools receive per student) also provides an incentive for schools to attract students from poorer backgrounds, or at least helps to remove the disincentive to do so. A key theme of this book is that schools in low income communities have to proactively challenge, correct and improve the expectations and outcomes of our students, so it makes sense that we should be provided with funding for the proactive intervention required.

While I'm in favour of the scrutiny and accountability generated by school league tables, it must be recognised that narrow and arbitrary government benchmarks have, at times, encouraged schools to focus on 'borderline' students at the expense of those on the periphery. For example, in England the key measure on which schools are judged is the number of students gaining at least five A*-C grades including English and maths. This has led to schools investing disproportionate amounts of time, energy and money at the C/D borderline, ignoring students at the top and bottom end. I know of a London school where all students take their maths and English GCSEs one year early to give them as many opportunities as possible to retake before they reach the end of Year 11. The problem is that a student who gains C grades in Year 10 has that grade 'banked' by the school, because there's no particular incentive for the school to turn that C grade into a B or an A, quite manageable with an extra year of tuition. This particular school has, on paper, transformed its results in recent years, mainly by squeezing C grades out of students who were previously gaining E and D grades. The problem is that the number of A*, A and B grades remained static. Without these higher grades it's very difficult to study A levels, and impossible to gain a place at a good university. So this particular school, despite apparently rapid progress, isn't actually equipping any more students to truly thrive in their future studies than before. It's tragic when incentives for schools are misaligned with the needs of students, but that's exactly what's happened here, and it's a story that's all too common. I would be lying if I claimed to ignore these headline figures, but we've worked hard to ensure that the needs of all of our students are being met, not just those who happen to find themselves working at the borderline.

Fortunately, since I started writing this book the government has announced a new framework of measures on which schools will be judged. These new measures will provide a more holistic indication of the success of schools, taking into account the progress that students have made between their arrival and their departure, as well as revealing their overall attainment. This means that schools will have an incentive to secure the very best grades for high-ability students, safe in the knowledge that an A* grade will gain more credit for the school than a C grade, whereas previously these two grades were both seen as 'high grade passes' and were therefore of equal value to the school as far as league tables were concerned. Similarly, schools will no longer write off students seen as incapable of gaining C grades, since all levels of achievement will now be recognised. So a student who is expected to gain E grades but gains D grades will gain credit for the school, encouraging schools to focus on the full ability range. It's right that the government strikes a balance between having high expectations of all students by judging all schools by the same standards, and recognising that some schools are starting from a much more difficult position.

This chapter has tried to suggest the optimal role for governments to play in a modern education system, based on the twin engines of autonomy and accountability. Above all, it's the job of the government to align the interests of schools, teachers, parents and students. The misleading claim on the website of the South London school provides a clear example of the need for transparency so that schools can no longer fool their own communities. A dashboard on the homepage of all school websites indicating the success of the school against a short list of measures (*eg* student attendance, % of students gaining five good GCSEs, % of students gaining five or more A-A* grades; most recent Ofsted rating) would be a welcome addition to the range of tools used to hold schools to account. When I first started teaching in Peckham, classroom teachers did not even know the school's exam results – a situation which seems incredible now. Clearly there is more to education than exam results, but in my view there's no better way of ensuring that schools are meeting the needs of its pupils than by revealing the performance of students and schools in well-designed and accurately marked tests.

One of the key points of contact between government and schools concerns the curriculum that schools deliver. Since 1988 England has followed a National Curriculum stipulating which subjects schools should provide and which broad topics should be covered (I say 'broad' because in truth the National Curriculum has always offered more flexibility than many educators acknowledge). Public debate about the composition of the school curriculum is a welcome reminder of the importance placed by society on the issue of what young citizens study at school. In the last year I've seen headlines arguing for a whole range of subjects and topics to be added to the school curriculum: financial literacy, citizenship, healthy eating, sexual health, social skills, the memory of 9/11, 'stillness', climate change, internet safety and British values. Such demands say more about the social concerns of the day than the inadequacy of the current school curriculum. In truth, we would all hope that a healthy awareness of finance, citizenship, democracy, nutrition, sex and social skills would emerge not from school, but from the home. That said, we live in an increasingly diverse nation, with London being one of a growing number of truly global cities, and we can no longer assume that young people are receiving sound advice from home about how to navigate some of the complexities of modern life. Although our primary focus will always be academic scholarship, I'm keen to provide students with a secure grounding in basic issues which will have a huge bearing on their life such as relationships and money. Young people often receive a particular perspective on such matters from their family, so it falls on schools to broaden the viewpoints of the students. The difficulty is finding time in the day for such provision. We must be wary of shoe-horning additional subjects into the school curriculum – no-one seems to suggest which subjects should make way for these new disciplines. We should also consider that without dedicated teachers and rigorous assessment materials these supplementary subjects risk being neglected by schools and teachers. At Burlington Danes we seek to develop all of the areas mentioned above, mainly in our personal, social, health, and citizenship education sessions led by tutors, but it remains a challenge to afford equal status to these pursuits as we give to our traditional curriculum.

As I touched upon earlier, the traditional curriculum has been bolstered in England recently by the introduction of the English Baccalaureate – a bundle of five GCSEs in traditional subjects: English, maths, science, a language and geography or history. Official league tables already reveal how many students at each school gain passes in these subjects, placing pressure on schools to deliver a traditional curriculum. It is hoped that this will prevent schools from padding out their headline figures by guiding students towards easier (often vocational) subjects. I fully support the introduction of the EBacc. Lots of headteachers have complained about it on the grounds that it penalises schools with large numbers of low income students. The problem with this argument is that it goes back to the old view that students from poorer backgrounds can't compete on equal terms in the traditional subjects against their counterparts from more affluent areas. The same headteachers who complain about the pressure this places on high-poverty schools would want their own children to leave school with decent grades in the traditional academic subjects, so why not for the students at their schools? I'm proud that Burlington Danes' EBacc figure compares very favourably with the national figure, as this shows that our success isn't based on a narrow focus on English and maths, supplemented by a clutch of low-status qualifications. There will always be a minority of students, perhaps 10–20%, for whom a traditional academic curriculum is unsuitable, but given recent economic trends, with rich nations such as the UK and US losing unskilled work to developing countries, it's difficult to defend a system where large numbers of students leave 11 years of full-time education without attaining decent grades in five academic subjects.

If my comments above seems disparaging towards less academic subjects then that's a reflection of the recent demise of vocational education in this country. Professor Wolf's 2011 report into vocational education in England was right to highlight the inadequacy of current vocational provision: 'The staple offer for between a quarter and a third of the post-16 cohort is a diet of low-level vocational qualifications, most of which have little to no labour market value' (The Wolf Report, Department for Education, 2011). Of course it shouldn't be like this. Germany is often cited as an example of a country where a vocational pathway needn't condemn a student to inferior career opportunities. The success of Germany's manufacturing sector would suggest that there is a place in the modern Western economy for high-end vocational training, and the government is right to adopt many of the reforms suggested by Professor Wolf. Thousands of students have been duped into following inferior vocational courses under the illusion that these courses are the equivalent of traditional GCSEs. For schools, these qualifications have been of equal value: they've gained the same points for the school in the national league table as academic qualifications. Yet for students, vocational courses haven't developed key skills or given them a qualification valued by employers and universities.

The almost farcical notion that most pupils should go on to university, popular under New Labour, was perhaps more damaging than it first appeared. Exams were watered down to allow access to university and students were told that BTEC courses in subjects like IT, health and social care and business studies were equivalent to GCSEs and A levels. A whole generation of children were led to believe that there was no value in traditional trades such as construction, plumbing, carpentry and welding. Why would a possible employer choose to undertake the challenge of training and developing the craftsmen and women of the future when a fully qualified, motivated workforce was available from overseas? It's no surprise that some sections of British society feel threatened by immigration.

That said, I get frustrated by those who criticise the school curriculum for being arbitrary and outdated. Howard Gardner, the American psychologist behind the theory of multiple intelligences, makes the following point:

> The time has come to broaden our notion of the spectrum of talents. The single most important contribution education can make to a child's development is to help him toward a field where his talents best suit him, where he will be satisfied and competent. We've completely lost sight of that. Instead we subject everyone to an education where, if you succeed, you will be best suited to be a college professor. And we

evaluate everyone along the way according to whether they meet that narrow standard of success. We should spend less time ranking children and more time helping them to identify their natural competencies and gifts, and cultivate those. There are hundreds and hundreds of ways to succeed, and many, many different abilities that will help you get there. (from interview quoted in Goleman 1995, p.37).

This chimes with some of the views of Sir Ken Robinson, whose YouTube video arguing that schools kill creativity has received more than seven million hits at time of writing:

If you looked at education as an alien, and simply looked at what the output was, who gets all the brownie points, you'd have to conclude that the whole purpose is to produce university professors (I used to be one). There's something curious about professors, they live in their heads, they live up there, and slightly to one side. They're disembodied. They look at their bodies as a form of transport for their heads. It's the way they get their heads to meetings.

Our education system is predicated on the idea of academic ability. The whole system was invented after the 19th century. The whole thing came into being to accommodate the needs of industrialism. The whole thing is built upon two ideas.

1. The most useful subjects for work are at the top. So you were probably steered away from things, as a kid, from things you liked, on the grounds that you would never get a job, doing that.

Don't do music, you're not going to be a musician, don't do art, you're not going to be an artist. Benign advice. Now, profoundly mistaken.

2. Academic Ability. which has really come to dominate our view of intelligence. Because the universities designed the system in their image.

If you think of it the whole system around the world is a protracted process of university entrance. And the consequence is that many highly talented, brilliant, creative people, think they're not. Because the thing they were good at at school wasn't valued, or was actually stigmatized. I think we can't afford to go on that way.

('Do Schools Kill Creativity?', Youtube, 6 January 2007).

Gardner and Robinson make some cogent points, and I agree whole-heartedly that schools should provide opportunity, encouragement and support for a wide range of interests and talent. This is especially important when students might not be exposed to art, music, drama, dance, sport or design at home. I take issue on two counts though. Firstly, I maintain that the most important task for a school system is to enable young people to master the basics of reading, writing, arithmetic, language, logic, and the empirical methodology of the sciences. These subjects are not arbitrary. The very fact that they are universal, and that schools in Singapore, Stockholm and San Francisco follow a similar curriculum, suggests that we've identified the subjects that matter; that prepare young people to think for themselves, to understand the world around them and to apply their skills to the field of their choosing. I enjoy meeting successful people in all walks of life, and when I talk to leading business people, such as the Google executive I met last week, I don't find them complaining about the lack of creativity of British schoolchildren, but I do hear concerns about mathematical knowledge, the ability to think logically and communicate coherently. Developing such skills need not dampen creativity. My second concern is that middle class preferences for creative pursuits take for granted the notion that young people will master the more traditional basics. This may be true in some middle class households but for the students I teach, I can't presume that they will become adept at the three Rs unless we rigorously develop these skills. So personally I think that the aliens of Ken Robinson's talk would be rather impressed by the subjects we teach in English schools, and I'm proud to offer a traditional curriculum at Burlington Danes.

There is another way in which central government can help to align the interests of different stakeholders in education, and that's by breaking down the arbitrary barrier between primary education and secondary education. In most parts of the country young people go to a primary school from the age of 4-11, before transferring to a secondary school for their 11-16 provision, then either staying on if the school has a sixth form or progressing to a specialist sixth form college for the two years preceding university. Introducing a sixth form to Burlington Danes has had a huge impact on the institution. The crucial point here is that creating a sixth form ensures an alignment of interests between our secondary provision and our sixth form provision, so that the skills required to take history at

A level, for example, are introduced and nurtured in our Year 7 history lessons. When students left us at 16 to pursue A levels elsewhere, there wasn't a huge incentive for the school to foster deep understanding and a passion for learning. Yet these two points – deep understanding and a passion for learning – are crucial for success at A level. In the first year of our sixth form we noticed that some students lacked these two requirements, and since then we've spent time and energy revitalising our Key Stages 3 and 4 provision, intellectualising lessons from Year 7 upwards. Consider this Year 7 English curriculum:

- *Oliver Twist* (original text)
- *Twelfth Night* (original text)
- *Frankenstein* (original text)
- Romantic poetry (Wordsworth, Coleridge, Blake, Keats, Byron, Shelly)
- Philosophy texts

A few years ago such a curriculum might have been reserved for older year groups, but we're seeking to stretch our students from day one and cultivate a love of literature and the confidence to engage with unfamiliar language. This has been triggered by the realisation of the requirements for success at A level. The process of taking students right through to university raises the intellectual ceiling of the school which, in turn, has a trickle-down effect on the whole curriculum. The curriculum must develop scholarship throughout the school rather than pursue short-term gains with key year groups. Thus we've invested a lot of time this year trying to intellectualise our Key Stage 3 curriculum. We've provided time and resources for heads of department to increase the challenge of their schemes of work so that teachers provide a rich, stimulating curriculum at all levels of the school. Teachers have been encouraged to create more opportunities for original thinking, and exams have been tweaked to stretch students. Through embedding these reforms in the lower rungs of the school we're seeking to minimise the need for intense intervention at the top end.

My drive to intellectualise the curriculum was sparked by a visit to local independent school Latymer Upper a few years ago. If you walk along Wood Lane you could be forgiven for thinking that the lush playing fields next to our site belong to Burlington Danes, but actually they were sold off many years ago to Latymer Upper – an impressive independent school based in Hammersmith. On the morning of this particular visit to Latymer I had observed a top set Year 7 English class at Burlington Danes. It was a strong lesson, but they were studying a teenage novel. At Latymer I saw students of the same age in an English class studying *Julius Caesar*. This changed everything. Our English curriculum was ripped up on my return to BDA as I asked the head of English to start from first principles and design a rigorous, challenging, intellectual curriculum from day one. My rationale for this is that students don't need our help to read a teenage novel. Thus began our drive to intellectualise our Key Stage 3 curriculum. All heads of department were given time to devise a new curriculum which would serve as a proper grounding for pursuing that subject throughout the key stages. I've heard people describe this as teaching the curriculum in an 'intellectually honest' manner, so that the Key Stage 3 programme of study is a true foundation for Key Stages 4, 5 and even degree-level study in that subject. As always, it doesn't take long for students to respond to these heightened expectations, and it's a reminder that it's the duty of all teachers and school leaders to 'pitch high and support below', rather than impose glass ceilings on the attainment of our students.

The extension of secondary schooling from 11-16 to 11-18 is a welcome recent trend and we must now turn our attention to another great divide: the chasm between primary and secondary. Primary and secondary schools remain very different animals in England. The average size of a primary school is 224, compared to an average secondary school size of 940. At primary school, students tend to stay in the same room, with the same teacher, for the majority of their lessons. This means an 11-year-old will spend July in a classroom with the same teacher and the same classmates for most of the week, then in September she will be at a secondary school, with more than 10 different teachers, and she will have to move classrooms throughout the day to find them. It is a seismic shift, but no more alarming to me than these practical differences is the fact that primary school teachers have no compelling reason to prepare their charges to thrive at secondary school. Once the students have left the primary school, they are simply not their problem. Just like when we were sending students off to sixth form without a clear awareness of the challenges they would face, primary schools are cultivating students ill-equipped to the demands of secondary school. My biggest gripe is standards of literacy. Official government figures in 2008 showed that

20% of 11-year-olds were leaving primary school 'functionally illiterate' (*The Guardian*, 20 May 2008). If we asked members of the public for their view on the biggest priority for primary education they would no doubt place literacy at the top of the list, so it's mind-blowing that so many students are failing to meet this most basic expectation after seven years of full-time education.

What does it mean to be ready for secondary school?

There's been plenty of talk recently about children being 'secondary ready' by the time they leave primary school. Here's what I would expect students to have grasped before their first day at secondary school:

- reading at their expected 'reading age'
- a structured piece of writing with sentences and paragraphs
- times tables up to 12
- correctly spell the 100 most commonly misspelt words
- discuss an author they've read several books of
- confident interactions with their peers
- express themselves in front of an audience
- competent with knives and forks
- be able to swim 25 metres
- able to look people in the eye and hold a conversation
- experience of some kind of responsibility *eg* register monitor

In the inner city the statistics can be much worse. I recall a Year 7 cohort joining us three years ago in which 85% of students scored below their expected chronological reading age in a baseline test at the start of the year. I'm sure that primary heads and teachers have their own views on these problems, but the boycott of national tests of 11-year-olds in recent years hasn't helped. Secondary schools have accepted that transparency is required in order to ensure accountability, and we've benefited from the rigour of standardised testing and league tables. Such measures must be rolled down to primary level, and the government should continue to encourage the development of all-through schools, serving students from 4-18, alongside the adoption of failing primary schools by strong secondary schools. Absorbing primary schools into bigger institutions would create opportunities for ambitious primary school teachers and leaders, who at the moment might feel that they have to work in secondary education if they want to accelerate in their career and earn a good salary. Integrating primary schools with secondaries would also make it easier for specialist subject teachers to work at a primary level, replacing the unacceptable *status quo* where the same teacher is expected to be able to stretch a 10-year-old in fields as diverse as science, history, languages, maths and English. I'm pleased to see that Teach First have now expanded into primary schools and I would welcome the spread of other initiatives that have enjoyed proven success at secondary level.

It's time for a root and branch review of how we select and train primary teachers. In the latter years of primary school it's imperative that young people have specialist teachers, rather than jacks of all trades. In fee-paying prep schools children benefit from a varied timetable with discrete subjects and specialist teachers. This specialism gives teachers confidence and enthusiasm. The appalling state of languages and PE teaching in particular is testament to the extent of the problem, and in my experience the same is true of science teaching, where the lack of lab access compounds the problem. A further problem with having one teacher for all subjects at primary is that if you get a mediocre teacher then you are stuck with that teacher every day, in every subject.

Perhaps the most alarming thing about the achievement gap between rich and poor students is that it's already evident at the age of five. A 2010 report by the Joseph Rowntree Foundation ('Poorer children's educational attainment: how important are attitudes and behaviour?') claims that, 'There are big differences in cognitive development between children from rich and poor backgrounds at the age of three, and this gap widens by the age of five'. A recent study found that: 'Gaps in cognitive development between better-off and disadvantaged children open up early on, with those from the poorest fifth of families on average more than eleven months behind children from middle income families in vocabulary tests when they start school' ('Cracking the Code, how schools can improve social mobility', the Social Mobility and Child Poverty Commission, October 2014). Much has been written about early years provision but on the basis of this evidence it would seem that we can't wait until primary school to intervene and we should redouble our efforts to reach out to poor families with high quality early years support.

All-through schools

Record numbers of all-through schools are set to open in the next few years. Many are start-ups; some, like BDA, are expanding existing provision to embrace ages 4-18 on the same site.

For these to work it is essential that the primary has its own identity as primary is very different to secondary.

The most exciting benefit of all-through schools is that specialist teachers and resources in modern languages, music (including instrumental tuition), art, and science can be stretched down to primary. How often is a pupil's education blighted not by incompetence but by the mediocre teacher who is so difficult to move on? All-through schools – thanks in part to economies of scale – have the chance to ameliorate this, increasing the sphere of influence and impact of your very best staff. An all-through school can share departments, such as SEN/EAL, the site team, finance office, gifted and talented provision, and thus offer to younger children opportunities that a primary school cannot usually afford.

I am also excited by the opportunity to track progress and map the curriculum from age four, the notion of education as a journey, with seamless transitions and no 'dips', that the school can shape and direct with a consistency of expectations, ethos and philosophy. This can only be dreamt of when some secondary schools have dozens of feeder primary schools. Opportunities for staff training and development are stronger too, plus the possibility of closer partnerships between the school and parents and the community.

Year 7 – the first year of secondary education – is a crucial year in education as students make that transition from primary to secondary. For the time being we have to accept that some students might start Year 7 lacking sufficient command of the basics in literacy and numeracy. But why should we let students progress to Year 8 without these deficiencies being rectified? I would propose that after one term in Year 7 schools should suspend the curriculum for those students who have not reached adequate levels of literacy and numeracy and that these students receive intensive tuition in these areas to enable them to progress to Year 8. If they fail to make rapid progress in these basic skills then they should repeat Year 7. Yes, these students would miss out on subjects like drama, art, humanities and languages for two terms in Year 7, but their whole secondary school experience will be hampered unless they get their English and maths up to scratch.

A chapter on the political framework surrounding schools would be incomplete without a discussion of the role of Ofsted, the government inspectorate. Let's start by recognising that schools and inspections aren't natural bedfellows. Like all communities, schools possess a distinct character, an amalgamation of the values and demography of the locality in which they're based, the history of the school and the character of the headteacher and the teachers. Furthermore, schools operate on an annual cycle, with a natural ebb and flow of activity and urgency throughout the year. The same school might glow in warm September sunshine and appear to be full of hope and promise, yet come back on a grey Tuesday in February and you'd gain quite a different impression. These seasonal variations are even more prevalent in the classroom, where assessment timetables will dictate the pace and purpose of learning at different points in the school year. As I've previously noted, a teacher forms a relationship with every class under his watch, and it's difficult to judge the success of this relationship in a 25 minute drop-in. There's an inherent tension between the rich tapestry of school life and a robust framework of inspection, because inspections must be based on consistent standards and empirical verification during the short period of time in which schools are observed. I'm not arguing for a second that schools should be left to their own devices. Teachers who don't mark books can't complain about students failing to take care over their work, and I've no doubt that standards would slip if schools were allowed to simply get on with things. People want praise, they want external validation for the efforts they've made, and this goes for schools and headteachers as well as students.

Ofsted materials from department leaders

As a school we have set up an Ofsted 'bunker': a room wherein all of our evidence and evaluation is stored and continually updated. Department leaders provide a department handbook which follows a consistent structure, as detailed below:

Introduction: Why study this subject? What is its intrinsic value? How does this department contribute, for example, to the academy's aim to equip all our students for adult life?

Section 1: Procedures

- staff list with qualifications
- timetable with setting arrangements with a chart (or list) showing how groups are arranged, who teaches which, whether any are parallel *etc*
- set (or teaching group) lists showing numbers and gender split, current performance data, SEN and EAL

- accommodation and general resources including administration, ordering equipment procedures; charging policy in department for lost books; use of the photocopier
- examination board(s) and paper reference numbers
- key departmental dates
- health and safety
- literacy strategy
- exemplary work and displays with photos
- education visits with exemplary letters, risk assessment *etc*
- professional development
- parental contact
- cross-curricular issues: ICT within the subject, contribution to students' spiritual, moral, social and cultural development

Section 2: Monitoring the work of the department

- homework and homework monitoring
- lesson planning: expected practice
- lesson observation and schedule
- peer monitoring and schedule
- marking and workbook reviews, exemplary marking and work at various levels
- raising achievement strategies/Intervention strategies
- using student data
- performance management
- behaviour support, strategies and rewards
- classroom support and EAL timetables and practice
- coursework deadlines
- previous Ofsted/HMI/Consultant's report on the department and the action taken as a result

Section 3: Policies and documents

- equal opportunities, for example, how does the department celebrate cultural diversity? Ensure that its materials promote equal opportunities?
- how does this department promote Every Child Matters?
- curriculum offer

- assessment policy and all assessment questions
- progress: current Year 9 and 11 achievement against predicted outcomes
- grade descriptors for students and parents
- department meetings proforma and minutes of meetings held this year
- staff absence: department policy and exemplary cover sheet

Section 4: Strategic planning

- Staff action plans
- Examination review
- Department SEF
- Department subject improvement plan and reviews of previous plans

Section 5: Schemes of work

- Examples of schemes of work from all Key Stages (these to be held separately)

Ofsted: Key questions for students

1. What level/grade are you working at now?
2. What is your target level/grade?
3. What have you got to learn in this subject to improve?
4. What do you find most difficult in this subject?
5. Are these lessons usually like this?

Like the National Curriculum, Ofsted was a product of the 1988 Education Reform Act, and I'm pleased to say that since its inception changes have been made to reconcile some of the tensions outlined above. It used to be the case that schools would receive several months' notice of an impending inspection, enabling them to adopt a range of strategies which sat on a sliding scale of moral and professional integrity, from giving the walls a fresh lick of paint to adorning the corridors with plants and flowers to granting leave to troublesome students for the period of the inspection. I even heard of one head granting leave to a couple of troublesome teachers. Such game playing is no longer possible as we now only receive 24 hours' notice ahead of a two-day inspection. I'm also pleased to see that Ofsted place greater emphasis on publicly held data and on the school's self-evaluation documentation, taking some of the pressure off the actual visit. This means that before the inspectors arrive at the school they already have a good idea of the performance of the school in relation to local and national norms, and the inspection itself is focused on validating the claims of the school. Some elements of game-playing remain though. For a school to gain the top judgement – 'outstanding' – a significant proportion of lessons observed during the two day inspection must be judged to be outstanding. Yet the classroom visits often consist of 25-minute drop-ins, and it's not always easy to judge the quality of progress being made by a class during such a short time window. For a maths or English teacher, for example, this 25-minute period equates to 0.25% of the time that the teacher will spend with the students in the course of the year. Furthermore, it could be that during the 25-minute observation the students would normally be engaged in focused, extended study, but such activity is unlikely to yield the evidence of progress that the inspector needs to see to judge the lesson 'outstanding'. So the canny teacher might interrupt the activity and lead a short dialogue with the class so that their progress can be evidenced. It's unfortunate when the task of passing an Ofsted inspection is different to the task of teaching a great lesson, or running a great school, however slight this difference is.

I'm glad that since I started writing this book Ofsted have loosened their obsession with judging individual lessons, and now go into classrooms to seek evidence which is later aggregated to inform a holistic 'teaching and learning' grade. Such is the depth of data held on schools these days that I would encourage Ofsted to focus on unpicking the stuff that exam results don't show. Do schools nurture the whole child? Do they develop leadership, citizenship and cultural participation? Is every student known and supported by at least one adult, do the students treat each other and their teachers with respect? On the whole I welcome the scrutiny of Ofsted and the judgements that it has cast on my schools over the years have become a source of great pride. Schools can be tempted to hide behind excuses and justifications for failure, for example by citing the background of the students they teach, and to play certain games to appear successful, such as entering student for a plethora of inferior qualifications which still carry currency in the league tables. That's why we need an inspectorate to shine a light on the true workings of our school. Once again, sunlight is the best disinfectant.

Ofsted and middle leadership: key questions to ask heads of department

Regardless of how good results are, there is a strong Ofsted focus on in-school variation. What evidence and intervention should you have?

- Literacy is a key feature of inspection. How can you demonstrate what your department is doing and that it is having an impact?

- SMSC (Social Moral Spiritual and Cultural) education is a strong Ofsted focus. How can you demonstrate what your department is doing and its impact?

- You need to be on top of sub-groups of students (based on gender, ethnicity, ability on entry, deprivation *etc*) identifying any under-achieving groups and intervening swiftly to support them. Be able to talk about individual stories.

- Ofsted say that the story is in the books. Conduct a trawl of student workbooks in your department: is marking fair and consistent? Does it support progress? Is there evidence of self and peer marking? What evidence and intervention should you have?

- Teaching and learning is the major focus. Monitoring, tracking and support. Is your key evidence accessible and clear?

- Ofsted seek out middle leaders who share vision and team work. What evidence do you have of your own impact?

- Ofsted will require outstanding schools to have outstanding teaching. What range of evidence do you have to support this?

This chapter has attempted to address relations between schools and government, and I've suggested how this relationship can by optimised to benefit our young people. One of the quirks of democracy is that education policy can change with the fortunes of the parties, and this sense of flux is exacerbated in England by the ministerial merry-go-round that we've seen in recent decades. It's the Prime Minister's prerogative to use cabinet re-shuffles to re-energise the government, or to shore up his own position, but the effect on schools can be quite unsettling, as this list of recent education ministers in Britain would indicate:

Kenneth Baker (Conservative): 21 May 1986 – 24 July 1989

John MacGregor (Conservative): 24 July 1989 – 2 November 1990

Kenneth Clarke (Conservative): 2 November 1990 – 10 April 1992

John Patten (Conservative): 10 April 1992 – 20 July 1994

Gillian Shephard (Conservative): 20 July 1994 – 2 May 1997

David Blunkett (Labour): 2 May 1997 – 8 June 2001

Estelle Morris (Labour): 8 June 2001 – 24 October 2002

Charles Clarke (Labour): 24 October 2002 – 15 December 2004

Ruth Kelly (Labour): 15 December 2004 – 5 May 2006

Alan Johnson (Labour): 5 May 2006 – 27 June 2007

Ed Balls (Labour): 28 June 2007 – 11 May 2010

Michael Gove (Conservative): 11 May 2010 – 15 July 2014

Nicky Morgan (Conservative): 15 July 2014 – present

With an average tenure of little over two years it's no surprise that while in office education ministers have tended to implement reforms with great urgency, and it's no surprise that school leaders have at times felt overwhelmed by the proliferation of policies and promulgations stemming from Whitehall. It is an obvious point to make, but if a school had experienced 12 leaders in two-and-a-half decades we wouldn't expect it to be in a great state. At worst, the speed and scale of reform leads to distrust about whether proposals will ever be fully implemented. Those involved in English schools in recent years will recall the fanfare following the 2005 reform of the 14-19 curriculum, with proposals promising pathways and diplomas for all students in the country. The reforms were due to begin in 2013, but they fell by the wayside with the change of government in 2010. Like a teacher promising an end-of-year trip to students but failing to deliver on the promise, such u-turns and broken promises quickly breed cynicism and contempt.

Schools are ill-suited to short-term tinkering: if the government changes the way that students are being assessed at 16 then we need to start preparing for this many years beforehand, and it's simply not acceptable for subjects to fall in and out of favour, as we've seen with ICT in recent years. I fully support David Laws, the schools minister, who recently pledged to protect schools from the 'whims of here-today, gone-tomorrow politicians'. There has been a dizzying amount of change in recent years, and although I support the spirit of Gove's reforms I fear that many school leaders feel lost in the new landscape. One student at Burlington Danes last year gained five GCSEs including English and maths but one of these was in business studies. This particular course did count in the headline measure in 2013 and will count again 2015, yet in 2014 it didn't count. Schools can't be expected to cope with this level of uncertainty.

The fickle nature of recent education policy has served as a reminder to headteachers to focus on meeting the needs of their students, rather than move with the shifting sands of central policy. But when schools are being scrutinised so thoroughly against these national expectations it's difficult for headteachers to take such a stance. My frustration with the fickle nature of recent education policy is exacerbated by the fact that I fully endorse most of the recent reforms. I don't want headteachers to boycott national tests, and I fully support the publication of school league tables as a means of ensuring transparency and accountability. Yet the nature of party politics and the short tenure of Ministers of Education offer ammunition to those within education who want the government to stay out of the way.

Currently in England we have a strange situation where the government has abolished National Curriculum Levels for Key Stage 3 and has explicitly encouraged schools to develop their own assessment frameworks to replace them. There are many areas in which I welcome autonomy for schools, for example when creating our home-school agreements and behavioural expectations. But when it comes to the macro issues – the big decisions like curriculum and assessment – we need direction from government. Teachers and school leaders in thousands of schools up and down the country are currently spending hours dreaming up new assessment systems, distracting them from their core purpose of improving outcomes for young people. Experts, not classroom teachers and school leaders, should be thrashing out these issues and creating a coherent assessment framework for students, teachers and parents to work under. To leave such fundamental issues to schools is a dereliction of duty.

Michael Gove was a man on a mission. I admire his zeal and his high expectations of students from all walks of life. Perhaps due to his own background, Gove had the courage to insist that children from the toughest of neighbourhoods can compete on the same terms as their more affluent counterparts. For too long, policy makers and educational leaders have created 'alternative pathways' for deprived students which in reality have meant soft and easy courses which they wouldn't accept for their own children. Michael Gove was pilloried by the profession but he has transformed the educational landscape, and mostly for the better. Siphoning 'weaker' students into pointless courses which gained credit for the school but not for the child exacerbated the chronic gap between rich and poor students. More students than ever before are now following an academic knowledge-based curriculum and Michael Gove deserves great credit for this.

In recent months there has been growing support for the idea of a Royal College of Teaching: an independent body, free from government influence, which could set the standards for the profession. Other commentators have called for the whole of education policy to be freed from government control. It reminds me of Gordon Brown's decision in 1997, just days after becoming Chancellor, to make the Bank of England independent, free from political control. This gave the Bank of England power to set interest rates and determine monetary policy free from political interference. Before this, governments could reduce interest rates before elections to win votes, potentially damaging the long-term stability of the economy for short-term political gain. Well, I wonder if it is time for the same thing to happen in education. This would mean that an independent education board would be responsible for educational policy, preventing the short-termism that we've seen in recent years. Education is too important to be left in the hands of fickle party-politics and career-minded politicians. Obviously there would still be a role for government, just like the government today sets our overarching economic objectives, but leaves the actual tinkering to the Bank of England.

I fully support the proactive engagement of government in our education system, but I would prefer a greater degree of continuity and consistency, with schools consulted and reforms planned out methodically. In short, government must cajole, nurture and energise the school system with the same care, and the same regard for long-term improvement, as a good headteacher applies to her school.

This chapter in a tweet: School leaders must accept and embrace the shifting sands of educational policy, whilst ensuring that they act in the interests of their students.

Lesson 11:
The pebble and
the mountain

'It isn't the mountains ahead to climb
that wear you out; it's the pebble
in your shoe' – Muhammad Ali

The quotation above captures the twin challenge that school leaders face. It's vital that we set out a clear long-term vision by presenting an engaging picture of the summit ahead. Yet at the same time we have to clear the current path of obstacles, and we need to be sufficiently in touch with the minutiae of school life that we notice when there's a pebble in the shoe.

When I arrived at Burlington Danes I was absolutely clear that the summit to which we would march was the creation of an outstanding school where the vast majority of students gained five or more good GCSEs. I made this vision crystal clear to everyone connected to the organisation and I repeated it on a daily basis. Furthermore, I offered reassurance that I knew what an outstanding school looked like, and I knew how to create one in this patch of West London. Throughout my time at Burlington Danes I revisited this vision and constantly judged our progress towards it. This involved disengaging myself from day-to-day challenges and catching a glimpse of the bigger picture. This enabled me to recognise, for example, when the time was right to switch from a transformative stage of leadership to a more systematic phase. The transformative stage itself had two stages. The first was what I would call 'intensive care': the patient's condition was critical and urgent action was required before stability was ensured. This involved tackling low expectations and removing a small number of failing teachers and dysfunctional students from the organisation. Some headteachers revel in this high-intensity transformative stage. Some get stuck there, unable to let go of the certainty that comes with the directive, decisive approach of the intensive care phase. But this state should only be temporary. What it possesses in potential for change, it lacks in trust and stability, and for long-term growth the prudent leader will gradually take the organisation into a more secure state – 'critical but stable', to continue the medical analogy. At Burlington Danes the critical state lasted six months, with the second state continuing for a further 12. The second state is still transformative but it's more developmental. After the initial removal of underperforming teachers and students the second phase involves winning the confidence of those who remain, convincing them that they can develop and succeed under the new regime. The fear that accompanied the first phase must be replaced by the trust which allows people to develop. In the first six months we asked for lesson plans to be submitted in advance of all lessons; in the next 12 months we focused on high quality inset to develop the skills of our teachers. In this second phase my own role was high on visibility and energy, as I sought to maintain the intensity we had generated since my arrival.

Our shared vision is of an academy that:

- is truly student-centred and places learning and teaching at its heart
- encourages our students to take responsibility for their own learning, achieve their full potential and enjoy their learning
- has the highest expectations of its students
- celebrates the unique talents of all its students
- listens to and acts upon students' views
- ensures its students are safe and secure and has an atmosphere of mutual support and respect
- helps students to develop the whole person – intellectually, physically, economically, culturally, socially, spiritually, morally and be part of a healthy community within which they feel secure, happy and valued
- encourages our students to understand equality and have a respect for all religions, cultures and ways of life, ensuring that students are sensitive to the feelings of others and are aware how their actions will affect themselves and others;
- allows students to discover that they are capable of more than even they themselves thought possible and success can be for everyone
- looks to the future without forgetting to enjoy the experience of today

After 18 months we entered a phase of development which we could call professionalisation. The focus here was on consistently meeting high standards in our planning, teaching, marking and communication. We shored up our routines and rituals, taking a systematic approach to all areas of school life. We began communicating with parents by text message. Cash transactions in the canteen were replaced by finger-scan recognition, which helped to remove the stigma for our students on free school meals. Leadership became more distributive, with working parties and student councils playing a more active role in shaping school policy. Performance management was overhauled so that all staff in the school, from lunchtime supervisors to heads of year, set meaningful targets at the start of the year and tracked their progress towards them throughout the year. Offering a subsidised Masters to our teachers reinforced the fact that we are a learning community.

The next phase is what we might call 'collaboration'. Having shored up our own systems and procedures we could start looking outwards, sharing good practise with other organisations. We opened our doors to interested parties from Britain and overseas. We expanded to include a sixth form, and began laying plans for a primary school. I became involved in various advisory groups and government committees, forging connections which I would use to enrich the Burlington Danes community. Our success gained the attention of national and international media which served to reinforce the confidence of the organisation.

The one phase missing from this is consolidation. The daily challenge of maintaining a vibrant school in a deprived community is so great that we will never reach a stage where all we need to do is consolidate. I'm also not sure that an announcement by a leader that we are approaching a stage of consolidation would have a very positive impact on the organisation. Students never fully master their scholarship, teachers never fully master their craft, and for schools the challenge of nurturing a diverse mass of energy is never fully met. So instead of consolidation I would call the final phase of growth 'renewal'. The role of the leader in this phase is to guard against complacency, to challenge the organisation to seek constant improvement; to eke out the small gains that could yet make a difference to a child.

Thus we remain in relentless pursuit of any possible advantage to secure the best possible grades for our students. I am fiercely competitive, and I liken our approach to that of of a sports team in a competitive field trying to gain any possible advantage, however miniscule. It's an approach familiar in the context of sport, where the smallest of improvements can make a difference over a long season. The Team Sky cycling team calls this approach 'the aggregation of marginal gains'. Before they reach a hotel on the Tour de France a member of the team will already have changed the riders' bed linen, replacing the hotel's standard sheets for the hypo-allergenic linen that the riders sleep in every night. A team chef will have taken over a corner of the hotel kitchen to ensure that the nutritional needs of the riders are met. Clive Woodward was similarly meticulous as England rugby coach, apparently seeking out 100 ways of improving performance by 1%, for example by replacing heavy cotton rugby shirts with tighter synthetic tops which were tougher for opponents to grip. In *Good to Great*, Jim Collins calls this 'rinsing your cottage cheese', in honour of the triathlon runner who rinsed his daily portion of cottage cheese to make it half a per cent less fatty. This approach works well in schools where we have millions of opportunities to support students over the course of their time with us, and it's particularly suited to exam season where the school's headline figure – such as 79% A-C including English and maths – is comprised of 180 students taking at least ten exams each. We therefore take advantage of every opportunity to improve students' chances, for example by offering free breakfasts during exam season along with bananas and water before exams, texting students to remind them of their exams and providing quiet areas around the school for individual revision.

Minor details can make a big difference in complex organisations and we make an effort to create an environment conducive to learning: flower beds, door stops, table tennis tables. Such attention to detail is examined by Malcolm Gladwell in his book *The Tipping Point*. He describes the man who was brought in to transform the New York subway in the mid-80s starting not with wholesale structural change, but by tackling graffiti (p. 141). This is based on the notion of 'broken windows', a criminological theory first proposed in 1982:

> Consider a building with a few broken windows. If the windows are not repaired, the tendency is for vandals to break a few more windows. Eventually, they may even break into the building, and if it's unoccupied, perhaps become squatters or light fires inside. Or consider a sidewalk.

Some litter accumulates. Soon, more litter accumulates. Eventually, people even start leaving bags of trash from take-out restaurants there or even break into cars. (Wilson and Kelling, 1982).

Gladwell links this theory to his own phrase, 'the power of context': 'Broken windows theory and the power of pontext are one and the same. They are both based on the premise that an epidemic can be reversed, can be tipped, by tinkering with the smallest details of the immediate environment' (p. 146). Such theories resonate with my experience of headship. The 'broken windows' theory strikes a particular chord because I'm told by our site team that before we became an academy we would spend tens of thousands of pounds per year replacing windows vandalised by students. Windows still break sometimes, and we always replace them immediately. We take the same approach to graffiti, which is one of those things you develop a sixth sense for as a headteacher while on walkabout. A piece of graffiti left exposed gives an impression of a lack of ownership and pride in our buildings, and it's an impression that will soon take root amongst the students.

As for the power of context, well for many of our teachers it's a recognition of the powerful influence of social and environmental factors which have inspired their decision to work in challenging schools, and the same is true of educational reformers. Michael Gove recognises the importance of his private education gained through a scholarship to Robert Gordon's College in Aberdeen, while pioneer of academies Andrew Adonis also cites the influence of attending a private school after he was placed in care as a child. The reforms pursued by Adonis and Gove have the feel of men who know how different things could have been, given their early experiences (Gove was adopted as a baby). In *The Tipping Point,* Gladwell provides plenty of examples of people being influenced by apparently insignificant contextual factors, such as the black students who performed worse on tests in which they were asked about their race, presumably as this reminded them of the low expectations associated with their ethnicity. Gladwell concludes that: 'We are powerfully influenced by our surroundings, our immediate context, and the personalities of those around us' (p. 259). Such theories – broken windows and the power of context – serve as humbling reminders that a deprived childhood should not mean deprived adulthood; the future does not have to resemble the past.

My fastidious approach towards the school environment is such that my team of caretakers often run away from me when they see me approaching. There's no excuse for shabby corridors, tatty carpets and floors pocked by chewing gum; managing your physical environment is one of the most basic tasks faced by any leader. We want students to take pride in their school, and this starts with the environment. A recent trip to the inspiring Bethnal Green Academy in East London reinforced my belief in the power of bright corridor displays – it's not just at primary school where bold, attractive murals and displays provide a stimulating backdrop to learning. It's also a tell-tale sign of a school in decline when displays show photographs of long-departed colleagues, or newsletters from years gone by. So I implore staff to renew their classroom and corridor displays, especially at the start of the year before supplies of energy are depleted, and before our annual cycle of open mornings and evenings in the first week of October. Of course a great building is no guarantee of a great school, but I fear for a head who struggles to maintain an attractive and stimulating physical environment.

School uniform is a powerful tool in establishing a distinctive identity for a school community. The uniform reflects the brand of the school, and wherever I've led a school I've insisted on a smart, professional uniform worn with pride by all students. A scruffy tie, untucked shirt or canvas plimsolls send out a subtle but clear message of defiance, and it must be tackled head-on at the first opportunity. Before I arrived at Burlington Danes, students without the correct footwear were issued with plain black plimsolls. This was intended to deter students from breaking the footwear code (formal black shoes) but predictably the plimsolls became something of a status symbol themselves: the exact opposite of the intended effect. It's said that the teenage trend of wearing low-slung jeans emerged in prisons where belts were removed from non-compliant inmates as a punishment, with the low waistlines then becoming a badge of honour replicated on the street. There are those who fret that uniform stunts individual expression, but in my view students don't need to express their individuality through their clothing. The challenge we face is creating a harmonious, coherent community, and we'll use all the available levers to accomplish this. Students complying to a smart, professional uniform provides a public show of unity, and a failure to gain compliance in this area can send out a message of weakness which some students will seek to exploit.

Norms and rituals are powerful tools for schools seeking to demarcate their own values from the values of the street. This is why we start the school day with every year group lining up, in silence, while tutors check their uniform and take the register. Heads of year oversee the process, scanning their charges from the elevation of a picnic table or other piecesof playground furniture. It might sound a bit regimented, but lining up 1,000 young people every morning sends out a clear message for the day ahead: school has started and our expectations are high. My natural tendency is to be more liberal than this orderly routine might suggest, but you don't have to work in challenging schools for long to realise the poignancy of that old maxim that order liberates; that structure allows freedom. I've seen many teachers with the most innovative lesson plans which falter in the delivery because they haven't established basic norms of respect and control in their classroom. No-one makes this point better than Sir Michael Wilshaw: "People say that we are strict. We give structure to children who come from unstructured backgrounds. If the boundaries haven't been set by parents or the community, you need to set them in school. We teach the children the difference between right and wrong, good and evil. They know that if they disrupt class or are rude to teachers, there will be consequences." (interview in *New Statesman*, 14 October 2011).

The sights and smells of Burlington Danes

Every school has its distinctive feel, we all recall the taste of school dinners, the smell of polished floors and the bad breath of our woodwork teachers. A stroll through Burlington Danes reveals its own melange of colours, shapes, scents and sights.

Memorable sights include huddled islands of teenagers; condensed breath rising into the chilly morning air as the sun rises during line-up; the bottlenecks at doorways and stairwells; a bevy of irate teachers crowding round a jammed photocopier with red lights flashing; bottles of water hanging out of bulging blazer pockets; the brisk step of a head of year going from a parent meeting to resolve a behaviour issue, a glazed look showing the merest hint of amusement at the trials of her day.

Smells include the pungent aroma of garlic at break time as the lunch time curry paste hits the pan; the stagnant air of a classroom recently vacated by Year 8 students (old enough to perspire, not quite savvy enough to deodorize); the musty scent of damp uniforms on a wet day; and the wondrous aroma of chocolate brownies baking in the cooking classroom, located conveniently below my office.

The soundtrack to our tour is provided by the ping and pong of table tennis balls; the incessant chug of the photocopier; the spritely pip of the school bell; the cacaphonous din of teenage conversations with large groups of youngsters talking over each other.

All of these sights, smells and sounds create a rich and memorable sensory experience and contribute to the distinctive rhythms of the school day, punctuated by the metronomic regularity of the school bell. Less perceptible, but far more powerful, is the ebb and flow of human energy, as 1,100 clusters of hormones, chemicals and endorphins go about their daily business.

There are some interesting tips on influencing behaviour in the book *Nudge* by Thaler and Sunstein, which offers advice on how governments and corporations can prompt citizens into mutually beneficial behaviour. They reference a study by Goldstein *et al* (2008) suggesting a hotel might seek to save on laundry costs by placing a sticker in the bathroom saying 'the majority of guests reuse their towels' (p. 472). We are heavily influenced by the behaviour of our peers so guests tend to respond to such 'norm-referenced' messages. Sunstein went on to work for President Obama at the White House, and it's said that David Cameron has his own 'nudge unit' at Number 10. It would be easy to dismiss such methods as political spin with no place in schools, but I think there's something we can learn. Alastair Campbell, the archetypal spin doctor, provides a blueprint when he says that 'OST is my first rule: objective, strategy, tactics. Get these the wrong way round and you are in trouble' (interview in *PR Week*, 3 October 2012).

In my case our objectives were clear: to restore pride to Burlington Danes through rigorous standards and exceptional results; the strategy was coming together – getting the right people in the right roles – and so I felt comfortable with the more tactical approach of nudging behaviour in the right direction. An example of a behavioural nudge can be found on the streets of Copenhagen, where painted green footprints point people towards litter bins. Nudging works on the premise that we're not as rational as we might like to think, and that our behaviour is in fact influenced by contextual factors; such as the conduct of those around us, the physical and environmental conditions in which we operate, and the expectations placed upon us. Schools therefore offer an ideal testing ground for nudging, since we're in the business of influencing human behaviour. So how do we nudge our students? One simple way is that criticism and correction takes place in private, while praise is done publicly. It's an obvious point, but my tannoy announcements and my newsletter commendations heap praise on worthy students, while those who fail to meet our expectations are dealt with in private. Similarly, the hundreds of photographs on display around the academy portray positive, responsible students working hard and enjoying their learning. Red tape down the centre of the carpet reminds students to keep to the left on the corridors. Our home-school agreement means that parents grant us permission to run same day detentions, enabling us to ensure that corrective consequences can be served quickly, and then put behind us – there's little point in setting a detention for not doing French homework if the student has to wait a week to serve it. Most of this is common sense, but cumulatively it helps to create a set of rituals and norms which set us apart from the community in which we are based.

So we've seen in this chapter the twin pressures that leaders face of keeping one eye on the mountain in the distance and one eye on the pebble on the path. A leader who is consumed by the big picture will lose the credibility of her staff. A dangerous disconnect will develop between the daily experiences of teachers and the lofty ambitions of the head. But a leader who is absorbed by day-to-day issues will soon find himself in charge of a rudderless organisation in which staff burn out because they lose sight of the long-term mission which justifies their daily efforts.

This chapter in a tweet: Leaders must always have one eye on the long-term and one eye on the present; they must grapple with the minutiae of school life.

Conclusion: Headstrong

'Kids who do well in school tend to do well in life, whether or not they come from poverty.'

Why Headstrong?

I called this book 'Headstrong' because it's my belief that a school is only as strong as its headteacher. Such a view is easy to criticise. It could be argued that it promotes an outdated organisational model, where corporate structures are linear and hierarchical, with disempowered staff expected to follow instructions from above rather than think for themselves. It could be argued that it underplays social factors and encourages 'superheads' to seek short-term gains and easy wins. Perhaps it ignores the myriad levers that contribute to school success, focusing instead on the most obvious one. Indeed it's rather unfashionable to suggest that leadership still matters. It would be easier to write a model for school success which didn't depend on the strength of the headteacher; where schools flourished due to the integrity and coherence of the systems followed. Yet the fact that there is no global formula for school success is an indication of the fact that leadership still matters in schools. I think there are two reasons for this.

The first is that no two schools are the same, and the leader of the school must therefore adapt the standard ingredients of school success to the local context. And this local context is a complex animal, made up of the history of the school (both recent and more distant), the culture of the staff room, the values of the playground, the demography of the local area, the strengths and weaknesses of the staff, the interests of the students, the facilities and resources, the quality of other schools in the area, recent exam results, local job prospects, the governing body. Headteachers must account for all these factors when they take on the mantle of school leadership, then constantly review them in order to pull the appropriate levers and flick the required switches.

The standard ingredients of school success

This book maintains that leaders must adapt their schools to the local context. But any good school will require a sprinkling of the following ingredients:

1. High expectations: actively believe and expect every student to make significant progress. Treat the bottom set like the top set

2. Great teachers who enjoy autonomy in the classroom

3. A headteacher who plays to her/his strengths

4. A coherent curriculum which develops students' knowledge over time

5. A progamme of assessment which accurately measures student progress

6. Transparent data revealing student (and staff) performance

7. Positive and caring ethos, developed through assemblies and student/staff interaction

8. Meticulous personalised intervention: support for weaker students; challenge for more able students

9. Robust organisational structure, giving staff clear roles and responsibilities

10. A programme of teacher development, nurturing the talent within

11. Decent facilities and resources; stimulating physical environment

12. Clubs and trips which develop the whole child

13. A pastoral system which ensures that every child is known

14. Clear and confident communication with parents and other partners

15. Strong community relations, embedding the school within the local context

16. Careers/university programme

17. Student council or similar system for harnessing views of young people

18. Clear and quick rewards and sanctions

19. Support and scrutiny from governing body/sponsor

20. Norms and rituals which provide familiarity and belonging

The second reason why leadership matters in schools relates to a recurring theme of this book: schools are intensely human organisations, almost tribal in their nature. By this I mean that schools are engaged in the fundamental exchange of knowledge and skills from adults to children, creating an environment of human intensity and vitality. In such an environment people seek the stability provided by a strong leader. Such a leader provides reassurance to students, teachers and parents. Almost everything that happens in a school is based on human interaction which is why schools are different to other organisations and rely more on human direction than systematic processes. If we go back to the John Lewis department store where we started this journey, the final link in the chain of their provision involves interaction between shop assistant and customer, but that's the tip of the iceberg, propped up by hidden systems and processes which are more formulaic than human. Buyers will consult historical pricing data to judge the optimal price of their wares, the logistical team will run algorithms to get these goods on the shelves. Yet in schools people are never far from the action, and this creates a delicate organisational dynamic which requires careful cultivation from a leader. In defending this 'headstrong' model I should also recognise that school leaders, like teachers, must play to their own strengths. Probably my most effective attribute is the ability to galvanise an organisation towards a common goal through establishing positive working relationships and a purposeful collective spirit. I set high expectations for students and staff and shine a light on the performance of the organisation through the transparent handling of data and rigorous attention to detail. Praise and recognition reinforce the achievements made by staff, and – before long – momentum builds and success becomes the norm. I acknowledge that there are other models of school leadership which don't rely so much on a strong figurehead, hence the importance of playing to one's own strengths and style.

So it's my view, after nearly 40 years in education, that the headteacher makes the difference between success and failure in school, particularly in challenging urban schools. It's the job of the head to be the shock-absorber: a source of stability, direction and reassurance in what can be a volatile environment. I'm yet to encounter a challenging school which is successful in spite of the headteacher: if the head is not good enough then the whole organisation is tempered by that. So is this model of leadership too top-down? My response to this would be that I expect all of my leaders in a school to be headstrong, and what is a teacher if not a leader of their classroom? Teachers must impose themselves on their classes in the same way that the head must assert herself on the school. Similarly, I expect my heads of department and heads of year to proactively direct their domains, taking responsibility to cultivate the values they wish to embed. So this model of leadership flows right through the organisation.

The test of effective leadership is always the state of the organisation in the absence of the leader. This test was applied at Burlington Danes in 2012 when I spent nine months acting as executive head of another Ark academy in Brixton, where I spent two or three days a week. I felt secure that standards at Burlington Danes would be maintained in my absence, such is the strength of leadership below me.

Leadership traits
Great leaders are:
• visible and accessible: leaders are the face of the organisation and must win the trust of key stakeholders
• morally upright and credible: they walk the talk
• proactive and strategic: they set out a clear and compelling vision
• able to shoulder responsibility: calm, authoritative, decisive – chief problem solver
• comfortable in their own shoes – fakes are easily spotted
• highly organised, with good time management skills
• team builders who create trust and nurture strong relationships
• able to adapt to context but not slaves to political fashion
• attentive to detail, taking the view from the balcony not the dance floor
• restless to improve
• willing to differentiate: not everyone is the same, but it's important to be fair

My time in Brixton reminded me of the fact that no two schools are the same. At Burlington Danes it had taken me a long time to establish positive relations with the students. They were mistrustful, angry and sullen. You could sense their feeling of betrayal; of promises broken, a school which mirrored the fractured world of the neighbourhood outside. I was shocked by the lack of warmth, which was such a contrast to the joyful and vibrant student culture that I had become familiar with at Sacred Heart. There, a large percentage of the students were from Nigeria and other parts of West Africa, and they actively shared the school's Catholic ethos, creating a mutual understanding between all parties. Burlington Danes is more diverse, with no dominant culture or ethnicity. In reception there might be a Muslim mother from Afghanistan next to a dad from Jamaica. It took longer to establish positive relations with the students, and even to this day I'm sad to say that they often give new teachers a difficult ride in the first term, before invariably accepting them later in the year. It usually takes a few years before our students actively warm to our teachers. The students in Brixton were far more ebullient. Even though I was a short-term executive principal they quickly warmed to me. In the same way that the old adage given to teachers that they shouldn't smile until Christmas is hopelessly blunt and ignorant of local circumstances, so too we must be careful not to create a blueprint for heads to follow in all situations.

The unique character of each school reinforces the need for heads to tailor their approach for the challenge they face. Even at the same school, headteachers will employ different styles at different times in their leadership journey. When I arrived at Burlington Danes I adopted a transformative style of leadership, providing direction and energy to banish the malaise which permeated the corridors. After the first few months I had gained the trust of my senior leaders, and they too had gained my faith in them. This enabled me to be more distributive, and to this day a large proportion of my time is spent in conversation with my senior leaders, checking in with them on the progress they have made on their areas of responsibility. In the twilight of my time at Burlington Danes I was more systematic, embedding the routines and procedures which will serve the school well for years ahead. Interestingly, a 2010 McKinsey report, entitled 'How the world's most improved school systems keep getting better', suggested that this tailored approach applies to national school systems as well as individual schools. The authors suggest different interventions required at different stages of an education system's journey, so a primitive national education system would benefit from 'scripted teaching manuals', whereas to get from good to excellent, schools should focus on 'cultivating peer-led learning for teachers and principals' (2010, p. 28).

I've noted above that a good test of effective leadership is how the organisation functions in the absence of a leader. But what about distance leadership? Say, for instance, if a struggling school in South Africa approached a successful British headteacher and asked for guidance on how to transform the school, would the headteacher be able to provide a model from afar which would improve the outcomes for that school? The headteacher would be able to suggest new systems and procedures. A performance management system might help to clear underperforming staff. Curriculum changes might enhance the learning experience of the students, and a data management system might shine a light on the workings of the organisation. But to really affect change you do have to be there yourself, developing relationships with key stakeholders, modelling the high expectations you seek to enforce, assessing the mood in the staff-room, checking that systems are being implemented as intended. This scenario reveals a key tenet of school leadership: the visibility of the head. When a head walks around the school they should carry with them at least a pinch of gravitas. I worked with one head who was a shadowy figure. He crept into classrooms anonymously, slinking around in the manner of a humble butler wishing to clear the plates from his master's banquet without disturbing the guests. I expect students to stand up when I enter their classroom, not for the sake of pomposity but because I'm the headteacher, and it's a role that needs to command respect for the school to function.

In short, leadership is like a tap turned on. You can't turn it off – you're doing the job all the time. The BlackBerry continues to buzz long into the evening. You miss the daily routines of teaching and the luxury of being able to close your classroom door and deliver a well-planned lesson, safe in the knowledge that you won't be disturbed for the hour ahead. Your privacy vanishes, and you have to develop the energy and stamina to convey positivity and reassurance at all times.

Power of context

You'll notice that many of the points above are focused on the role of the head in challenging schools, and it's my belief that in the inner city the headteacher plays a far more pivotal role than in more comfortable contexts. The reason for this is that in the inner city, schools must proactively instil change. We must alter the direction of travel for our young people and it's this intervention which is so difficult, so energy sapping, and so complex. The problem of public education has been that schools have reflected their neighbourhoods, which is fine in affluent areas. So the challenge for a headteacher of a middle class, suburban school is to manage a stable learning environment, safe in the knowledge that the students in his care will most likely end up fine whatever the school does. You could say that the school's job in this situation is simply to do no harm! Headteachers can therefore take a *laissez faire* approach, maintaining a steady ship and allowing their teachers to get on and teach. It's a fundamentally different proposition to the role of a head in a challenging urban school, where proactive intervention is required to change the direction of our charges. Unless we create a rich, loving, positive culture, the values of the street will take hold. Unless we provide challenging, engaging, pacey lessons, student progress will continue to fall short of national norms. Unless we offer personalised intervention based on rigorously tracking student progress, pupils will fail to meet their potential. Unless we impose impeccable expectations of behaviour, and immediately sanction non-compliance, disaffection and subversion will take root.

Schools in tough areas have to work harder than schools with a more affluent intake to gain the same results. In short, we have to be better. England has some fantastic private schools, but it is my view that they are successful largely because of the students who walk through their doors each morning. These students are more likely than my students to benefit from a stable family life. They are more likely to have been exposed to stimulating conversation, books and a wide range of cultural experiences from a young age. They are likely to live in neighbourhoods free from crime and the temptation of gangs. Furthermore, their parents have actively chosen to send their offspring to independent school. This suggests (a) that their parents are affluent; and (b) that their parents value education. With these two criteria in place, young people are likely to do well whichever school they go to.

The difference between the culture required in a challenging school with that of a more affluent school is like the difference between the intensive care ward and physiotherapy ward of a hospital. In the physio ward the supervisor can keep a low profile, allowing her physiotherapists to get on with their job, whereas in intensive care the margins are much smaller, and the manager must run a tight ship, with clearly defined roles and expectations, a culture of accountability and transparency, with severe repercussions for any non-compliance. Of course, the headteacher of any school could decide to lead in a transformative, proactive style, but this is likely to fail if there's no sense of the necessity. And if students are gaining good results and progressing to good universities, then it's difficult to convince people of the urgency for reform. I saw this for myself on a recent conference on school leadership in Norway. I shared with the headteachers in the audience my view of headship, and the rigorous approach we take at Burlington Danes, but I struggled to convince them that our measures were appropriate for their stable, successful schools.

The influential American educator E.D. Hirsch makes a similar point when he criticises the view that schooling should be 'natural'. He suggests that the American school system suffers from the misplaced view that the acquisition of knowledge and skills is a natural process, requiring passive support from schools rather than rigorous intervention: 'Yet the romantic concept of education as a natural unfolding – by far the most influential idea in the history of American education – has small basis in reality when it comes to reading, writing and arithmetic. On current scientific evidence, the notion that the job of schools is to foster the natural development of the child is only a half-truth' (2006, p. 7). The problem, as Hirsch recognises, is that a hands-off, non-interventionist approach exacerbates the achievement gap between rich and poor because affluent students are more likely to gain knowledge and skills through their daily interactions with well-educated family members, whereas students from poorer backgrounds have no other source of this tuition beyond school.

Once again, the challenges being faced by schools in challenging areas is fundamentally different to those faced by schools in more comfortable circumstances. Our students are being swept along by a tide of underachievement and low expectations. We need to halt their flow, take them to a more placid stretch of water with fewer currents and rapids, then gradually equip them with the skills to swim against the oppressive torrent, avoiding the hazards and pitfalls they will be sure to face on the way. Conversely, most students in more affluent schools are being carried on a current of success, and the role of the school is simply to help the students stay afloat and remove the occasional obstacle. In fact, such is the ease of the passage that some independent schools intervene to make it more difficult. I'm reminded of the private girls school in a well-heeled part of South-West London where the headteacher recently introduced a 'Failure Week' to give her girls a taste of adversity, which she felt they lacked. The week involved presentations on resilience from guest speakers, and encouraged girls to embrace activities beyond their existing skill set. I applaud the ingenuity of Failure Week, but – to be blunt – when it comes to adversity most of my students have had their fill. The reality, of course, is that most of us swim along with the tide in which we find ourselves. Played out across a whole society this serves to reinforce inequalities dictated by accident of birth. Thus, the task of leading a challenging school is radically different to the task of leading an affluent school and requires a headstrong leader who can galvanise the organisation to proactively alter the life chances of our young people.

Closing the gap

Let's explore in more detail what can be done to close the achievement gap between rich and poor students, a gap which should be anathema to a liberal society. As one academic study puts it, 'the yawning gap between the educational achievement of poor children and their more affluent peers remains a complex and seemingly intractable problem' (Perry and Francis, 2010, p. 5). One of the biggest obstacles to closing this gap is a failure to recognise that schools have a role to play, and that schools in challenging areas can secure great results given the right conditions. E.D. Hirsch makes the point well:

> I completely concur with the desire to gain greater equality of social circumstance for all children. But that pressing social goal does not have to be used as a distraction for our schools' failure to make a dent in the reading achievement gap between demographic groups. It does no practical good to attack the economic status quo by defending the educational status quo. If schools themselves can do a far better job of narrowing the achievement gap in reading, that will be a supreme contribution to the social aims that Rothstein and many others desire. (2006, p. 15).

On both sides of the Atlantic some commentators have portrayed schools as mere microcosms of society, the implication being that schools in challenging areas are destined to churn out poor results, a situation described by Hirsch as 'demographic determinism'. Let's remind ourselves of the conclusion of the influential Coleman report, published in America in 1966: 'That schools bring little influence to bear on a child's achievement that is independent of his background and general social context; that this very lack of an independent effect means that the inequalities imposed on children by their home, neighborhood, and peer environment are carried along to become the inequalities with which they confront adult life' (1996, p. 325).

Or take this extract from a 2006 article in the *British Journal of Educational Studies*, which argues that the view that schools can make a difference is in fact the source of the problem: 'The prevailing fallacy for much of the past two decades has been that schools can make all the difference necessary. The school effectiveness and improvement movement was hegemonic long enough to have a number of lasting effects. The focus was to be on teachers and within school and particularly within classroom processes. If we can only make teachers good enough, equip them with sufficient skills and competencies then the wider social context of schooling is seen as unimportant' (Reay, 2006 p. 291).

Isn't it incredible that in the minds of some academics the 'enemy' is the view that schools can make a difference? I was alerted to this and similar articles by members of my senior team who were embarking on a Masters in education management at King's College London. They suggested to me that this view of the powerlessness of schools to combat educational disadvantage continues to dominate in the educational establishment, a view reflected in a 2007 study by Butler and Webber: 'These findings suggest that so long as pupils' GCSE performances are so strongly affected by the type of neighbourhood in which they live, a school's league position bears only indirect relationship to the quality of school management and teaching" (p. 1229). And in case we're in danger of getting excited about a few exceptions to the rule of the achievement gap, another academic brings us back to reality: 'teachers and school leaders should resist the urge to draw inspiration from media accounts of heroic teachers and principals winning against the odds in 'tough' schools. Closer inspection invariably reveals the reality is not as impressive as the story' (Thrupp, quoted in Reynolds and Teddlie, 2001, p. 99-113).

Such defeatism is brought to life in Andrew Adonis's 2012 book *Education, Education, Education*. Adonis describes a visit to a failing school in the North-East, and his incredulity when he heard this pearl of wisdom from one of the teachers: '"Twenty years ago", he said, "when the boys left here, they walked down the hill and turned left to get a job in the shipyard or right to go down the mines. All those jobs have now gone. They might as well walk straight into the sea". I didn't know how to respond. It seemed too obvious to say that, if they got a decent education, they might prosper on dry land' (p. 22).

Like an alcoholic denying his addiction, it's difficult to reform a system which doesn't recognise the potential for reform. All of the quotes above reveal a deep defeatism, with teachers and academics resigned to the notion that schools in tough areas must necessarily be inadequate, and that we shouldn't expect any different until society itself is reformed. This latter point – the need for social reform – hints at the fact that educational defeatism is found more on the left than the right of political commentary. It's ironic that some of the boldest reforms to tackle the achievement gap, such as George Bush's 'No Child Left Behind' policy, and the drive for accountability and rigour championed by Michael Gove, have emerged from the right. Of course schools alone can't close the achievement gap, but the evidence of successful schools in the last decade should finally put to bed the pessimistic claim that schools cannot make a difference.

I have seen this for myself. In 2007 35% of students at Burlington Danes gained five or more A*-C grades in their GCSEs. In 2014 this figure was 79% (46% of students gained the English Baccalaureate) enabling this cohort to gain places at top universities such as Oxford, Bristol and LSE. The ethnic and social composition of our students has hardly changed in this time (66% of our students currently qualify for pupil premium, and the social deprivation indicator for our Year 8 cohort is more severe than for our Year 11 cohort), and we haven't relied on easier vocational qualifications to boost our grades, as evidenced by the fact that our English Baccalaureate pass rate is higher than the national average. Fortunately some members of the academic community recognise the difference that schools can make, in spite of ongoing social disparity: 'I completely concur with the desire to gain greater equality of social circumstance for all children. But that pressing social goal does not have to be used as a distraction for our schools' failure to make a dent in the reading achievement gap between demographic groups' (Hirsch, 2006 p. 15).

In his book *How Children Succeed*, Paul Tough claims that 'kids who do well in school tend to do well in life, whether or not they come from poverty' (p. 188). Again I'm reminded of the figures quoted earlier about the woeful literacy levels of British prisoners. Throw the forces of globalisation into the mix, where unskilled jobs are being lost to the developing world, and we're left with a toxic blend of factors which combine to create bleak prospects for those who leave school empty-handed. Surely we have to question the justice of a society where success is the norm in some schools and failure is the norm in others. Six years ago, two-thirds of students left Burlington Danes without a decent set of qualifications. Now three-quarters leave our gates having acquired this. It would be absurd to argue that those students who left six years ago were somehow less able or less deserving of a sound education. It seems strange that we've tolerated such failure and allowed the prospects of so many young people to be dependent on the state of their local school. Even in America, probably the world's most individualistic nation, there is widespread commitment to equality of opportunity: 'Since 1987, when Pew started asking these questions, between 87% and 94% of respondents in every poll have agreed with the statement 'Our society should do what is necessary to make sure that everyone has an equal opportunity to succeed' (Tough, 2012 p. 186). We can't do everything, but no institution is better placed than the state school system to deliver on this democratic entitlement.

What we must do therefore is strike a balance between recognising that schools in tough areas face an immense challenge to gain good results, though one which can be overcome with the right approach, while seeking to tackle some of the social ills which stack the odds against such schools. This book has suggested that schools can succeed even in the toughest of social contexts, but I don't deny that the effort required to bring this about is not far from Herculean. A recent staff consultation at Burlington Danes revealed that teachers work an average of 12 hours each day during the week, then spend at least one day at the weekend preparing for the week ahead. They cheerfully cover lessons for absent colleagues, sparing us from the blight of supply teachers. I'm blessed with a senior team who think nothing of working through their lunch break every day, or receiving calls from me on a Saturday morning or Sunday evening. But I appreciate that this 'emergency room' mentality is difficult to replicate. We must recognise that schools can only do so much, and this is not to make excuses but to face reality. A good school cannot solve all the ills of society or make up for the challenges that many children are exposed to in the home and on the estates. The home matters, parents' attitudes matter, society's respect for education matters. So alongside school-based reform we should pursue structural changes which level the playing field between the social classes.

A good starting point would be to deny the right of private schools to claim charitable status, a legacy of the time that independent schools really did serve those in need, but which now serves to entrench the privileges of the few who can afford private schooling. Many independent schools have paid lip service to their charitable obligations, for example by offering a smattering of free places to gifted poor folk. At the other end of the spectrum I've welcomed the introduction of the pupil premium by the coalition government, a subsidy of £900 paid to schools for every student in receipt of free school meals. For a school like ours, with two-thirds of students eligible for the pupil premium, this provides us with hundreds of thousands of pounds in additional capital each year, which we use to fund our intervention programmes and target students in need of particularly intense support. The 2010 US documentary film on urban education *Waiting for Superman* revealed the value of government investment in challenging schools by exposing the cost of failure. The average US prisoner (of which there are over two million) absorbs $35,000 of taxpayers' money per year, less than the cost of a year's tuition at a top private school. It's a simplistic equation, but the implication of course is that investing in education will save money in the long run by cutting crime and reducing the need for costly remedial intervention later in life. I hope this book has revealed the extra lengths that challenging schools go to in order to intervene in the lives of our young people, and it's absolutely right that additional funding is provided for these efforts. Quite frankly I'm sure we could educate middle class students for half the money required for every student from a challenging background.

How we spend our pupil premium

Curriculum and staffing

- additional group in timetable blocks for all subjects Year 7-11 and seven tutor groups for all year groups; bottom group has only 15 students
- use of teaching assistants for intensive literacy intervention
- literacy lead on SLT; pupil premium lead on SLT; literacy post holder on staff
- staff providing support related to attendance and welfare
- The Sanctuary for vulnerable students every lunchtime

Additional resources/teaching time

- resources to support learning, including hardware and software – *eg* Lexia, Accelerated Reader, class sets of reading books/Achievement for All
- intervention through the colour-coded groups in Key Stage 4: *eg* resources for revision and immersion sessions directly linked to final examinations

- curriculum enrichment (Gifted and Talented) *eg* Into University, 'debatemate', first story, life classes
- subsidised music peripatetic lessons – over 300 pupils per week
- GCSE booster sessions/weekend learning/holiday learning and associated materials
- 'GreenHouse' table-tennis coach working with our low attaining and less confident students/boxing coach/rugby coach – all raising self-esteem through small group and individual coaching

Mentoring and support

- early morning and lunchtime targeted literacy mentoring and reading buddies/reading booster; Lexia computer license
- peer mentoring literacy scheme at lunchtimes with free lunch provided
- assertive mentoring Year 11 and Year 13
- homework club
- free healthy breakfast in exam season
- Jamie's Farm trips
- parent(s) meetings with underachieving students in Key Stage 3 with principal with uniform voucher incentives to attend.
- cultural Capital trips to museums and galleries throughout London

Finance and training

- financial support provided to allow students on FSM to access extra-curricular provision (*eg* history battlefields trip, Barcelona, theatre trips).
- incentives and rewards/travel costs

Alongside funding, admissions policy is a key tool in closing the achievement gap. Admissions matters because of the influence of peer pressure. I've previously noted that most of us drift along with the flow of those around us (psychologists have labelled this tendency to gravitate towards those around us 'the magnetic middle') and the fact is that in more affluent schools this peer pressure is conducive to learning. When it comes to exam season, students recognise that the stakes are high; they change gears and they study. They don't need compulsory Saturday classes, one-to-one mentoring, or revision notes painstakingly compiled by their teachers. They understand the link between effort and attainment, and they have faith in their ability to improve their own life chances. A critical mass of motivated, self-reliant students galvanises the whole school. Consider the difference between going to the gym and working out on your own, compared with going to the gym and joining a scheduled class, or having a personal trainer. Anyone who's been to a gym class, or trained one to one or in a group, will know that you work far harder when being pushed by someone else, and when other people around you are working towards the same goal. This is what good schools in low income areas do; they provide the motivation, conditions and positive peer pressure that cajoles young people into working hard and make rapid progress.

We don't have that critical mass of self-motivated students at Burlington Danes, hence the 'intensive care' required to affect change. Strangely enough, we do have plenty of middle class streets in our locale. The house where the Cameron family lived before moving to 10 Downing Street is closer to our gates than the White City estate which many of our students call home. Yet our more affluent neighbours are drawn to the selective faith schools, suburban schools or independent schools such as Latymer Upper, whose lush playing fields border our own Wood Lane site.

I would like the social composition of schools to reflect the composition of their neighbourhoods (which obviously presents problems where the whole locality of a school is deprived, again showing the interplay between social issues and urban education), but despite our success we still struggle to attract more affluent members of the local community. I suggested earlier that Ofsted could shine a light on these figures, perhaps denying the 'outstanding' rating to schools whose own social composition is significantly higher than that of their neighbourhoods. Like the Pupil Premium, which provides additional funding for schools serving more deprived students, this would help shift the incentives which currently encourage schools to attract well-to-do students. A 2014 study by the Social Mobility and Child Poverty Commission ('Cracking the Code') suggests that we need to refocus our efforts on schools with average proportions of disadvantaged children. There is evidence that these children tend to do okay in schools where they are in the majority and also when they are in a small minority, but struggle in schools with 'middling proportions' of disadvantaged young people.

Independently monitoring admissions processes would also prevent schools from playing games which favour more 'desirable' applicants. One town in North Carolina offers an example of a radical approach to school mix. Such was the disparity between the rich suburban schools and the deprived inner city schools in the town of Raleigh that the local authority intervened to create a perfectly balanced social mix across all of its schools. This was based on the view that every school would benefit from possessing a critical mass of engaged, motivated, compliant students: 'Schools with a majority of middle-class parents will not tolerate incompetent teachers, or drinking fountains that don't work, or restrooms with no toilet paper' (Grant, 2009, p. 106). The results were striking, though it's difficult to imagine public support for such drastic measures, not least from more affluent constituents.

Parents too have a part to play in ensuring social mix in schools, though I recognise from my own experience the huge parental drive to do what's best for your own children, and I wouldn't expect parents to subdue this drive in favour of the greater good. Instead, schools must convince aspirational parents that they share the same high expectations for their children, and they have the expertise to stretch the most able students. I love reminding our prospective parents about the number of our teachers who went to Oxbridge, about the links we have with top firms and universities, and the wide range of enrichment activities which would rival the extra-curricular provision of most private schools. On any given week students could take part in first story, where they write their own book alongside an established author, then star in the Ark Schools spelling bee, before taking the stage in our West London debating club, where students will face peers from Latymer and St Paul's. This year we've introduced 'Oxbridge' interviews for our brightest students in all year groups, providing them with a taste of the type of questions they can expect when they apply to Oxford and Cambridge. The benefit of attracting aspirational parents is that they provide another layer of scrutiny and support. If their son or daughter doesn't receive homework one day, or if their books haven't been marked for a few weeks, these parents will be emailing the school and speaking to me. I've said before that our parents are very supportive, but it's more of a passive support than proactive, which means that it's down to us as a school to provide all the accountability and scrutiny when it comes to homework and marking.

For their part, state schools need to ensure that they really do stretch the most able students. A 'gifted and talented' programme is all well and good, but our brightest students (like all students) need to be challenged in the classroom in every lesson. Last year I marked submissions for a national essay writing competition. It was painful to see the gulf in quality between the essays written by students in independent schools and their counterparts in state schools. It reminded me that our most able students need to be exposed to excellence outside of our own school, lest they think that by being in the top set at Burlington Danes they would also be in the top set at a top private school. A national exam for high performers might make grim reading for some state schools but at least it would show high-achievers from state school the standards that they need to reach to compare with their peers in independent schools.

A few years after introducing our sixth form provision we proudly sent a few students off to Oxford and Cambridge for their admissions interviews. They didn't receive offers. We discovered that our students weren't getting into Oxbridge because their interview exposed a lack of cultural and intellectual dexterity. When it came to being historically aware, culturally curious and engaged by science and technology, our students fell short. So we set about trying to cultivate cultural literacy from Year 7 through our Oxbridge Project. There were two parts to this project. The first involved inviting 120 students from Years 7-10 to take part in 'Oxbridge interviews' which probed them on their awareness of current affairs, unseen poetry and philosophical dilemmas. Successful applicants were then invited to weekly talks and seminars from experts in a range of academic fields in subjects as diverse as platonic philosophy, marine biology, nanoscience, the economics of apartheid, the refugee convention, the UK's energy crisis, microfluidics, myth and the Middle East, the aeneid and communication in the digital age. The Oxbridge project was led by one of our English teachers Dr Natasha O'Hear. She captures the spirit of the project in a report that she wrote for me on conclusion of the initiative:

> This is an unashamedly elitist project designed to go some way towards levelling the playing field (in national terms) for the top 5-10% of our students. They are a group of very able students who, at present, are not in a strong position to compete for places at the top universities with their peers from more fortunate backgrounds because, through

no fault of their own, they lack the intellectual roundness and finesse that students from more uniformly academic schools naturally acquire. These qualities cannot be developed overnight, but must be nurtured over years. Preparation for the top universities, not in terms of UCAS forms and references, but in terms of a more intellectual and rigorous way of thinking, must start for our students in Year 7 and continue throughout their time at BDA. I hope that the Oxbridge Project is starting to fulfil this role and that it will also serve as a gateway to intellectual emancipation as a goal in its own right.

These last few pages have focused on the importance of school mix: recognition of the power of peer pressure within schools. I think schools could do more to tap into this peer pressure and mould it towards positive ends. Simple measures like students wearing the school colours when playing football against another school, creating a house system and flying the flags of the six houses in the playground, distributing water bottles with the school crest on, all serve to create a sense of belonging. For seven hours each day students and staff are contained in a small area, offering a great opportunity to influence spirits through displaying positive visual stimuli and tweaking the physical environment. Similarly, norms and rituals provide powerful cohesive glue. Reading the academy prayer together in assembly, lining up in silence at the beginning of the school day, finishing every term with a religious service, these norms and rituals serve to create a sense of belonging, moulding the disparate motives and values of our students and staff into a purposeful body.

One phrase that I've used sparingly in my suggestions for closing the achievement gap is the phrase 'levelling the playing field', which might be associated with positive discrimination towards students from disadvantaged backgrounds. I've always believed that it's our job to equip students from low income backgrounds to compete with those from more affluent families, rather than to lower the bar in their favour. In 2013, fully one-third of our sixth form leavers gained places at russell group universities. In our fourth year since the sixth form opened we've only just secured our first Oxbridge place, but I don't blame Oxford and Cambridge for maintaining high standards for all students. In fact, through their Widening Participation programmes, top universities have never done more to reach out to students from challenging schools, but it's important that our students gain places at these institutions on merit.

The achievement gap between rich and poor would also benefit from closer collaboration between different public services. Mental health problems in challenging schools are critical, and often go untreated. I'm also concerned that the criminal justice system is too lenient when it comes to youth crime, sending out a weak message to young offenders. Pupil Referral Units have rightly been the subject of recent commentary. These units provide education for students excluded from schools, but in my experience the clustering of dysfunctional children only serves to exacerbate their exile from mainstream society. I've rarely seen evidence of the rehabilitative potential of such units, and there seems to be little expectation for these units to deliver an education for their students.

The key responsibility of governments is to align various stakeholders behind the interests of the child. When schools have been judged solely on the number of A*-C grades, some students capable of gaining A and A* grades have been ill-served. When arbitrary divisions have been created between the primary, secondary and sixth form years, schools have been encouraged to seek short-term gains rather than equip students for the challenges that lie ahead of them. Indeed, primary and early years education would benefit from the same level of scrutiny and accountability which has transformed much of the secondary sector in recent years. Having worked in education for nearly 40 years I'm on the verge of working with pre-11-year-olds for the first time, as Burlington Danes opens its own primary school in 2015. I don't underestimate the challenge of primary education, but I'm convinced that my knowledge of the skills and character required by children at the age of 18 will enable me and my colleagues to provide a primary experience which equips children to thrive at secondary school and beyond.

Call to arms

If this book has attempted to emphasise the importance of school leadership then the other side of this coin is that I would love more people to aspire to the incredible privilege of leading a school. It's been widely noted that many headteachers are on the verge of retirement, and concern has been raised about the willingness of younger school leaders to fill their shoes. Take the first few lines of this *Daily Telegraph* article:

> More than a third of primary schools and almost a fifth of secondaries struggled to find a head after advertising the position last year, it was revealed. Roman Catholic schools are being left with the most acute shortages because they traditionally restrict recruitment to believers. Headteachers' leaders blamed rising workload, the target culture in schools and a real-terms cut in pay, saying that teachers were reluctant to take on the extra pressure of headship. It comes despite the publication of official data earlier this year that showed 700 heads or deputies now earned more than £100,000. But Russell Hobby, general secretary of the National Association of Head Teachers, said the report showed "worrying trends in the school labour market at the very top level" ('Schools facing head teacher shortage in pay row', 13 December 2011).

Such concerns don't account for the fact that there's been an influx of ambitious teachers coming into the profession in the last ten years, with Teach First and Future Leaders both actively cultivating their recruits for future school leadership, and within my own senior team at Burlington Danes, four of my assistant principals have only just turned 30. There's a growing pool of headteachers who have advanced to school leadership at an early age, so in reality I don't expect there to be a shortage of headteachers and there's no reason there should be, given the wonderful opportunity offered by the role.

My message to those considering headship would be that you can be a headteacher *and* sleep at night. Stress is often caused by a sense of powerlessness, yet as a headteacher you have more opportunity than anyone else in the school to change things. Yes, schools are placed under great pressure these days, but anyone who has successfully won control of their class and then their year group, or their department, will be able to transfer these skills to school leadership. I would be especially keen for more women to aspire to the role. Perhaps I'm old-fashioned, but I do think that men and women tend to possess different leadership traits, and I think the school system would benefit from more female leaders. A sense of authority seems to fit men more naturally in my experience, but I think women are better at recognising the complexity of situations, a handy attribute in tough schools. I would advocate expanding the use of executive heads who might oversee several schools, with a designated associate head working within each school. This gives the associate head a taste of leadership with the security of an experienced head above them. People worry about being up to the task of headship, but it's easy to forget that the role itself confers plenty of authority on the holder: when you become a headteacher *you become a headteacher*! Much of headship is common sense and I would encourage people to back themselves and get on with it. On a good day I can't think of a better job. I love the frenetic buzz and familiar rhythms of school life, and I cherish the energy and talent that confronts me in the staff room every morning. As head you feel like you're having a strong influence on people's lives and I relish the opportunity to implement my plans.

A winning mentality is central to my model of headstrong leadership. On that first day at Burlington Danes I told the staff that I knew how to create an outstanding school, and if they trusted me and played their part, that's what we would become. I remain extremely competitive, and the scrutiny and accountability provided by Ark and national league tables fuels this desire to succeed. I enjoy being the figurehead of the organisation, the galvanising force bringing everyone together. I constantly reinforce my high expectations with students and staff. I can be quite blunt in my communication, but more often than not my words are full of praise and positivity, as I seek to impart my determination to others. Visibility remains important to my model of leadership, though in recent years this facet has diminished slightly as other commitments have affected my daily presence at Burlington Danes. I have a restless drive to improve by borrowing ideas and practices from other schools and other professions. An eminent surgeon spoke to our students recently and he stressed the importance in the medical profession of keeping up with the latest innovations and theories, a point which somehow seems less relevant in education, yet there's no reason why it should be. Dylan Wiliam's observation that there are bigger variations between classrooms than between schools is an interesting one, and has been used by some to argue that the best way to improve schools is to focus on teachers and classroom practice rather than school leadership (www.dylanwiliam.org). But this argument fails to recognise the role heads play in recruiting the best teachers and then providing the conditions in which they can thrive. So, is school leadership an art or science? The National College of School Leadership and other school leadership development programmes such as Future Leaders would appear to subscribe to the view that leadership traits can be taught and acquired. But leadership is about character as well as competence, and when you examine the details of these leadership programmes you realise that they recognise the importance of emotional intelligence and personality traits amongst the competencies that the programmes also seek to develop. One of the key tests of leadership is whether or not a leader really seems comfortable in his or her own shoes. This authenticity and integrity is impossible to fake, and it's one reason why I'm slightly sceptical of the notion of leaders in other fields being parachuted into school leadership. I support accelerating progression to headship, but it's vital as a headteacher that you can relate to the teacher struggling to control his class; the head of department seeking to develop her team; the parent concerned about her son's progress. My confidence in dealing with such situations comes from my own experience as a teacher, a head of department and a mother. It's not until you've written a timetable, supported a struggling teacher or excluded a student that you gain a full awareness of the tensions and pressures at work within a school. It's also vital that school leaders remain connected to classroom practise. Inevitably you become de-skilled as a teacher when you leave the classroom to enter school leadership, but it's still important that you've cut your teeth in the classroom, that you understand the joy and pressure of teaching six periods in a day, and that you can quickly judge the quality of a lesson and offer advice to the teacher concerned.

I encourage all of my staff to keep themselves fresh, energised and inspired by doing things they love outside of school, whether it be yoga, football, travelling or reading. I think it's vital that those of us who work in schools have rich personal experience to draw on, and one of the rules of leadership has to be the ability to take ideas and inspiration from other leaders. I've borrowed something from all of the headteachers I've worked with. From Colin Garvey at Sacred Heart I learned about team-building and collegiality, and the importance of the moral integrity of the leader. From Sir Michael Wilshaw I've noticed the authority that comes from a leader with a proven track record. Success breeds success, and provides huge leverage for the leader. Like an investor starting with a million pounds compared to one starting from scratch, it's much easier to make money once you've already acquired some, and it's much easier for a leader to gain support for his plans once he's got a proven track record. My chair of governors at Burlington Danes, Lord Fink, has an infectious desire to serve others, to send the elevator down to those below. I admire his humility, and his determination to improve the life chances of others. To borrow a phrase that Stanley used at one of our prizegiving nights, we should all hope that at the time of our passing someone could say "the world is a better place for him passing through it". British politics has thrown up some interesting models of leadership too. I admire Blair's conviction and his bullet-proof confidence in his own ability and judgement. Confidence can be a fickle friend, and too much of it can of course be dangerous; legend has it that on their triumphal marches Roman generals were followed by a slave whispering in their ear: "remember you are mortal". I write this just a few weeks after the death of Margaret Thatcher, a leader whose individualism never quite chimed with my own views, but I admired her grit and decisiveness. I marched with the miners back in the 1980s, and tend to prefer leaders who appeal to hearts and minds before driving change.

My book on headship would be incomplete without mentioning that there are two headteachers in my house, with my husband Serge, who took up the post I vacated when I left Sacred Heart. From Serge I've learnt the value of tackling behaviour head-on. If your relationships with students are secure enough then you can be brutally honest in your criticism of their behaviour. So I'm quite direct with children and, perhaps more importantly, with their parents. They know I want what's best for their children and I won't let poor behaviour interfere with their progress, or the progress of the community. Some people shirk at the idea of mixing work and family, but for me it comes naturally; I guess my hand was forced after I married Serge at Sacred Heart. In any case, I think the fact that I'm comfortable working with members of my family makes me appear more human. There happens to be four husband/wife relationships at Burlington Danes, indicative of the tight community we've nurtured. Our children have become used to having two headteachers in the house. My youngest son gets fed up with the constant nagging about his homework, and of course headteachers can have problems with their own teenagers too which helps me empathise with parents. One big difference between my home life and my school life is that at school the children don't answer me back.

My family have shared the highs and lows with me. My most treasured career moments would be celebrating exam results with students and staff, cherishing the joy on the students' faces as they see the fruits of years' of labour. I'll also never forget the scenes in the staff room at Burlington Danes in 2009 when I revealed to staff that Ofsted had just judged us as 'good' in every category, and in 2013 when the judgement from the inspectors was 'outstanding'. Tears, hugs and yelps immediately filled the staff room. It's difficult to convey the feeling on paper, but for teachers who had spent years working hard at the school, only for their efforts to be hampered by failing standards and lack of direction, this validation brought incredible relief and pride. It's only when you've experienced the tragedy of a failing school that you can truly appreciate the sheer beauty of its resurgence. Of course, once you achieve excellence you soon feel the pressure to maintain those standards, and one of my worst career moments happened in August 2012 when a shift in the GCSE grade boundaries sent our headline figure tumbling from 75% five A*-C with English and maths to 66%. I felt physically sick as I sat in my office with a few colleagues trying to work out what had happened. The pain of an unexpected dip in results is an occupational hazard for a headteacher today, but such bothers are trifling compared to another occupational hazard: the death or serious illness of a student or a colleague. Such events strike at the heart of the school, and it's at these times that you realise the true value of a school community.

The future of schools

Our journey of headship started at that department store in Chelsea when I was asked to revive a flagging school after submitting a cursory application form. It seems strange that Burlington Danes Academy – a place to which I had no experience or attachment – has since absorbed more than six years of blood, sweat and tears. In that time I've seen that schools can be transformed; that strong leadership can improve the life chances of our children. Thankfully, our transformation has been matched by several other schools and I would like to think that there's no place any more for that defeatism which accepted school failure as the inevitable result of urban poverty. It's not just individual schools but also networks and clusters of schools which have shown that transformation can really happen. Let's start with Ark. In 2012 the average GCSE pass rate with English and maths across the network was 56%. Seven years ago the average pass rate in the predecessor schools, before conversion to Ark, was 19%. Not all academy chains have enjoyed such success, as Christopher Cook from the *Financial Times* notes here: 'All in all, it appears that among the multi-school academy chains, Ark is the best. And some, if you look, are struggling. To be clear: these chains mostly took over failing schools to begin with. But some have really struggled to turn them around' (7 January, 2013).

The fact that some academy chains have struggled is an indication of the difficulty of the task of school transformation. After all, these chains are purpose built for school resuscitation. But again, we shouldn't mistake the *difficulty* of the task for the *impossibility* of the task. Strikingly, London as a whole has managed to transform the educational outcomes of its young people. In 1997 just 16% of students attending London state schools gained five or more good GCSEs. Today that figure stands at over 60%. In a city of the size of London it's impossible to argue that this improvement is down to a few isolated success stories or changing demographics. So the challenge now is to roll out these reforms across the country, to turn these exceptions into the rule. Aspirations can be so low outside of London. Ask London children what they want to do in the future and they will say 'doctor', 'lawyer', 'businesswoman'. Outside of London you're far more likely to hear 'footballer', 'beautician', 'hairdresser'." It's time for squads of teachers and school leaders to be transplanted from the cities to the regions. These pioneer teachers, attracted by higher pay and a relocation allowance, would alleviate the shortage of talented, ambitious teachers in regional towns, particularly in shortage subjects such as maths, physics and languages. Now that Teach First has a decade of participants to draw on, it's not far-fetched to suggest that some of these ambassadors – as Teach First call them – might be ready to leave the big city but not ready to see out their career in a leafy suburban school. A scheme which lured these teachers, middle leaders and senior leaders to Lincoln, Hull, Ipswich, Swindon, Middlesbrough, Preston, and Portsmouth could have a huge impact.

The London Effect

'Schools can make a decisive difference. The best evidence for this comes from the experience of London. Just one in a hundred of the bottom fifth of schools for poor children in Figure 2 is found in the capital. Commission-sponsored work has previously looked at evidence on the dramatic changes in educational outcomes for children in the capital. In 2002, London was the lowest performing region in the entire country but now performs better than any other for disadvantaged children, with these children 38% more likely to get five good GCSEs including English and maths than children elsewhere. The advantage is even higher at higher grades, with disadvantaged children in London three times more likely to get eight A*-B grades at GCSE than those elsewhere. Part of the London effect is likely to be down to demographics – for example, the concentration of children from ethnic minorities. However, research suggests that this explains only about a fifth of the London advantage.'

'Cracking the Code, How schools can improve social mobility', The Social Mobility and Child Poverty Commission (2014)

I started the book with that Nietzsche line, that 'in large states public education will always be mediocre, for the same reason that in large kitchens the cooking is usually bad' and it's interesting to note that the states which are lauded for their public education tend to be small states – Singapore, Finland, Hong Kong – or provinces within larger nations, such as Ontario. I think this proves the power of context and the fallibility of any identikit model of successful schooling. This is why we need to encourage more great teachers into headship, so that we can create a generation of heads who realise that that to create a successful urban school in the 21st century you have to proactively create a counter-culture: an educational culture of love, endeavour, resilience and scholarship.

This is an incredible moment for public education. There is a global interest in what it takes to create great schools in the toughest of areas. At Burlington Danes we've recently welcomed delegations of educators from Japan, China, California, Norway, Denmark, Israel, India and Brazil. No-one denies that great teachers are critical to the success of any education system, but beyond this there is disagreement about the precise ingredients required for that elusive gold standard of school success. Progress at Burlington Danes has been thanks in part to rigorous testing and the transparent display of data, whereas in the much-heralded schools of Scandinavia testing is rare and students' awareness of their own progress appears to be minimal. When Michael Gove suggested that a longer school day and shorter holidays would raise standards in English schools, only for others to point out that, 'Finland, which ... excels in most education league tables, subjects children to fewer hours of teaching a day than any other country in the developed world' ('Asia's teachers say copying their school hours won't help Britain', The Daily Telegraph, 21 May 2013). Others see salvation in technology, but recent evidence suggests that technology is no panacea, and only raises standards when combined with a holistic approach to school improvement. A recent 'one laptop per child' programme in Peru seems to confirm that you can never take the human element out of the mix required for a great education: 'If teachers are telling kids to turn on computers and copy what is being written on the blackboard, then we have invested in expensive notebooks' ('A disappointing return from an investment in computing', *The Economist*, 4 April 2012).

Fly-on-the-wall documentaries such as *Educating the East End* have raised awareness of the challenge of urban education, but the reality is quite different. I feel that these shows look for the worst in young people, and reduce the role of teacher to that of social worker and counsellor. The reality is that most children at a British school today do not present significant emotional and behavioural challenges. Children want to do well and they need talented teachers in front of them to bring the best out of them, to have higher expectations of them than the children have of themselves. These TV shows are happy to show teachers struggling to contain a child with ADHD but they don't show the staff room conversations which actually make a difference to a young person's future: two science teachers grappling with the challenge of bringing the theory of relativity to life in their classroom, or maths teachers tweaking the Year 7 curriculum to ensure that it serves as a foundation for the enhanced rigour of the reformed maths GCSE. I've let plenty of film crews into Burlington Danes but I'm pleased that I turned away the producer who pitched the idea of *Educating White City* to me a few years ago.

I've previously quoted the French educator Daniel Pennac, who says this about teaching: "Teaching is not a military art, it's an orchestral art. A good teacher is a good conductor... He can't just neglect the third violin. The orchestra is made up of all the instruments, some of them extremely simple instruments, but they participate in a general complexity" (interview in *The Independent*, 17 September 2010). It's this 'general complexity' which has prevented me from offering a fool-proof blueprint for school success. Heads must embrace the organic, delicate nature of schools and adapt their approach to the resources and needs that they encounter. The human element can never be removed from the mix, which makes human variables such as confidence, mood, momentum and hope so vital in schools. And it helps explains why teachers are so essential to the success of a school. headteachers must bend over backwards to attract, cherish, cultivate and retain great teachers. The need for proactive, people-oriented leadership is particularly acute in areas of social deprivation, where schools must swim against a vicious tide of low expectations and entrenched underachievement.

I write this in May 2013. Next week will be the final week of school for the students who joined us in September 2006, when Burlington Danes Church of England School became Burlington Danes Academy. The transformation of the school was not immediate, so these students remember the pain of a troubled school – the frustration of chaotic classrooms, the agitation of unruly corridors. But that memory is fading. Perhaps the most pleasing thing about what's happened at Burlington Danes is that success has become the norm, it's become expected. In the staff room too, nearly three quarters of our teachers have no memory or experience of Burlington Danes as a failing school. So when our sixth form students leave next week the collective memory of a dysfunctional school will go with them. It's been quite a journey.

This chapter in a tweet: Schools, especially those in tough areas, require steadfast leadership in order to overcome contextual disadvantages.

Epilogue

I leave Burlington Danes on 79% five A*-C including English and maths – our third consecutive year of 75% or better. Yet there is still plenty of room for growth in that patch of West London between the A40 and Wormwood Scrubs. Successful schools have to raise the bar all the time. Management consultants call it the Sigmoid Curve: the tendency for growth and improvement to tale off over time. The solution is constant renewal – fresh impetus and new areas of focus. So my successor at Burlington Danes should focus on the A*-B grades, basing all tracking and intervention on these higher grades. There's also work to be done on ensuring that students are ready for the longer and more challenging terminal exams which are replacing modular units and coursework. This will require a Key Stage 3 curriculum which develops and consolidates the accumulation of knowledge over time. For the older pupils, the school can support preparation for longer terminal exams by providing revision space for students after school – all the more important for children who might not have access to a quiet place to study at home.

My departure from Burlington Danes has given me a chance to reflect on my proudest achievements there. I remain proud of the rank orders that we introduced in my first term. It is controversial to publicly display the attainment of all students against each other, but these rank orders were transformational in switching the focus from behaviour to learning. The key challenge for any assessment system is that it has currency with parents and students. Throughout the decades that I've spent in schools, nothing comes close to rank orders in meeting this challenge. Parents might not realise that a Level 4 in Year 8 means that their child is working below expectations for their age group, but the alarm bells will soon be ringing when they find out that their child is 130th in the year group. Similarly, if the same child is 80th in the year group the following year then the parents will know that they have made real progress. All parents, no matter their own educational background or their grasp of the English education system, understand their child's progress in relation to other children. Such progress is far more tangible than saying that a child has progressed from a 4a to a 5c. A hidden benefit of rank orders is that it forces teachers to work together within their departments to devise rigorous tests and then mark them accurately through standardised mark schemes and robust moderation. Teachers do this because they know that the outcomes of the tests will impact the students' position in the rank order, so they better make sure that all students are given a fair crack of the whip. This is accountability in the purest sense: teachers striving to support the students in their class because they know that the students care about their own progress. Furthermore, parents are empowered by rank orders because they understand them. We're approaching a point where we have different assessment systems for primary school and then each of the three Key Stages from 11-18. That's four different systems for students, parents and employers to understand, and it's another reason why I'm immensely proud of the uniformity and consistency offered by rank orders.

Of course, rank orders on their own achieve very little – it's the opportunity for follow-up and intervention which makes them so potent. I'm still shocked to find parents of students in Year 7 who are surprised to find their children languishing in the lower reaches of the rank order. After seven years of primary school they had no idea that their child was struggling. So rank orders empower parents by lifting the veil on their child's progress and giving families a chance to respond. I love seeing parents walk away from school with a clutch of library books and study guides after a sobering parents evening has lifted the veil on their child's performance. If there's an assessment system which can match rank orders for power and immediacy then I would love to see it.

I'm also proud of what I call the 'intellectualisation' of our Key Stage 3 curriculum. It has always been my belief that students from all backgrounds can thrive in traditional, academic subjects. We would all want our own children to do well in English, maths, the sciences, languages and humanities, so it would be wrong of me to shoe-horn my students into easier but less valuable courses. Plenty of schools take this easier route, and until recently the league tables haven't exposed them. Students have been able to secure C grades at English and maths and a pass in a couple of vocational subjects and their school appears to be riding high. Beneath our headline figures I'm proud that nearly half of our students gained the English Baccalaureate in 2014 (A*-C grades in at least five traditional subjects) – way above the national average. At A level, in 2014 58% of all A2 grades were A*-B. The basis of this success is the rigour that we apply to Key Stage 3, with students following challenging programmes of study which develop their core knowledge and skills in an intellectually honest manner. In short, the work that students do in a Year 7 history lesson is a scaled down version of the work that we hope they will be doing six years later in A2 history. It's a far cry from the days of building paper mache castles in Key Stage 3 history.

Above all, I'm proud of the sense of community that we created. We truly serve the local community. Despite being a Church of England Academy with a specialism in maths, and despite being massively over-subscribed, we apply no selection criteria. We could select by religious faith or aptitude for our maths specialism, but we don't. Distance from the student's front door to the school's front gate, along with the presence of siblings already at the school, remain our only selection criteria. This creates a rich sense of community and with five years of outstanding results behind us we can now legitimately say that we've had a positive impact on the community around us, improving the life chances of hundreds of young people and their families.

Beyond the exam results, I'm immensely proud that these young people will hold doors open for people, give up their seats on the bus and address their elders as sir and madam.

Postscript

An awkward curtsey and an 'outstanding' judgement...

Since I began writing this book I was honoured to made Dame Commander of the Order of the British Empire (DBE). "You're the Head of one of those schools that has been transformed," said Her Majesty the Queen as I collected my award, though a fit of nerves meant that my knees were knocking so loudly that I could barely hear her. The video that my husband took reveals that I proffered an awkward ballet-style curtsey as I approached our head of state. Later in the same year – 2013 – the inspectors finally called (it had been almost five years since their previous visit) and Burlington Danes was deemed to be outstanding in all categories. The report begins with the following observations:

- The mission to provide the very best education for every pupil within a caring and safe environment has become a reality in this outstanding academy.
- Students, staff and parents are proud to be part of this mission and speak very highly about the academy.
- The inspirational leadership of the principal, who is well supported by all of her staff, has resulted in a relentless pursuit of excellence.
- Given their starting points students make outstanding progress resulting in above average attainment, especially in English and mathematics.
- Students who are eligible for additional government funding (the pupil premium) are supported very well both academically and pastorally. As a result, the gap between their attainment and that of other students has narrowed considerably.
- Students' behaviour is exemplary. They are courteous, polite and respectful to each other and staff. Students enjoy being at the academy and are happy and feel very safe.

- The overall quality of teaching is outstanding.
- Teachers' subject knowledge, planning, marking and their thoughtful use of questioning are particularly strong.
- Careful monitoring and intervention systems ensure that all students achieve their ambitious targets. However, in a very few lessons there could be greater challenge for the more-able students.
- The academy's provision for the teaching of literacy is outstanding.
- The promotion of students' spiritual, moral, social and cultural development is outstanding and permeates all of their activities.
- Governors effectively monitor and support the academy's work and use the pupil premium wisely to help those eligible.
- The sixth form is outstanding. Students' progress in the sixth form is outstanding as a result of highly effective teaching and the implementation of effective study programmes.

The report can be found in full at: www.burlingtondanes.org/ofsted-and-performance-data

TES Outstanding Academy of the Year nomination, 2014

A 'comprehensive grammar' in the heart of White City, London, Burlington Danes Academy proves that great schools can do more than achieve excellent grades; they build and enrich lives. The academy has rightly earned a national reputation for giving its students an outstanding start in life. Its stunning success is a collaborative effort with both the ARK Schools network and the Church of England.

Every student matters. Every lesson counts. Formal, scholarly and courteous; sport and creativity flourish and are actively encouraged. A Christian community, the academy believes in no excuses. No matter your background, circumstances or ability, you will succeed. Manners and courtesy are profoundly important.

The significant rise in results, both at GCSE and A level, underpins the academy's success. Indeed, data interrogation is a major strength. Staff know with pinpoint precision the progress of their groups. The school's thorough models of intervention are equally as precise.

Five A*-C grades including English and mathematics: 2013: 77%.

AS A*-B grades: 2013: 47%.

A2 A*-B grades: 2013: 44%.

An overwhelming proportion of BDA sixth form students who apply to russell and 1994 group universities go on to achieve places. Offering over 20 different courses, the sixth form provides a diverse and expansive education, with an emphasis on independent study. A key part of the wider school community, it retains a rich and vibrant identity of its own.

The academy adopts a 'tough love' approach, where each individual is clear about what it takes to achieve. This is not to say that it is all about results; developing character matters as well as academic success. Of course, the two come hand-in-hand.

In November 2013 Burlington Danes Academy was inspected by Ofsted and judged 'outstanding' in all four categories: 'The mission to provide the very best education for every pupil ... has become a reality in this outstanding academy.'

Far from viewing this as the end of the journey, the academy is now seeking 'Teaching School' status and has become a 'Leading Edge School' and in 2015 an on-site primary school will open.

Both the academy and the Ofsted report appreciate that the remarkable turnaround of a school in 'special measures' in 2006 is thanks to an impressive collective will-power. An amazing team of staff consistently rise to the challenge of teaching outstanding lessons: 'The commitment of all staff in this academy to the continuous improvement of teaching and learning is exceptional. They ... learn from each other.' (Ofsted. 2013).

Governors actively support learning and pupils take great pride in their school. Ofsted noted 'overwhelmingly positive' student feedback:

"Learning is brilliant at this school" (Year 8).

"Teachers really support us to meet our ambitious targets" (Year 11).

"We are given so many opportunities to really prepare us for the best universities" (Year 13).

The SLT provides drive, focus and direction to help both staff and students flourish. We do not accept excuses for underachievement. Our aim is to make Burlington Danes not just outstanding but exceptional.

Bibliography

Adonis, A. (2012) *Education Education Education*. London: Biteback.

Bambrick-Santoyo, P. and Peiser, B. (2012) *Leverage leadership*. San Francisco: Jossey-Bass.

Belbin, R. (1996) *Management teams*. Oxford: Butterworth-Heinemann.

Blair, T. (2008) *A journey*. London: Arrow.

Butler, T. and Webber, R. (2007) 'Classifying Pupils by Where They Live: How Well Does This Predict Variations in Their GCSE Results?' *Urban Studies*, 44 (7) p.1229-1253.

Coleman, J. (1966) Equality of educational opportunity [summary report]. [Washington]: U.S. Dept. of Health, Education, and Welfare, Office of Education.

Collins, J. (2001) *Good to great*. New York, NY: HarperBusiness.

Csikszentmihalyi, M. (1990) *Flow*. New York: Harper & Row.

Dweck, C. (2006) *Mindset*. New York: Random House.

Gladwell, M. (2000) *The tipping point*. Boston: Little, Brown.

Gladwell, M. (2009) *Outliers: The Story of Success*. London: Penguin.

Gawande, A. (2010) *The checklist manifesto*. New York: Metropolitan Books.

Goldstein, R., Cialdini, R. and Griskevicius, V. (2008) 'A Room with a Viewpoint: Using Social Norms to Motivate Environment Conservation in Hotels' *Journal of Consumer Research*, 35 (3), p.472-482.

Goleman, D. (1995) *Emotional intelligence*. New York: Bantam Books.

Grant, G. (2009) *Hope and despair in the American city*. Cambridge, Mass.: Harvard University Press.

Hargreaves, A. and Fullan, M. (2012) *Professional capital*. New York: Teachers College Press.

Hirsch, E. D (2006) *The knowledge deficit*. Boston: Houghton, Mifflin, Harcourt.

Hyman, P. (2005) *1 out of 10*. London: Vintage.

Kelling, G. L. and Wilson, J. Q. (1982). Broken windows: the police and neighborhood safety. *Atlantic Monthly* 249(3) p29–38.

Kennedy, A. W. and Kennedy, E. (2013). *The alpha strategies*. Indiana: Xlibris.

Kirkup, C. (2005) Schools' use of data in teaching and learning. Annesley: DfES Publications.

Lareau, A. (2003) *Unequal childhoods*. Berkeley: University of California Press.

Marlowe, B. and Page, M. (1999) 'Making the most of classroom mosaic: A constructivist perspective' *Multicultural Education*, 6 (4) p.19-21.

McKeown, M. (2012) *The strategy book*. Harlow, England: Pearson.

Muller-Hill, B. (1994) 'The Idea Of The Final Solution And The Role Of Experts,' in Cesarani, D. (ed) (1994) *The Final Solution Origins and Implementation*. Routledge: London. p. 62-70.

Pennac, D. (2010) *School Blues*. London: MacLehose Press.

Pink, D. (2009) *Drive*. New York, NY: Riverhead Books.

Pirsig, R. (1974) *Zen and the art of motorcycle maintenance*. New York: Morrow.

Putnam, R. (2000) *Bowling alone*. New York: Simon & Schuster.

Rogers, B (2011) *Classroom behaviour*. Third Edition. Sage: London.

Reay, D. (2006) 'The Zombie stalking English Schools: Social Class and Educational Inequality' *British Journal of Educational Studies*, 54, (3). p. 288–307

Reynolds, D. and Teddlie, C. (2001) 'Reflections on the critics, and beyond them'. *School Effectiveness and School Improvement* 12 (1), p. 99-113.

Rosenthal, R. and Jacobson, L. (1968) *Pygmalion in the classroom*. New York: Holt, Rinehart and Winston.

Sahlberg, P. and Hargreaves, A. (2011) *Finnish lessons*. New York: Teachers College Press.

Seligman, M. (1991). *Learned optimism*. New York: A.A. Knopf.

Smith. J. (2012) *The Learning Game*. London: Abacus.

Smith, M. (2002) 'The School Leadership Initiative: An Ethically Flawed Project?' *Journal of Philosophy of Education*, 36 (1), p.21-40

Syed, M. (2010) *Bounce*. London: Fourth Estate.

Thaler, R. and Sunstein, C. (2008) *Nudge*. New Haven, Conn.: Yale University Press.

Tobin, K. Roth, W, and Zimmerman, A. (2001). 'Learning to teach science in urban schools' *Journal of Research in Science Teaching* 38 (8), p. 941-964.

Tough, P. (2012) *How children succeed*. London: Arrow.

Wilkinson, R. and Pickett, K. (2010) *The spirit level*. New York: Bloomsbury Press.

Wooden, J. and Tobin, J. (1972) *They call me coach*. Waco, Tex.: Word.